Henrietta Louisa (Farrer) Lear

The Revival of Priestly Life in the Seventeenth Century in France

Henrietta Louisa (Farrer) Lear

The Revival of Priestly Life in the Seventeenth Century in France

ISBN/EAN: 9783744659154

Printed in Europe, USA, Canada, Australia, Japan

Cover: Foto ©ninafisch / pixelio.de

More available books at **www.hansebooks.com**

RIVINGTONS

London............................ *Waterloo Place*
Oxford............................. *High Street*
Cambridge......................... *Trinity Street*

THE
REVIVAL OF PRIESTLY LIFE

IN THE

Seventeenth Century

IN

FRANCE

A SKETCH

BY THE AUTHOR OF
"A DOMINICAN ARTIST," "LIFE OF S. FRANCIS DE SALES,"
"HENRI PERREYVE," ETC. ETC.

RIVINGTONS
London, Oxford, and Cambridge
1873

TO

The Reverend John Daubeny

CHANCELLOR OF SARUM CATHEDRAL

AND PRINCIPAL OF HER THEOLOGICAL COLLEGE

WHOSE LIFE IS DEVOTED

TO THE SUBJECT OF THIS LITTLE BOOK

IN ENGLAND

IT IS DEDICATED

WITH THE WARMEST AFFECTION

AND GRATITUDE

Preface

THE following pages must only be read from the point of view from which they were written—*i.e.* as a mere sketch of one part of a very important period of Church history. They do not in the smallest degree affect to comprehend the great subject placed at their head; enough if they should lead people to read and study for themselves some parts of a mine of information not readily exhausted. But perhaps in these days, when so many hearts are depressed by a keen sense of the evils surrounding Christ's Church in the various shapes of unbelief, misbelief;—and imperfect practice,—even where theoretically belief may be sound,—some consolation may be gained from seeing how the like clouds hung darkly over their forefathers, and out of what abuses and corruptions God has not failed to bring His Church. Thank God that each carefully studied page of history does but confirm us in our strong unfailing trust in His unfailing Promise, "Lo, I am with you always, even to the end of the world."

We are all fast hastening on to the individual end of each, as far as this life goes. May His Grace enable us to be faithful in our respective callings, to give up all for His Sake joyfully, to fear no evil, certain that His Arm is round us, His Right Hand succouring us.

"And then it shall be said in that Day, Lo! this is our God, we have waited for Him, and He will save us: we have waited for Him, we will be glad and rejoice in His Salvation."—Isa. xxv. 9.

CONTENTS

CHAPTER I.
CHARLES DE CONDREN 1

CHAPTER II.
S. PHILIP NERI AND CARDINAL DE BERULLE 31

CHAPTER III.
DE CONDREN'S INNER LIFE AND LETTERS 51

CHAPTER IV.
THE ORATORY AND ITS SYSTEM 157

CHAPTER V.
S. VINCENT DE PAUL AND THE LAZARISTS 213

CHAPTER VI.
SAINT SULPICE AND JEAN JACQUES OLIER 252

CHAPTER VII.
PRESENT TIMES 305

PRIESTLY LIFE IN FRANCE.

CHAPTER I.

CHARLES DE CONDREN.

A TIME of great darkness is generally also a time in which some great and dazzling light is seen; the stars never shine so brightly as in the darkest sky; and when the heaviest clouds of negligence or profligacy have lowered with the most seemingly hopeless density over God's Church, He has ever vouchsafed to cause His rainbow to appear, telling those whose hearts are well nigh failing for fear "that there is light in Heaven." So it was in the particular period of French Church History here touched upon. The sky was dark with clouds of unbelief, ignorance, neglect, sensuality, and avarice, enough to scare the bravest heart; and yet through it all there bursts upon our sight a galaxy of light which casts its brightness over the Church to this day, and will cast it so long as history endures.

Some names, known and loved wherever true hearts beat with love of Christ and His Church, will readily occur to every one's mind in thinking of that period, but amid the "bright particular stars" which shine forth so gloriously in the Church of the latter part of the sixteenth and earlier part of the seventeenth centuries, the name of Charles de Condren is probably unknown to many who are familiar with those household objects of love and veneration, S. Francis de Sales, S. Vincent de Paul, or even with the scarcely less revered names of Cardinal du Perron, Cardinal de Bérulle, and M. Olier. This is as he himself, the Père de Condren, would have wished; for the one most striking characteristic of his singularly holy life was its intense humility—the real desire to "efface" himself—to penetrate his whole existence with the spirit of S. Paul's words, "Not I, but Christ in me."

"Would have wished" may be said advisedly; for who can for a moment doubt that when the mortal puts on immortality, when the flesh ceases to cumber the spirit with its weakness, when every motion of sin, of pride, or self-consciousness has fallen before that Light in which the freed soul sees light for ever, there can be but one desire even in the humblest heart, *i.e.* that God may be glorified; and if His Glory can be promoted by setting forth how His upholding Grace was vouchsafed to any of His children here on earth, so as to bring them nearer than is common to our Dear Lord's Likeness, would they not now joyfully assent to any such manifestation, re-echoing the cry, "Not unto us, O Lord, not unto us, but to Thy Name give the glory!"

Lowly as he was, marvellous in his gift of humility, and veritably counting himself all unworthy of any place among those who have done good service to the Church, Père de Condren can scarcely be overlooked by those who study the history of the Church in the sixteenth century. Foremost themselves in the revival of a higher tone among the clergy of France, the Oratorians were so distinctly the progenitors of those great works which—as so often occurs in the order of God's Providence—subsequently overshadowed their source, that, while acknowledging the services of the Lazarists and Saint Sulpiciens, these latter must be traced backward to the Oratory; and, though not the founder of that Congregation, few members had so important a share in shaping and directing its course as de Condren. The Director of Cardinal de Bérulle and of Jean Jacques Olier—whose great work as founder of the Seminary of Saint Sulpice was mainly de Condren's doing—left no slight stamp on his times, to say nothing of his influence upon the King of France (Louis XIII.) and his unruly brother Gaston d'Orléans, or what he did as Superior of the Oratory.

Yet all the while, as the image of Charles de Condren rises before one, it is still more as the saintly Priest, whose whole life was spent in seeking to imitate the Example of our Blessed Lord, than as the able ecclesiastic, or wise director, or active superior. There is a singular sense of repose as we dwell upon his history; the turmoil of Church politics—certainly not less stirring then than now—the manifold engrossments and occupations of his office, literary, spiritual and administrative, never seem to disturb the calm steadfast bent of his soul, or that clear current of his life which swept onward like a deep river towards the sea, straight for Paradise. There is none of that restless hurry and scattering of power to be traced in de Condren's life, which led one of his noblest descendants—the modern restorer of the Oratory, Père Gratry—to write: "The world moves on with ever-increasing rapidity, movement becomes intensified in every shape, moral, intellectual, and physical; and beneath this surface movement I fear one discovers that there is a slackening of central impetus—we whirl about more, but we advance less. . . . It is a universal blot, every living thing finds the difficulty of self-recollection, of gathering itself together, and abiding steadfast at the heart's core. . . . It is the *degenerare tamen* of Virgil; it is that which S. Bernard has called 'evisceratio mentis,' the disembowelling of the soul.

... Life hurries on, spreads itself far and wide, but the source of life dries up. ... In days of old there were men whose whole life was absorbed in their great Centre—God; and who found peace, light and happiness therein. To them it furnished the motive power, the life of all things. But in these days where shall we find such calm, deep minds, dwelling in the Invisible, and rapt in heavenly things, ever facing eastwards amid the whirl of life? ... All our strength [as priests] lies in prayer and faith, nourished in our souls by recollection and retirement, by the habit of that interior life which alone fosters holiness, light and love. We shall never become useful ministers of the Gospel by multiplying our surface efforts, or by accumulating good works; that can only be done through the mighty power of a humble heart which leans on God, of a thoughtful soul which drinks deep of Him."[1]

Père Gratry might well have had his predecessor's life in mind as he wrote these words,—for if ever a man's good service sprang from that mighty power, "a humble heart which leans on God, and a thoughtful soul which drinks deep of Him," it was his of whom it has been written,—"He was a very marvel in his detachment from creatures and his union with God. His great freedom from creature engrossments

[1] Life of H. Perreyve, p. 173.

left a clear space for the workings of Divine Light, and he was filled to overflowing with its brightness."[1]

Charles de Condren was born December 15, 1588, at the Château de Vauxbuin, near Soissons. His father —a soldier—held a good position at the Court of Henri IV., and the test and standard of merit in his eyes was military capacity, physical courage and endurance. Apparently Madame de Condren's horizon was less limited; for before her child's birth, and on his first entrance into the world, she offered him specially to God—an offering upon which the future Oratorian looked back gratefully as having influenced his future career in no small degree.

"I had the blessing," he wrote, "of being dedicated from my birth to God, like the first-born of the Children of Israel, but I had an advantage over them in that the law of substitution has ceased to be, and I am not exempt from myself fulfilling the conditions of my dedication. . . . I thank God for this,—I do not covet a dispensation—I am only too happy to serve perpetually in the Temple of God." But the soldier-father had no intention of making a Levite of his boy; and, lest nursery caresses and influences should enervate his first formed character, the baby was taken from women's care for all save that which rougher handling scarce could afford; and, while still

[1] Boudon.

in arms, he was carried about by one of his father's soldiers, who amused Charles with warlike play, made military songs his lullaby, and taught him to look upon drums and trumpets, swords and harquebusses, as natural toys. As soon as the boy could walk he was dressed in miniature uniform, and supplied with tiny weapons of war. No wonder that the military tendency thus early developed clung to de Condren through life, so that to the end, through all his years of self-devotion in a very different service, it was still hot within him; and he would smile sometimes at his own soldier-like nature. One or two childish feats of courage and prowess, still recorded, gave intense delight to his father; all the more that one in which, by a deftly dealt blow, Charles parried the onslaught of a buffalo in the Parc de Monceau, was witnessed by Henri IV., and the King was not chary of his notice and praise.

However, M. de Condren had the wisdom not to confine his son's education to strictly military matters; and the natural gift of a remarkably powerful memory, so that he could repeat even difficult things by heart after once reading them—and alluding to which he once said that he "thought he had never forgotten anything since he was eighteen months old"—made his progress rapid and easy. Only one thing—more necessary perhaps for a gentleman's complete education then than now—young de Condren could not learn—the art of dancing. He was always taken ill when this process was attempted! and later on, when constrained by his father to take part in Court entertainments, the same result invariably occurred. The future ascetic was also foretold in his childish displeasure with a very pretty portrait which had been taken of him. Conscious of the danger of vanity, he assaulted the picture privately with a big stick, but unfortunately found it altogether beyond the reach of his small arm; whereupon, true to his military training, Charles watched his opportunity, and contriving to shut himself into the room where the offending picture hung, with some arrows he shot at the impromptu target till it was satisfactorily defaced! Besides these traits little concerning de Condren's childhood is on record, save his strict truthfulness and accuracy. His tutor, M. le Masson, a Canon of Soissons, bears testimony to the purity of his childish life, and adds that his ability and orderly ways made it pleasant to teach him.

It was an understood thing in the family that Charles was to be a soldier, and when at about the age of twelve he began to feel a powerful drawing to a different career, he foresaw that any change of vocation would be unacceptable to his father. Nevertheless a stronger power than the boy could resist led him on;—the Love of God grew warm in his heart, and with that the spirit of sacrifice, which henceforward coloured his whole life so deeply, took possession of him. Already he grasped the great doctrine of our Dear Lord's One Perfect Sacrifice; and out of that grew an intense desire to unite himself to It in dying daily; and this he conceived he could best do as a priest, although his high estimate of the dignity of that calling and his own unworthiness thereof became continually more marked. According to his own account, a clear voice resounded within him, "I will that thou be a Priest to serve Me and My Church;" and he then and there prostrating himself, offered his future life to God, and never henceforward felt the slightest doubt as to the course which lay before him. Consequently henceforth, while studying diligently, he looked upon all his secular studies as only so many means of preparing himself to serve God better, and the talents, which he could not but recognise in himself, as gifts to be used for His Glory. M. de Condren removed his son after a time from school, wishing him to study at home, and then the ease and rapidity with which he learnt (he is said to have mastered the science of mathematics in the most wonderful fashion) enabled him secretly to devote his leisure to theological studies. Sometimes he went out professedly shooting, but as soon as he was well away in the woods, and some presentable bag made to avoid exciting suspicion, the young sportsman laid aside his gun, and a volume of the Fathers (S. Augustine was his favourite author) or the Summa of S. Thomas Aquinas was drawn forth, and the rest of his day was spent in study. He had another ingenious device to the same end. With the connivance of his own personal attendant, a German valet, who would do anything his master wished, and who undertook never to let any one save himself make Charles's bed, young de Condren cut away a hollow place in his mattress, and kept his theological books, the sight of which would have given sore offence to his father, therein, gladly cutting short his hours of sleep on behalf of this chosen study. It must have been rather difficult to work hard and pray much in that bustling cheerful family house, always full of company, and with constant interruptions from Court gaieties and the like. But from the time that Charles left school he made recollection and advance in the spiritual life his great aim, and while so doing he learnt to offer the very interruptions which otherwise would have fretted him to God, and thus by patience turned them to his soul's profit instead of hindrance. His sister accidentally took up a sheet of paper some time later, which contained his general confession for the two years and a half elapsed since he came home from school, and though on seeing what it contained she immediately put it down; her passing glance shewed her that the first point of her brother's self-examination was recollection of the Presence of God, and that he must have been able to preserve this in a very marked and unusual manner.

But this sort of thing was not at all what M. de Condren desired. His ambition that his son might win military renown had by no means decreased, and as soon as Charles's studies were considered to be finished, the old soldier prepared to send him to join the army either at Calais, where Devic was in command, under whom Henri IV. had expressed a wish that his young protégé should serve; or in Holland, which was supposed just then to be the best school of military discipline. It was a time of sore struggle to the young man, for notwithstanding his strong drawings to the priesthood, and his firm belief that it was his vocation, he had no slight inclination for the army; and his own natural tastes, developed as they had been by early training, quite fell in with the course which respect for his father's wishes prompted him to take.

It was a question only to be solved by much prayer, and in that, accompanied by fasting, de Condren sought for light as to his real and highest duty. His father saw that there were breakers a-head, and with kindly consideration he called in the assistance of a relation, M. de Briqueville, Chevalier de Malte, whose personal piety gave him a certain weight with Charles. This gentleman did not fail to urge upon his young cousin the paramount duty of obedience to his father, as well as the probable displeasure of the King if his wishes were lightly set aside. De Condren assented to all this, and moreover he frankly admitted that he had a passionate delight in the calling now urged upon him. He did not refuse active service, only asking that he might be sent to Hungary to fight against the Turks, rather than to Holland or Calais, and adding, " Nevertheless, if I had my choice, I would do neither, for my one sole ambition is to serve God in His Church."

M. de Condren was greatly irritated when de Briqueville reported his son's views, and for a time he even refused to see Charles, accusing him of cowardice and bigotry. Those were trying days, and the issue seemed doubtful, when an unexpected solution to the difficulty was sent, in the order of God's Providence, in the shape of a severe illness, which ran its course so fiercely that before long the doctors pronounced the case hopeless. Charles had already thoroughly grasped the spirit of sacrifice, which was later on so marked a feature of his character; and seen from that point of view, he was ready to accept life or death, as it pleased his Master to appoint. But when he heard his father's bitter lamentations, and his appeal to God to spare his child, there came upon him a strong impulse, which he obeyed, beseeching M. de Condren to make a willing sacrifice, and adding that possibly, if he were to offer his son willingly to the priesthood, God might yet see fit to raise him up to health.

Greatly touched at this, which to all appearance was a dying request, the old man out of the abundance of his heart offered his child freely, adding, "Since the very thought of our earthly court kills him, perhaps the promise of the Heavenly Courts may revive him;" and from that moment he became as full of hope as he had been of despair.

The father's hopes were fulfilled, and Charles recovered; but for fear his changed prospects should be forgotten with his changed condition, he insisted on putting on a cassock the first time he left his bed, and henceforth there was no further question as to his destination in life. Having once conceded the point, M. de Condren was anxious to promote his son's views heartily, and made no difficulty about sending him to study at the Sorbonne, where Charles was the pupil of Philippe de Gamache and Duval, under whom he speedily distinguished himself.

His natural ability made his work comparatively easy, and much time was spent by the young student in prayer, so that he was looked upon with great respect, and some little awe, by his companions, who notwithstanding found plenty to admire in his intellectual and physical capabilities. Always subject to severe illness, de Condren was again attacked by a one-and-twenty day fever while studying at the Sorbonne, A.D. 1609, and when the crisis came he was so reduced that the last Sacraments were administered to him by the Abbé Hébert, afterwards Archbishop of Bourges. He was supposed to be in the last agony, when de Gamache, meeting his class as usual, felt so absorbed in the condition of his favourite pupil, that instead of the intended lecture, he could only speak of the dying youth, on whose earnest life and stedfast preparation for death he dwelt lovingly; and as he himself and his listeners waxed warmer and more full of regrets, he entreated all to lift up their hearts to God, if it might be that He would yet restore de Condren. Together with their professor the whole class knelt in prayer—and it was granted—the longed-for turn in the malady came, and once more de Condren turned back to life from the very edge of the grave.

According to the rule of the Sorbonne, when de Condren had completed his course of theology, at the age of twenty-three, he was sent as professor of philosophy to the University of Paris, and he applied all his energies to fulfilling the task well. He began by carefully writing all his lectures, but the ill health which became increasingly his lot, hindered this greatly, and he was obliged to give up the habit and often to trust to his memory as sole preparation; but notwithstanding he continued to distinguish himself by the ability with which he lectured.[1]

A prayer was found which he had written for himself to be used habitually before entering his classroom, in which he asks light and knowledge of God, to enable him to impart them to others, ending with these words, "Shed out Thy Light upon Thy children through me, but may they never impute to me the light, the truth, or any other gifts which are solely Thine; may they ever keep Thee in Sight as the One

---

[1] Habitually de Condren looked to God for the words he should say or write for the benefit of others. Thus we find him writing to a certain M. de Silleri, who had asked him for spiritual instructions: "I have set myself to write several times. I have offered your intention to God, and told Him how bound I feel to help you, and have besought grace to do so, very earnestly for several days, but so far He has not been pleased to vouchsafe me anything to say to you. 'We had the sentence of death in ourselves, that we should not trust in ourselves, but in God which raiseth the dead' (2 Cor. i. 9). I may well apply the Apostle's words to myself, for I have found nought in my own mind save a great void, and the sentence of death. . . I need not marvel that I can do nothing without Christ, since it is my duty to desire nothing save His Will, but I must humble myself because I cannot always find that strength I need in Him."
—Letters, No. lxxiv. p. 273, edit. Pin.

Only Principle of all truth, and help me always to acknowledge Thy Light, and my own profound darkness."

There were certain rules which de Condren made for himself in this new phase of life, one of which was to watch carefully over his eyes, and not let them habitually wander, and so form an unrecollected habit of mind. On arriving at the door of his lecture-room, he used to pause an instant in ejaculatory prayer, and then making the sign of the Cross, he began his work as in God's Sight. He was on the watch for passing movements of self-satisfaction, vanity or speculative tendency as he taught, diligently checking them; and one special point in his self-examination had reference to the inner spirit as well as the outer way in which his lecture had been delivered. Already de Condren had subjected his daily life to a carefully studied rule, in which the examination of conscience filled an important place. Taking our Saviour's words—" Without Me ye can do nothing " —as a guide, he examined himself as to whether he had striven to fulfil every duty in Christ's Strength ; how far he had given good heed to the whispered inspirations of the Holy Spirit ; whether he had given way to his natural impulses, or if self-love had in anything prevailed over the Love of God; whether friendship or complaisance had induced him to lose sight of his first duty to God ; whether he had resisted God's

Holy Will, or been relaxed and cold in devotions, or in his highest aim after a holy life? All these points were duly weighed, his omissions confessed with contrition, and a fresh dedication of his whole being made to God. He was wont, later on, to recommend those who are striving after the hidden life to make a brief self-examination three times a day, namely, in the morning—looking forward to the duties of the coming hours, and back upon the faults of the day past, so as to guard against their renewal, and specially consecrating all the little details of life to God:—and at noon and evening reviewing the past in the same spirit with which Bishop Andrewes says, "Evening is come; the evening of life is old age."

He sought to lie down to sleep, making an act of dying to the things of this life, and surrendering his body, soul and spirit to God during the season of helplessness, uniting his own natural rest in intention with the Rest of God and His Saints. His first waking act was to be one of self-oblation;—himself, every faculty and action, offered absolutely in union with God's Will. All through life de Condren looked upon the first thoughts in waking as a most important point of self-watchfulness.

"Members of the Incarnate Word," (he wrote to a priest under his guidance,) "and pledged to live in

Him Alone, we should begin that life daily, as we begin our material life anew each day on waking. It is of His Grace that we shake off the bonds of sleep, which is a kind of deathlike void, and begin to serve Him afresh; and I believe that moment of waking to be a very important one, which gives the tone to our whole day. Beware of letting the natural indolence of your first awakening master you, or indeed any other temptation or passion :—we should cultivate the habit of waking up zealous for God's service, striving to fill our hearts with His Presence by the help of some holy thought, so that there may be no room for the world or the devil to enter in, or for our own evil propensities to coil around and hinder our work. While asking God to keep us in His Holy Hands at the beginning of the day, it is well to dedicate our waking to the Unchanging Watchfulness of God. 'He that keepeth Israel shall neither slumber nor sleep.' (Ps. cxxi.) Even as God has given us rest as an image of His Eternal Rest, so our wakeful hours are an emblem of His Vigilance, and we should honour Him in both alike. . . . It is well too, on first waking, to worship the Word, Who accepted human life in the Incarnation. We should make an act of self-renunciation, and offer ourselves to Him to whatever purpose He will use us; putting aside all that enslaves us to self or the creature, and seeking to enter into

His Mind, forsaking all which He rejected, and striving to drink as deeply of His Spirit as we can."[1]

And again: "The soul should wake to God as promptly as the body wakes to life—as soon as the material light gladdens our eyes, the Sun of Righteousness should enlighten our hearts. Sleep calms the mind, and prepares it for new beginnings, but directly that sleep has passed away we are specially alive to all manner of impressions, be they for good or evil. A holy thought faithfully grasped then will abide with us through the day's distractions; but if we yield to evil thoughts in our first waking moments, the devil and self-love will conspire to disturb our devotions and hinder us all day long."

So carefully was de Condren's rule of life framed, that it prescribed that he should dress quickly, fixing his thoughts the while on that fall of man which first led to the need of garments to cover him; and bearing in mind that his cassock was the livery of God, an emblem of the "Coat without seam;" a warning to enfold his soul as closely in Christ as his body was enfolded by its vesture.

In like manner de Condren's devotional exercises were minutely arranged. Long since he had made it a rule to himself never to begin to pray, or come into God's Presence, without an act of con-

[1] Lettres, lxxviii.

trition. Of course, he went daily to Mass, and as it has been said, that was his life, his Heaven, his All.[1] He never wearied of repeating that a good Communion implies the reign of God within the soul; and in later years, when he had to teach his spiritual children how best to use this great and precious Gift, he always loved to dwell upon the desire our Dear Lord has that we should come to Him in His own Blessed Sacrament, in order that we may be one with Him—that we may dwell in Him, as well as He in us;—urging that men should communicate, not for their own soul's benefit alone, but for His Glory, and to satisfy His exceeding longing after us.[2] In the same way he was always anxious to prevent people testing the fruitfulness of their communions by their conscious delight or consolation therein, or even by more apparently substantial results. Such earnest desire for warmth of feeling and tangible effects has more of self-love in it than the love of God, he used to say.

De Condren's rule was that when the bell rang for any meal, he made an act of self-oblation, asking that the food he took might be taken for God's Glory, and thanking Him for it—so that the natural satisfaction of eating and drinking might be secondary to his Master's service. In society and seasons of recreation

[1] Vie, Abbé Pin, p. 71. [2] Lettres, lxxvi. lxxx. &c.

one of his strictest rules was never to speak ill of any one, and as far as might be to screen the faults of others. Another rule guarded him against too free intercourse with the world and its foolish tittle tattle, —but meanwhile all this secret vigilance did not make him stiff or constrained. His manners were open and attractive, so his contemporary biographer (the Père Amelote) says; his conversation was especially bright and varied, as might be expected of one gifted with such a power of memory; he was always cheerful, and the centre of cheerfulness to others, and his gentleness and consideration won the hearts of all who knew him.

When the appointed year of his Professorship ended, de Condren determined on spending that which was to follow in the strictest retirement and preparation for his ordination; and as a preliminary measure he renounced his position as eldest son (his brother was a soldier, as we find by an allusion in one of his letters),[1] signing a formal legal act to that effect, and only consenting to receive a small yearly allowance from his father, a practical form of self-renunciation which touched the elder de Condren's heart deeply, and seemed to make him realise the intensity of his son's vocation more than he had yet done. If he might not give Charles money, at least he might give him

[1] No. lxxxviii.

the books which, though not equally attractive to the old soldier, he knew to be his son's delight; but after a time even the costly library thus formed frequently underwent losses, and the books he loved de Condren often sold to relieve the poor. "It is better to let my intellectual craving fast than that the poor should lack bread," he would say.

The proposed year of solitude and preparation—a prolonged Retreat virtually—was spent in the country, and at length, September 17, 1614, the great desire of his life was fulfilled, and de Condren received Priest's Orders. This was immediately followed by a retreat of three weeks, with a special view to his First Celebration. Probably its results may be held as expressed in a letter written some time later to a priest under similar circumstances.

"Take counsel with those about you," he says; "they will, I imagine, find more need to restrain and simplify your mind than to pour in anything fresh. God will fill it the more abundantly in proportion to the simple content with which you accept whatever it pleases Him to give you. Always begin your preparation by an act of purification as in the Presence of Jesus Christ (the One Sovereign Priest, and the Fountain Head of all priestly intentions) from sin, from self, and from the world—the three things which are liable to usurp His place in our hearts, and fill them by excluding Him. After an act of humiliation, of contrition, and of abnegation with respect to these three hindrances, pray that He would Himself cleanse you. It was before the First Celebration that He washed His disciples' feet, and He told S. Peter that except He should wash him he would have no part in Him. We cannot be worthily prepared for this Great Sacrifice unless He wash us in His Precious Blood, unless we spiritually cleanse ourselves therein. Then give yourself wholly to Him, to offer up the Sacrifice with His Mind and Intention, in His Name and as His representative. We should seek utterly to efface ourselves in this great act—to be merely members of Jesus Christ, offering what He offers, and doing what He does, as though we ourselves were nothing. We can never sufficiently ignore ourselves in this Sacred Office, or say simply enough with Jesus, 'This is My Body.' Next, offer Jesus to God's Divine Majesty, as a sin-offering in honour of His Greatness; as a thanksgiving for all His Blessings vouchsafed to His Church and to all creation; as a satisfaction for all offences against that Majesty; as an acknowledgment of the worship due to that Infinite Perfection, to the boundless Love of God, and as an act of reparation for all the insults men heap upon Him.

"Further, offer the Lord's Body as comprising the

Church's whole voice in prayer together with your own:—Jesus sums up in Himself and is all that we can possibly desire or ask of God, and the best and fullest prayer that we can offer is that Jesus may be perfected in us and in others. In Him is all our grace, and in Him it will be fulfilled with the greatest perfection that we can ask or seek. In Him all the holiest intentions both of the creature and the Creator are combined.

"Bear in mind too that the Sacrifice which you offer is not merely the Sacrifice of the Son of God—it is also the Sacrifice of the Head and the Members, that is to say of the Perfect Redeemer, of Jesus Christ in His Church, which is His fulness; for our Divine Head communicates His Priesthood to His Church, offering Himself with her, teaching her to offer herself with Him. 'We in Him and He in us.' At the Altar you are a partaker, a member with Him and with the Blessed Virgin, with all the Saints in Paradise, and all the faithful yet militant on earth. Hence it beseems you to forget yourself in them, and to offer the Holy Sacrifice in, for, and with them."[1]

Prescribed routine required de Condren next to return to the Sorbonne, to take his Doctor's degree, and during this sojourn in Paris he made himself remarkable by his earnest preaching—taking (under

[1] Letters, No. lxxiv.

obedience, for he always shrank from coming forward voluntarily) an Advent course or "Station" at Saint Nicholas du Chardonneret, the Lent Station at Saint Honoré, and the Octave of Corpus Christi at Saint Médard, and filling up his time—though indeed one would not imagine there could have been much to spare—by going forth to evangelise and teach among the poor population of the suburbs.

When the Collegiate forms were all fulfilled, de Condren, who had but one aim—the total dedication of his life to his Master's service—hastened to present himself before Monseigneur Hennequin, Bishop of Soissons, placing himself at his absolute disposition, and asking only to be employed in the humblest offices of the Church, wheresoever he could be of use. So little was this the usual tone of the young clergy of those days, among whom too frequently preferment and profitable office was the great object, that the Bishop received de Condren's declarations as merely a courteous way of asking for a benefice, and while giving him the reception due to his worldly position, expressed his regret that no cure of souls suitable to the young priest's connexions and expectations was at his disposal. Much distressed at being so misunderstood, de Condren endeavoured to explain that nothing was further from his wishes than to hold any benefice whatever, and that all he asked was to be usefully but humbly employed. The good bishop was not a very enthusiastic person probably, and he could not wake up to a perception of the young man's real meaning, so the interview ended by de Condren's taking leave of Monseigneur Hennequin, considerably disappointed, but trusting his future to God's Providence, prepared to do whatever His Will might indicate. To his old tutor, M. le Masson, de Condren remarked that he had hoped to be allotted the post of curate in some country parish, where he would have worked heart and soul, but he supposed he was unworthy of such a post—unfit as yet to do any real good to the souls of other men; and he then adopted as his rule, and followed to the end of his life the conviction, "when there seems no opening for any new undertaking which one desires, one should remain quietly where one is, seeking to glorify God to the utmost in the position He assigns one for the time being, until it shall please Him to call one to some fresh work."

The result of this check to de Condren's ardour was that he spent another year at the Sorbonne, during which, in spite of almost continued ill-health, attended with much real suffering, he worked indefatigably both among the poor and in hospital and prison visiting, so that some of his friends said that practically he was the curate of several parishes instead of one only! But while resolutely persevering in all this external work, a conviction was day by day deepening in de Condren's heart, that his true vocation was an interior one, and that it was in the Religious life that God meant to claim his service. While refusing no toil which was allotted to him, he treasured times of private study and meditation increasingly, and drank more and more deeply of Patristic theology and Holy Writ, which last he habitually studied on his knees. Naturally too, he frequented religious houses, pondering within himself as to what Order God would have him join. His love of poverty made him seriously think of joining the Franciscans, while the life of prayer and silence led by the Carthusians attracted his fervent spirit with powerful influence. He was in the habit of frequenting their house in Paris, and at times his desire to enter that community became very urgent, and many a day he knelt before the Blessed Sacrament offering himself to God as a follower of S. Bruno if such was His Holy Will. But somehow the answer to his fervent prayers did not lead him on in this direction—and a strong conviction was impressed on de Condren's mind that it was not in either of these Orders that God required His service. With characteristic humility, he believed this to be because he was unworthy of them, and while giving up any choice in the matter, he continued to offer himself before God for any community He might assign.

"There are four conditions on which one's mental attitude must be shaped with reference to the work of one's life," he used to say: "1. To do all things whatsoever for the love of God; 2. To be content to do nothing at all, if it is His Will; 3. To bear everything for Him; 4. To be content to have nothing to bear if He is pleased to withhold the Cross for a time."

No wonder if those who watched him took a different view from his own of de Condren's worth and powers. An official personage came to ask the venerable Head of the Sorbonne, André Duval, to send de Condren as confessor to a certain convent, implying that it was not necessary to select any one very special for a parcel of women—if a priest could hear their confessions and give them absolution, no more was needed.[1] But the old Doctor turned sharply upon his visitor, and assured him that M. de Condren was worthy of a cardinal's hat, and that no ministry could be found in the Church for which his mental capacity and personal holiness would not amply fit him. Nor was this estimate of the young priest's worth confined to those who immediately surrounded him. While he was thus labouring and praying, believing in his

[1] Even this was not necessarily what every priest could do at that period; a French Bishop a few years later declared sorrowfully that the greater number of priests in his diocese did not even know the formula of absolution!

humility that it was because of his own unworthiness that as yet he could not see plainly whither God would have him go, his vocation was being made out for him elsewhere. Père de Bérulle, Founder of the Oratory in France, had heard of de Condren, had watched him, and was deeply impressed by him, and believing that such a man would do infinite service for God in the Community he was founding, was not only praying himself, but had asked the prayers of a great number of pious people, both Religious and in the world, on behalf of his desire, *i.e.* that if it was indeed, as he believed, God's Will, de Condren might be led to the Oratory. For three years Père de Bérulle had been praying thus, when, as though in answer to his prayers, de Condren being pressed within himself by an urgent desire to come to some definite knowledge as to his vocation, it came into his mind that he would go into retreat at the Oratory, and if possible obtain the privilege of the Père de Bérulle's help during it as his spiritual guide.

No need to say that this was thankfully afforded, and during the retreat the Father's impressions were daily deepened. It was a season of severe trial at first to de Condren. Dryness and darkness, weariness, interior desolation, a seeming impossibility of seeing his Dear Lord—all these and other searching spiritual trials, such as it pleases God sometimes to lay upon

His chosen servants, came upon the young priest. He found a tender and experienced director in de Bérulle, and was able himself to say at the most trying moment of the storm: "It is well—I need not to wake my Saviour—enough that I know Him to be with us in the ship—I know that He shares every peril—and after all, while He seems to sleep, I know that His Loving Heart wakes for me."

At the end of a week the darkness passed away. Charles de Condren knelt peaceful, satisfied, in full faith before the altar, his prayers answered, his vocation decided. God had spoken within His servant's heart, and he had no longer any doubt as to whither he was called.

"Be it unto me according to Thy Word," was his answer, and on June 17, 1617, de Condren entered upon his noviciate, taking the habit of the Congregation of the Oratory on the 25th November following.[1]

[1] Archives, p. de l'Oratoire, m. 626.

CHAPTER II.

S. PHILIP NERI AND CARDINAL DE BÉRULLE.

IT was with a view to remedy the existing state of things among the clergy which is illustrated by de Condren's unsatisfactory visit to the Bishop of Soissons, that the Oratory had been founded in France by Père de Bérulle. But he was not the first founder of the Congregation. An ignorant, degenerate, too often demoralised clergy, and the abuses which as an inevitable result penetrated all sections of the Church, ecclesiastical and lay, led to the Reformation, which in its turn lowered the standard of sacerdotal dignity and reverence in many quarters. Wars of religion, luxurious courts, apostate priests—these and many another blot defiled the Bride of Christ, and as usual, the reaction stirred up the hearts of those who were "faithful unto death," and urged them on in their several ways to do whatever in them lay to counteract the overwhelming floods of misbelief and laxity, and to maintain a body of pure-minded Catholics, ready to give themselves even to death for Christ's Sake. Of such were Ignatius Loyola, S. Teresa, S. Vincent de Paul,

S. Francis de Sales, and S. Philip Neri, the first founder of the Oratorians.

There is something peculiarly attractive in the character of "sweet Father Philip," as it reaches us. He was a Florentine of noble family, born in 1515; and even in his boyish days, when he delighted to relieve the monotony of school hours by visiting the celebrated Convent of San Marco in Florence, drinking in holy thoughts and visions from Fra Angelico's marvellous frescoes, he was familiarly known as "il buon Pippo"— so pure and earnest were his ways. Sent when eighteen to Naples, in order that he might become partner and heir to a wealthy merchant uncle, Philip gave the world a fair trial for two years, and then, with the same bright cheerfulness which marked all his actions, he severed himself from all his brilliant earthly prospects, and travelled on foot to Rome, begging his bread as he went, "for the love of holy poverty." The ascetic and devout life which he led there, feeding on vegetables and fruit, studying theology with ardour, and yet praying even more than he

[1] Throughout his long life, S. Philip Neri practised an abstinence which he would not permit his spiritual children to imitate. He used to say with a smile, that he was "afraid of growing fat!" but to the other Oratorians he enjoined eating what was set before them, sometimes saying that it was better to take a little more rather than a little less, as those who ruined their health by prolonged insufficient nourishment could very rarely make up the lost ground."—Vie de S. P. Neri, Abbé Bayle, p. 226.

studied, was not with a view to preparation for Holy Orders—for that Philip held himself all unworthy—he only aimed at offering his own body and soul in daily sacrifice to God, and forwarding the purification and sanctification of the world so far as the pure and holy life of each separate individual, lay or ecclesiastic, must do. After a time, finding that his best school was devout meditation and communing with God, he sold his library, all save the Bible and Summa of S. Thomas, and gave the proceeds to the poor. It was at this time that his heart was said to have been so dilated by love of God and man as to have materially altered his physical conformation. "He was so carried out of himself by the Love of God, his zeal was so mighty and so vast, that the world itself was too small to fill his heart, while that heart itself was too narrow to contain the immensity of his love." So writes the Eagle of Meaux of S. Philip Neri.[1]

Such a man surely had a special work to do in the Church, and in humility yielding to the call of God and the advice of his spiritual superiors, Philip was ordained Priest in 1551, when aged thirty-six.

Already a few priests in Rome had joined together in a sort of Confraternity, the object of which was mutual edification and support. Philip Neri soon became one of them, and under guidance he devoted

[1] Oraison Funèbre, P. Bourgoing. Bossuet, Œuvres, xii. 649.

himself chiefly to the confessional, where nearly all his days, and not unfrequently a large part of his nights too, were spent. "I do not wish to call any hour my own, or even any moment," he was wont to say. His special gift was in dealing with young men. The natural freshness and beauty of his own mind both attracted him to the young and exercised a singular fascination over them; the playful mirth and poetic grace which bubbled up in his pure and loving heart was such a contrast to the careworn earthly absorption or meretricious worldly gaiety of most men, that they hung around him spell-bound. The grass plot on Monte Janiculo, near to San Onofrio, where S. Philip Neri used to resort with his goodly company of young companions, and where he promoted their games, shared their confidences and wild imaginations, and led them on to the Love of God with the wiles of true human love, may still be seen—or might—in the Rome we have all known and loved; that Rome of which one of S. Philip's worthiest descendants, Henri Perreyve, says, "It is really a dreadful thing to have lived two years running in Rome! Henceforward every day brings back anniversaries which plunge one's heart into whole oceans of longings and regrets!"[1]

[1] Lettres, 2nd edit. p. 269. "Vous êtes donc à Rome? C'est terrible, savez-vous, que d'habiter deux années de suite à Rome! Chaque jour ensuite ramène ces anniversaires qui jettent l'âme dans des océans de regrets et de désirs!"

These outpourings of intimacy and fellowship were not all. The young men who thus gathered round Philip Neri for the pleasure of his society, also gathered round him for instruction, and he was soon obliged to seek a spacious hall to receive all who sought to profit by his teaching. This was informal. They read aloud, they discussed difficulties, they prepared little orations—Baronius, the celebrated historian, brought his historical learning to bear upon the subject in hand,—they sang hymns and motets, composed and led by Palestrina, who was one of Philip's disciples; and from these gatherings, and the musical performances he encouraged at them, we derive our name "Oratorio" for the sacred musical dramas, which are now once more beginning to be used as S. Philip Neri used them, not merely for the delectation of musical taste and criticism, but as an expression of, and stimulus to, devotion and fervour. Such was the beginning of the Oratory, and the few priests who first lived together at San Geronimo were its first members. It is amusing to read of learned men going to consult the already famous Baronius, and finding him washing the dishes or preparing the homely meals of the little Congregation[1]—for into a Congregation the rapidly

[1] Baronius wrote playfully over the chimney of the kitchen where he displayed his culinary powers, "Cesar Baronius, coquus perpetuus;" but in mercy to the digestion of his brother Oratorians it is a comfort to know that his office was *not* perpetual !

increasing band developed; and in 1575 Pope Gregory XIII. gave them canonical authorisation as such, and assigned them Santa-Maria-in-Vallicelli, as their church. They were then upwards of 130 in number. The spirit of their Congregation was liberty, mutual help, zeal for souls. They had few rules—they lived and prayed together, they sought to support and edify one another by good example, to give strength to isolated exertions by companionship and sympathy. They set a perfect fulfilment of the priestly life and office before them as their aim and object, and while neglecting none of the bodily or spiritual necessities to which it behoves Christ's servants to minister, they specially devoted themselves to the spiritual welfare of men and boys—seeking to win the young from the snares of sinful pleasure by teaching them the charms of holiness and charity, by making religion lovely and winning in every possible way, by using the gifts God gives to man—music, painting, beauty in art and nature of every kind, to draw souls to the Source of all Beauty. Such was the aim of S. Philip and his Congregation of Oratorians:

"Omnia vestra in caritate fiant."

It was not intended as a new Religious Order. S. Philip Neri believed that there were already sufficient Orders in existence, and he continually repeated his wish that his Congregation should be secular priests, free from vows and special obligations. "His object," writes one of his descendants, "was, above all, to form a congregation in which, amid a licentious corrupt world, men might follow the path which leads to a blessed Eternity, but without leading an austere life, without severe bodily mortifications, without wholly severing themselves from earthly ties; rather following a moderate line, adopting pious habits, and using earthly things well and wisely. Any one who studies this object as the keynote to the whole will see that it is of the very essence of our Congregation to maintain a happy medium among extremes. Its chief merit is its moderation."[1] When certain members of the new Congregation wished to introduce vows, S. Philip, though strongly against any such introduction, referred the question to the Pope, who emphatically decided against them. Not that this implied any excessive liberty. There were certain simple rules which were voluntarily accepted by the members of the Congregation, and thenceforth steadily and conscientiously kept. Such involved the obligation always to seek personal sanctification and the edification of others by diligent exercise of the Christian graces—obedience, humility, poverty, simplicity, and charity. Liberty and obedience to rule were

[1] Abbé Bayle, Vie, p. 188.

closely and inseparably bound up together, so that when S. Carlo Borromeo visited the Oratory he inquired admiringly of the Founder how he obtained such obedience as he—the Cardinal Archbishop—never had been able to win from his priests? " I impose but few commands," was the answer; "a Superior's example does more than any words and rules. The best way of ruling anybody subject to one is to do oneself that which one requires of them." He objected to a community of goods in his Congregation, and when certain members thereof brought him a memorial asking to establish it among the Fathers, S. Philip wrote in the margin, "Habeant, possideant."[1]

While inculcating simplicity and frugality, he was also strict as to neatness and personal cleanliness, often quoting S. Bernard, who said that he had "always loved poverty, but dirt never!"

The Superior was to be elected every three years, but, by common consent, the Congregation elected their Founder as Superior for life, and he fulfilled the office till two years before his death, when, by reason of his advanced age, he induced his spiritual sons to elect Cesar Baronius in his stead. The celebrated author of the Annales has written at length upon the objects of his Congregation, and the summary of these, as gathered together by a distinguished living

[1] Vie, p. 192.

member of the Oratoire de France, seems so well fitted to the existing needs of the Church in the nineteenth century also, that it may well be quoted: "To wrestle against the errors which assail faith by seizing their own weapons and turning these against themselves; to set against a false, exclusive, self-seeking science, the most loyally true, the most liberal, the most disinterested learning: never to allow the enemy to pitch his tents and take possession of any point of human intelligence, but apostle-like, to send forth missionaries into every branch of science, shedding upon all the light of revelation, and constraining all to promote the advance of Christ's Kingdom; to accept this permanent struggle under whatever changing circumstances may arise in different periods and different stages of civilisation; to become all things to all men, in order to win every mind to the faith, every heart to the Love of Jesus Christ; and, as a necessary consequence, to do battle one while on the platform of Holy Scripture and Biblical exegesis, another while on that of philosophy, history, or natural science; or again, if need be, to track the winding evolutions of modern thought, refusing to allow antichristian science to confiscate the domain of social and political science, and monopolise it on behalf of reason, as revolting against faith; and to this end, unremittingly, never discouraged, never wearied, to go on blending prayer with study, sanctifying labour by meditation; spreading out to reach all wants, and reducing the discordant notes of mere human learning to the great harmony of the One glorious Gospel of Christ. Such is the course which, in his far-seeing solicitude for the interests of truth, S. Philip laid down for the members of the Oratory amidst the impassioned strifes of the sixteenth century."[1]

It is a course which has been filially pursued by S. Philip's descendants, amid whom occur many names well known to science and literature, worthy of their great predecessors—such as Cardinal de Bérulle, de Condren, Eudes, Bourgoing, Senault, Gault Bishop of Marseilles, Malebranche, Thomassin, Mascaron, Massillon, Houbigant, Gratry, Perreyve, Perraud, and others—not to speak of other nationalities.

S. Philip Neri repeatedly declined a Cardinal's hat, and endeavoured with a persistency difficult to realize for such as ourselves, to shun everything approaching to honour or even any reputation for holiness or wisdom. He died May 26, 1595, at the age of eighty, surrounded by his faithful children in the faith. Just twenty years before, Pierre de Bérulle, destined by God to carry the work of the Oratory into France, was born, on February 4, 1575, one year earlier than S. Vincent

[1] L'Oratoire de France, P. Adolphe Perraud, p. 24.

de Paul, who in his turn was to do so great a work among the Clergy of France. De Bérulle had a strong vocation to the religious life, and being educated by the Jesuit Fathers—his director a Carthusian, and his dearest friend, the confidant of all his thoughts and aspirations, a Capucin monk—it might have seemed probable that he would have joined one or other of those Orders. But God had other work in store for him, and after making due proof of his vocation in each, de Bérulle was counselled both by his Carthusian director and the Provincial of the Jesuits to wait and see to what destiny God was reserving him, for clearly none of these was his resting-place—much as he prized them all;—neither these or any other religious Order corresponded entirely to his needs, whether of grace or nature. Ordained in 1599, de Bérulle gave himself zealously to the work immediately pressing upon him in Paris. His success among the Huguenots was great, and he made many conversions; so that Cardinal du Perron made one of his telling remarks, so often quoted, "If you want to *convince* a heretic, bring him to me; if you want to *convert* him, take him to M. de Genève [Francis de Sales]; but if you want both to convince and convert him at once, take him to M. de Bérulle!"

Henri IV. conceived one of his hearty likings for the young Priest, whose controversial talents interested him; and he successively pressed the Bishoprics of Laon, Nantes and Luçon, and the Archbishopric of Lyons upon him. It is always hard for great people to understand a man's indifference to position and wealth, and Henri IV. was not a little perplexed at de Bérulle's steady refusal of all his offers. " You will not receive what I offer?" the King said petulantly one day, " then I shall get some one else to order you to do so !" meaning, of course, the Pope. " Sire," de Bérulle answered, " if your Majesty presses me thus, I shall be constrained to quit your kingdom." The King turned to Bellegarde, saying, " I have done everything in my power to tempt him and have failed; I don't believe there is another man in the world who would resist so firmly!"[1] " As to that man," he used henceforth to say, " he is a very saint, he has never lost his baptismal innocence !"

Long before his ordination de Bérulle had been an intimate friend of Madame Acarie, and had known all her wishes concerning the Carmelites, and her ardent desire to bring the reformed daughters of S. Teresa into France; and when at last the wise and holy men with whom her counsels were shared decided that the time had come for making the attempt, it was agreed to send M. de Bérulle to Spain with the object of bringing a colony of Carmelites to Paris. It was a

[1] Vie S. V. de Paul, Maynard, i. 63.

wearisome, difficult task, so many hindrances sprang up, so much opposition; but after patiently bearing with all, the work was accomplished, and de Bérulle took charge of the Order in France as Superior General. This however was not to be his great sphere of labour for God. The condition of the Clergy in France at this time was such as to fill the heart of any devout man like de Bérulle with consternation. Vincent de Paul said that he had found numerous priests whose ignorance was so great that they could not say mass correctly, and did not know the ordinary form of absolution. A Bishop writing at that period was forced to say, "I shudder to think that at this moment there are some seven thousand priests in my diocese either drunkards or of impure life—utterly without vocation;" and another Bishop wrote, "Except the *chanoine théologue* belonging to my church, there is not a priest in my diocese capable of any ecclesiastical office."[1] "You are a mere priest!" was a common form of reproach, Abelly says, at that time, and Amelote says that the world held the name to be synonymous with ignorance and debauchery. Such a state of things could not fail to press heavily on a man such as de Bérulle; nor was he one likely to rest satisfied with deploring an evil unless he were also striving to remedy it.

[1] Vie S. Vt. de Paul, vol. ii. p. 11.

Two years after his ordination, de Bérulle was saying his office, when one of those peculiar and unaccountable impressions which most of us have experienced some time or other was made upon him as he repeated the words, "Annuntiate inter gentes studia ejus," "O praise the Lord Which dwelleth in Sion; shew the people of His doings." (Ps. ix. 11.) A strong desire was kindled in his mind to see a company of priests arise whose mission should be to preach and teach the Love of God among all people, and from that time he kept in view the aim of beginning such a work, discussing it with his most intimate friends, among others a saintly woman, Madlle. de Fontaines-Marans, later a Carmelite nun. Like S. Philip Neri, he did not wish to found a new religious Order, nor even a regular Congregation bound by the three vows. The Congregation which de Bérulle wished to see at work was to be altogether priestly, and in nowise monastic. The priesthood is not essential to a monk's profession; but all members of this Congregation were to be priests, and their Ordination vows alone should bind them, the Bishops should be their superiors. Such, he thought, was the most likely way to achieve his object,—the revival of discipline and spirituality among the clergy of France. The Oratory seemed to fulfil all that he desired, and after some years of mature deliberation and prayer, a French Congregation bearing that name, and substantially the same as that of S. Philip Neri, was founded.[1]

De Bérulle had neither the wish nor intention of being himself the Superior of his Congregation. Admiring and reverencing Francis de Sales as he did, and knowing how earnestly he had the reformation of the Clergy at heart, he hoped for a time to induce the Bishop of Geneva to be founder and head of the work. But the Bishop was not to be persuaded; and later on, when certain persons found fault with him for devoting himself to the Order of the Visitation, saying that his time would have been much better bestowed on training Clergy, he answered that "God's faithful servant, M. de Bérulle, was much fitter for that work than he, and was doing it well," adding, with characteristic humility, "I am disposed to leave great undertakings to great men."[2] He used sometimes to say that if he were to begin wishing to be anybody else rather than himself, he should wish to be M. de Bérulle, and that he would very gladly

[1] The first Oratorians, as founded by S. Philip, were entirely local—each house independent of all other houses, having its own superior and noviciate, but de Bérulle's opinions as to the needs of France, and perhaps too the national tendency to centralisation, led him to alter this part of the Italian system, and to concentrate the government of all French Oratories under one Superior-General.

[2] Spirit of S. Francis de Sales, p. 384.

leave his present condition in order to live under that saintly man's guidance.

De Bérulle tried to find other heads for the Congregation, and was only at last overruled by the Archbishop of Paris, de Retz, to take the responsibility himself. At length, on the eve of S. Martin's Day —November 11, 1611—six priests took possession of a small house, the Maison du Petit Bourbon, in the Faubourg S. Jacques. The following morning Madame Acarie and two other devout women communicated in the new Oratory; the six members spent their morning in prayer, and thenceforward led a community life—but all their rules and customs were gradually planned and discussed, rather than entered upon at once.

In one of his early Conferences de Bérulle sets forth the obligation of the Priesthood as of Divine Institution, *i.e.* to aim at the highest standard of perfection, the Example of Christ; to look upon every priest as the channel of His Grace and Mind, and therefore bound to set them forth in his life and his whole conduct, seeking above all else to promote Christ's Kingdom among men; and further, the obligation to preserve and confirm that special union with our Dear Lord, which He vouchsafes to His faithful ministers as the very centre point of all their strength—the essential quality of a power greater than that committed to the Angels of Heaven.

"We must ever remember," he says, "that one of the offices of our Lord Jesus Christ is His Eternal Priesthood, such as none else can hold; therefore we must always recognise Him as our Founder and Chief; we must refer whatever good we may be enabled to do to Him, as the sacred and abundant Source of all good." The letters patent of the Congregation describe the Oratory as "a Congregation of priests living together, with the main object of promoting primitive perfection in the priesthood, of teaching the doctrine of Jesus Christ in town and country, undertaking whatsoever ecclesiastical functions their Bishop may assign to them, superintending whatever good works he may commit to their care, and generally doing their best to make a good use of the Grace of God committed to them in the holy office of the priesthood."

In May 1613, the Oratorians received Pope Paul V.'s Bull solemnly confirming their Congregation. This Bull expresses that the object of the Congregation "is to be composed of pious priests, specially devoted to fulfilling the duties of the sacerdotal life with the utmost attainable perfection, . . . bound as they are by the closest ties to Jesus Christ, our High Priest Eternal according to the order of Melchisedek, the Chief and Head of all Christian Priesthood." The name of Oratory was to be taken in honour of the Divine Redeemer's prayers during His earthly sojourn; the members professing a special devotion to the memory of His nights and days spent in prayer for mankind. The Congregation was to live together, subject to rule, in a constant spirit of humility, as the servants of the Most High; to be subject to the Bishops in their ministerial work; and in cultivating science and learning, their object was to be less that of seeking these for their own sakes than for the use to which such knowledge can be applied in the service of Christ.[1]

The Oratory increased rapidly, branch houses were established in various quarters, and their numbers increased in 1619, when a considerable part of Cesar de Bus' Congregation, known as the "Doctrinaires," joined the Oratorians. In their early days they had retained the ordinary prefix of Monsieur—soon however they took the title of Father; and in order to stifle any pride of birth and high name, de Bérulle decided that the Fathers should only be distinguished by their baptismal names. Eventually this could not be continued.

In the early beginnings of the Oratory, Vincent de Paul came to Paris, sent on a political mission from

[1] "Sacerdotum insuper aliorum ad sacros ordines aspirantium instructioni, non circa scientiam, sed circa usum scientiæ."

Rome, and he and de Bérulle first met in the Hospital of la Charité, where both were labouring for God among His suffering children. S. Vincent's supernatural gift of charity had already begun to make itself felt, and de Bérulle was anxious to know one whose heart was so akin to his own. They quickly contracted a warm and lasting friendship, and S. Vincent, who was anxious to escape from the perilous notice and honour which were already gathering round him, as well as from the flattering proposals of office and position coming from the Court, sought shelter in the Oratory, not with the intention of becoming a member of the Congregation—for though yet unshaped in his mind as to this his future vocation, S. Vincent felt that God was leading him on towards a definite work, in the same direction with, yet apart from, that of de Bérulle—but as a retreat from the world, and in order to benefit by the spiritual advice and guidance of de Bérulle, who had no small part in developing his plans, and leading him onwards in the great work of his Mission.

For two years S. Vincent remained at the Petit Bourbon in the Faubourg S. Jacques, during which time its Superior-General became confirmed in the opinion that he was destined to a great work for God in training the Clergy to a higher standard, and though for a while other works took precedence of this in

S. Vincent's career, the first seeds of the Mission may justly be considered as having been sown there. When S. Vincent left the Oratory, it was in compliance with the request of de Bérulle, who wanted to find a fitting successor to François Bourgoing, parish priest of Clichy, then about to join the Oratory. S. Vincent undertook the charge with hesitation and misgivings as to his own fitness for its responsibilities, which for a time he fulfilled with his usual devotion and ardour. He rebuilt the church of Clichy, which remains now substantially as he left it.[1]

[1] Vie S. V. de Paul, Abelly, ii. 24, Collet, i. 35.

CHAPTER III.

DE CONDREN'S INNER LIFE AND LETTERS.

SUCH was the Congregation in which Charles de Condren found his appointed work, and of which he proved one of the most valuable members. Père de Bérulle had not over-estimated the merit of his new associate. At the end of his first year, de Condren was sent to found a house at Nevers; in 1619 another foundation at Langres was committed to his hands; and in 1621 a third at Poitiers. A letter from thence to his former tutor, M. Masson, expresses de Condren's mind as to all his various destinations.

"I believe I am to be here for some months, possibly longer. God is everywhere, and there is no place whence one cannot see Heaven and work for the Church, so that all abodes alike should be acceptable to those who seek God Only, and aim only to reach Heaven. A Christian is satisfied everywhere, so long as he knows that he has no earthly dwelling-place save wheresoever God sends him to serve His

Church. So you are content to serve Him at Soissons in prayer and works of charity for souls; and I am content for the present, and for as long as God pleases, to be at Poitiers. We are in absolute peace in the midst of surrounding war, of which however scarce even the rumours reach us; and in truth it does not beseem us to busy ourselves about the news of the day."[1]

Before long, however, Père de Condren was recalled to Paris, in order that he might be Superior of the Séminaire de Saint Magloire,—the first attempt at a, strictly speaking, Theological College, having for its special object to train and fit men for the office of the Priesthood. This was the first link in the chain of providential circumstances which led to the foundation of the great work, the Seminary of Saint Sulpice, though as yet de Condren and his spiritual son, Jean Jacques Olier, had not been brought together.

The time during which de Condren governed this new house was one of extreme trial to his own soul. That strange struggle which is so often permitted by God's all-wise Love to beset His chosen servants came upon the Father. Once he had been full of light and joy, conscious of and rejoicing in an abiding quickening sense of God's Presence; but now darkness, dryness, and a deadly oppression banished this happiness.

[1] Lettres, xcix.

All his vast stores of learning, theological and other, so needful to his present work, seemed lost, and a kind of mental paralysis fettered his thoughts. He might hunt vainly after an idea, or a train of reasoning, the livelong day, for all his intellectual faculties were numbed. Meanwhile he had to give constant lectures to the students of Saint Magloire, to preach in their chapel (and it had become the fashion for royalty and the Court, as well as for the faithful generally, to attend the Oratorians' services), and to deal with a multitude of souls who brought their troubles and perplexities, individual and ecclesiastical, to him.

Père de Condren entreated the Superior, de Bérulle, to allow him to resign the office he felt so unequal to exercise, but in vain. Père de Bérulle, himself so deeply versed in the mysteries of the hidden life, knew well that, amid all this dryness and desolation and seeming incapacity, a great work was going on both in de Condren's soul, and through him upon those who listened to his instructions. After this it became a matter of obedience to persevere; but de Condren said that every time he was going to preach he expected utterly to break down, and he habitually offered to God the humiliating failure he felt likely to make.

"I used to go into the pulpit," he said, "with such a total want of mental perceptions, that I had not the least idea how to begin; and when God vouchsafed me some good thought, I did not know at all how to go on, or what to say next."[1] But nevertheless the preacher did not betray this inward distress to his auditors. There was never the slightest incoherence or hesitation to betray his secret discomfort, and while himself conscious of nothing but dulness and dryness, his words conveyed light and life to the souls he taught.

Other spiritual trials, active as well as passive, were added to these which beset his intellectual being, temptations which sometimes are so mysteriously permitted to beset the pure in heart, and which led him to think himself unworthy to approach the Altar of God. These temptations were hidden in the depths of his own sorrowful spirit, but it pleased God to make known to two saintly persons that de Condren was thus suffering, and that his sufferings were wholly free from sin; neither should he abstain from celebrating the Blessed Sacrifice because of his conscious unworthiness. The Religious to whom this communication was made imparted it to de Condren, who, amazed at so minute and detailed a knowledge of his unspoken troubles, such as could come only from a special design of God's Providence, accepted the lesson with the utmost humility, and obliged the per-

[1] Vie, Amelote, p. 135.

son in question to give him a faithful account of all God's message, himself listening to it on his knees. From that time he fulfilled all the duties of which he still felt so unworthy, endeavouring, as he said, to "suffer in holiness."

Unfortunately none of de Condren's published letters are dated, and it is only by the help of internal evidence that one can refer them to their rightful period. It seems probable, however, that it was during this season of spiritual trial that he wrote to one under his direction as follows :—

"Be content that God should be God in all things, and that being to you, as He is, a Jealous God, He should not tolerate any rival. Give yourself up to God in Jesus Christ, and to Jesus Christ in union with His own abandonment to His Father; so that, divesting yourself of any desire to live for yourself, or to be anything whatsoever, your sole wish may be that God should dwell in you, and that He may guide you with reference to all things whatsoever. . . . . Your being should be wholly absorbed in Him, there must be nothing left for the creature, less still for yourself; the consummation of all things should be for you in Jesus Christ through the Holy Spirit—in short, in God—His directing, guiding, perfecting Hand. You have nothing to do save to give yourself up to His Will with respect to you, willing only what

He wills, desiring only His Glory, until all things are swallowed up in the unity of that Glory."[1]

After a time these distressing trials and temptations were removed, and not unnaturally de Condren's gifts and powers in the guidance of souls were found to have increased greatly through their sharp discipline. From this time he seems to have been endowed with a very remarkable power of reading souls, and of making God's Ways plain to those who sought to advance in the interior life.

About this time the marriage of Henrietta Maria of France with King Charles I. of England was in contemplation, and Père de Bérulle was chosen by Louis XIII. to go to Rome and negotiate the necessary dispensations, after which he was sent to England as the Queen's Confessor, whence, however, Louis XIII. recalled him in three months to assist in certain complicated negotiations concerning the Valtelline. The King was anxious that this chosen counsellor should obtain a Cardinal's hat, and in spite of Père de Bérulle's sincere entreaties that he might be excused bearing this dignity, it was conferred upon him by Pope Urban VIII. in August 1627.

"The courier who was taking these tidings to the Court, then at Saint Germain," (say the Annals of the Congregation,) "left a note as he passed for our

[1] Lettres, iv.

General, containing the announcement. One of our Fathers happened to be with the R. P. General when he read the note. Seeing him after reading it kneel down in prayer, from which he rose with a sorrowful downcast expression, the Father asked 'What is the matter? You seem troubled. Have the English taken the Ile de Ré?' The General only answered, 'No, thank God, nothing of that sort has happened;' and without saying anything more he began again to pray, and remained so occupied until the arrival of the Nuncio who brought official tidings that he was a Cardinal."[1]

It was in 1625, when the General of the Congregation began to be so much occupied by external duties, that he recalled de Condren from S. Magloire to the Mother House in the Rue Saint Honoré, and to those who knew them both it was no surprise to see the elder man place himself under Père de Condren's direction. He was wont to say of the latter that "he must have been born imbued with the spirit of the Oratory," and he used to remark that " while the Congregation obeyed its General, that General obeyed Père de Condren." So great was his veneration for his saintly disciple, that as he passed Père de Condren's room Cardinal de Bérulle would kneel down and kiss the floor where he was wont to tread.

[1] Vie du Père de Bérulle, p. 60.

The Father's direction was sought largely. Men of the world, men of science, proud of their own attainments, met with a mind fully able to cope with them in the humble Oratorian. His extensive reading, assisted by his marvellous memory, gave him a very unusual command over most subjects, literary, philosophical, or scientific, and all his knowledge was held as a trust from God, to be faithfully used in His Service, for which due account must be rendered hereafter. How entirely this was the controlling motive of his mind may be seen in a letter on the subject of study to a friend.

"I would that we were all holy enough to desire no knowledge save to know Jesus Christ according to S. Paul's words, 'Non judicari me scire aliquid inter vos nisi Jesum Christum, et hunc crucifixum.'[1] He realised that all the knowledge of this world will perish before the Judgment of God, when nothing will endure save Jesus Christ, and that which has come forth from Him. Men have given birth to their various schools and systems, but all these will perish with them. Latin and Greek came forth from Babel, like other tongues; they were the offspring of sin, and they will perish when sin is done away with for ever. Even the study of God's

[1] "I determined to know nothing among you save Jesus Christ and Him Crucified." 1 Cor. ii. 2.

Works, the knowledge of His Creation, from Heaven to earth, from the cedar of Lebanon to the hyssop, was owned to be but empty and vain, a mere weariness of the spirit, by the Wise King whom it pleased God to enlighten. If we were to be gifted with the like Spirit of Divine Wisdom, we should see it as he did, and it would be a weariness to us to apply to anything save to Jesus Christ, instead of delighting and finding satisfaction in other studies. An excessive devotion to human science is too common a blot among literary people, who therein rather imitate what Solomon called the vanity of vanities than the wiser conclusions he came to under the guidance of the Holy Spirit. But we are Christians by God's Mercy, and more bound than was Solomon to despise the world and its wisdom. We know as he did not that Jesus Christ Alone is the Science of Saints, we are disciples in God's school, wherein we receive Jesus Christ the True Wisdom, and we must learn that all else is vanity and vexation of spirit.

"I do not say all this with a view to deter you from study, but rather to lead you to study after a Christian fashion, and without losing sight of the pure instinct of the Spirit of God. I say it to prevent you from yielding too far to the vanity of human intellect, or the love of profane literature, which cannot be blameless in any soul dedicated to God, but which is specially to be avoided in the case of us who are priests, and who as such are set apart to the Lord. By our priestly consecration we separated ourselves from all profane and even all purely secular interests, in order that we might minister at God's Altar, teach His Wisdom to the world, do His Work in it, stablish His Kingdom, and above all cause Jesus Christ to live in the hearts of our people. We must not withdraw from these holy duties for the sake of any delight whatsoever in secular literature; it would be a distinct damage to our sacred calling. Therefore the first rule you should adopt in your studies is not to let yourself be led away by them, not to seek your greatest happiness in them, not to make them your chief object, not to prefer them to your heavenly birthright, not to look upon them as the most important kind of knowledge after which you are bound to aspire, since they are but human. On the contrary, you should count the trammels of secular learning as a humiliation which your intellectual being has to endure willingly for the Love and in honour of the Son of God, Who vouchsafed to come on earth and to lay aside His Divine Omniscience in order to use the language and thoughts of men.[1] Such an attitude

[1] Rom. viii. 23.
"For the thoughts of mortal men are miserable, and our devices are but uncertain. For the corruptible body presseth down the soul, and the earthly tabernacle weigheth down the

of mind in study with respect to Him Who came among us 'in similitudinem carnis peccati,' will preserve you from danger.

"Our one first aim will be to serve God Alone, to live in Him solely, to keep apart from earthly things. But if we give ourselves heartily to our Dear Lord, entering into the spirit of His Incarnation, we shall, without losing anything of that original attitude, go forth as He came forth from the Father, and apply ourselves to earthly matters; hearken to the words of men, albeit sinners, learn their languages and accept rather with patience than with self-seeking or complacency such application to secular studies as is needful for God's Glory. But in order to do this in holiness and according to the Mind of Christ we must give ourselves wholly to Him, and entreat of Him to keep us free from self-esteem, and the other mental infirmities which beset those much given to literary pursuits.

"Our reverend Father and honoured Founder was always very anxious that since it has pleased God to give our Congregations educational work to do, it

---

mind that museth on many things. And hardly do we guess aright at things that are upon earth, and with labour do we find the things that are before us; but the things that are in Heaven who hath searched out? And Thy counsel who hath known, except Thou give wisdom, and send Thy Holy Spirit from above?" Wisdom ix. 14-18.

should be done in the Spirit of His Dear Son; I feel bound to urge his wishes upon you, and to warn you against allowing your studies ever to diminish aught of that Spirit or of His Grace in you."[1]

And again,—

"You will never find any real settled peace so long as you delight in study and science out of mere self-love. Christ cannot endure any ruling motive save His Own pure Love in the hearts He cherishes and guides. While working diligently at the studies which are necessary to your earthly calling, you must inwardly long for the blessedness of the future life, wherein God will be our Light and Knowledge. Study is but a consequence of our fallen life and a humiliation arising out of our fallen nature which has lost its original light. We ought to study in a humble spirit, and nothing that our own understanding requires or men teach us should usurp God's place in the heart. If you feel that the vain love of science is getting hold of you, turn to God and resolve that He Alone shall be your Light and your Glory— the sole Object of your satisfaction and rest. It is of His Mercy that He will not permit your mind to find rest elsewhere than in Him. If He left you to yourself your studies would engross you and distract you from Him, as they have done with many another, without

[1] Lettres, vi.

your realising the mischief that was at work. Look upon study as a necessary labour in your present condition, to be borne with in a penitential spirit, the object of which is rather to give God glory than to make you learned. Do not be disturbed if you are beset by the love of learning, although you are striving to be detached from it. Be satisfied to renounce self in the matter from time to time, and for the rest wait in humble patience till God gives you the grace of perfect detachment."[1]

Elsewhere, writing to the members of a branch house concerning their duties as students, he says, " If we have Cicero on our lips, at all events let us strive to have Jesus Christ in our heart, and a great zeal for souls in our will. Let us not be filled with the love of profane elegance in literature, but let us therewith combine the love of simplicity and Christian humility. Let Jesus be the God of all the studies in your house. . . . We must not make a mere Parnassus of His house of prayer, His Oratory. Secular studies should be no more than one way of practising charity to us, and we should make these exterior works a means of winning souls, whose salvation is the great desire of the Saviour. True Christian perfection, far from despising such means of benefiting one's neighbour and of glorifying God, seizes them gladly, and turns

[1] Lettres, No. cvi.

them to a good purpose, working them earnestly and boldly. But to do this, you must drink deep of this spirit of charity, at its Fountain Head, Jesus Christ —in order to be able to carry out such work in the true sense of sacrifice—in His Name, and to remain uninjured by the vanity of human intellect in study.

"Of old heathen poets and philosophers invoked Apollo and the Muses, and verily the Evil One, worshipped under such names, inspired them frequently with vanity and licentiousness. But in the school of Jesus we must know no inspiring '*furore*' save the fervour of His Love, nor any guiding spirit in our studies save Himself. We must walk by His Light, Who is the God of Truth, and rely upon His Help, the rather that His Love is as boundless as His Ruling Power. Let us work in that Strength, with full confidence and a hearty diligence worthy of Him and His Love, on behalf of those who come to us for instruction. It would be a fault worthy of His Judgment, if we were to be more careless or slothful in the studies which He assigns as our duty, and to which His Holy Spirit calls us, than were heathen men of old in their schools where false gods only were invoked."[1]

But while Père de Condren's learning and wisdom

[1] Lettres, vii.

were so great that Cardinal de Bérulle was wont to write down his sayings on his knees; and Saint Vincent de Paul declared that "there was no one like him—*non est inventus similis illi;*" and Sainte Jeanne de Chantal was heard to say that "if God had sent Francis de Sales to teach men, Père de Condren seemed fit to teach the Angels;"[1] the Oratorian Father himself was as ready to devote the vast stores of his spiritual mind to the humblest as to the most elevated of souls.

"God made de Condren expressly for the Saints," wrote Cloysault, "and gifted him with the power of leading them to the highest perfection; there was no path of holiness too marvellous for his immediate apprehension, and indeed he was so versed in such ways that he used to say he believed there to be as many saints living in our day, though more secretly, as in the primitive times of the Church."[2]

There was all the difference between him and most other men, it has been remarked, that there is between one who relates to you the things he has seen with his own eyes and one who only repeats what he has been told. Naturally this deep personal insight into spiritual things gave him great perception not merely of ordinary character, but of the spiritual mind and capacity

---

[1] Vie de M. Olier, p. 60. [2] Vie, Abbé Pin, p. 144.

of those he had to deal with, but so far from relying in any way on this, de Condren was always slow to accept the direction of souls. He held that the One Sole Director is God, and he was unwilling to assume that he was God's chosen delegate in the direction of any individual soul, until much prayer on both sides confirmed the belief that it was so. " They could find endless earnest men every one of whom is fitter than me for the office ; " he was wont to say. But when once the office was undertaken, its duties were most faithfully performed, as a direct trust from God. His great object was to teach his penitents to look from him to Jesus Christ as their real Director, and it was remarked that while Père de Condren's holiness and gentleness and exceeding sympathy bound his spiritual children to him with the strongest ties, he never yielded to any of the natural affection which so often binds souls together, and the real love which he felt for them was singularly governed by an almost unearthly detachment. " He loved them," says one of his biographers, (after remarking that de Condren's spiritual children were freer from all natural clingings and attachments to their director than is usual;) " solely in and for God, and thus either their natural affection for him died out for lack of meeting any return, and so they left him, or more frequently it became purified and supernaturalised, similarly to his affection for them. The result was, that while loving his spiritual children with a boundless love, he was perfectly detached from them, and they from him."[1]

There is certainly something warmer and more attractive in the winning demonstrative affection shewn by S. Francis de Sales or S. Vincent de Paul for those under their guidance, and human nature somewhat recoils from the process by which de Condren caused his penitents to attain to such exceeding detachment. Possibly the eager, warm-hearted Sainte Jeanne de Chantal had some such thought when she spoke of her own beloved spiritual Father as sent to guide men and women, while Père de Condren was fit to deal with angels; and some hearts may feel that warm human affection visibly displayed and felt has helped them the better to draw near, and realize the exceeding vastness of that Love which permits, nay encourages, such an intensely familiar approach from the creature It has created and redeemed. It is impossible to deny that the glowing words of affection which fell from Francis de Sales' pen the moment that he took it up to address a child in the faith, draw one in a more confiding spirit to him than the grave, measured, utterly undemonstrative letters of Père de Condren, amid which anything like an expression of affection can rarely be found. But S. Paul has said that "there are diver-

[1] Vie, Pin, p. 148.

sities of gifts, but the same Spirit, differences of administrations, but the same Lord, diversities of operations, but it is the Same God which worketh all in all" (1 Cor. xii. 4); and doubtless those souls, which through the seemingly chilling system of the one holy man, yet attained the goal we all seek, will equally give God thanks with those who have been led by a more gentle, humanly attractive system.

From the same point of view Père de Condren refrained scrupulously from giving any direction which seemed to come from himself or his own mind. "It does not pertain to me," he used to say, "to pour anything of my own into a soul. It is a sanctuary wherein God dwells, and whatsoever enters without His orders dishonours and profanes it. It is the exclusive right of Jesus Christ to appoint the work of His servants, His right to speak to hearts; it is the Father's right to teach His children;—He converts and renews them as the potter a vessel. He Only makes them new creatures; He regenerates them by His Spirit and His Word; He gives them ears to hear, and a heart to love. It pertains to the Head to prompt every movement of the members." He often drew attention to the way in which our Lord dealt with souls, tarrying, awaiting the right moment to act upon them, professing His inability as Man to do anything without the Father. And above all, he would do nothing without much prayer. Did some penitent, rich or poor, seek Père de Condren's guidance? —on his knees he besought God to shew him whether it was the work intended for him to do, and the penitent in like manner was bidden to pray earnestly to be guided by God's Will alone in the matter. The charge once accepted, his system was quiet and slow; he disliked pushing new practices, suddenly changing religious habits, or forcing minds into channels which might not be best adapted to their special needs. "To be conformable to Jesus Christ," he used to say, "we must lead souls on gradually—giving them such instruction and such discipline by degrees as they are able to bear,—watching their progress, and regulating our steps by their needs. It was thus that our Lord led His disciples gradually on, until they were ready to receive teaching for which at first they had no capacity. It seems to me that you should from time to time leave the souls you are training almost entirely to God;"—(Père de Condren is writing to a priest who had asked his advice in dealing with certain persons,) —"so that they may learn to find all you have taught them, in Him. We must not look to him that planteth or him that watereth in God's work, but solely to Him that giveth the increase. If it was needful for His Disciples that Christ should go away in order that the Holy Ghost might come upon them, we ought to be ready to believe that our personal efforts are not indispensable to those we teach, nay, even that sometimes they may be hurtful. All that men can do for souls will be simply injurious to them, unless God bless their efforts; and we are never really useful to anybody without His Divine Guidance. His Hand Alone heals and succours, and the remedies man applies without reference to Him are never efficacious."

The Queen Mother, Marie de Medicis, applied to Cardinal Bérulle to recommend a suitable confessor for her younger son, Gaston d'Orléans, who was already a source of trouble and difficulty to her, and whose various escapades were a constant source of offence to his brother Louis XIII. and the imperious Prime Minister, Cardinal Richelieu. The Superior of the Oratorians had no doubt in his own mind as to the man he would select for this delicate office, but knowing de Condren as he did, the Cardinal hesitated to promise his services rashly; so he only told the Queen that there was a member of his Congregation who was endowed by God with every qualification for the task, but that the only hope of obtaining his good offices lay in God's Grace, and that he must pray for guidance in the matter. Accordingly, with much prayer, Cardinal de Bérulle sounded Père de Condren, and found him, as he expected, intensely reluctant to accept a post which would necessarily withdraw him in a measure from the retirement he loved so much, and renew those ties to the Court which he hoped were broken for ever. However, being pressed by his superior, and feeling that a priest has no right to evade responsibility however unwelcome, if God lays it on him, the Father did not persist in a refusal, and de Bérulle informed the Queen that he was prepared to give her "his heart's treasure, Père de Condren," as her son's director. Nevertheless the latter still hoped to be set aside for some fitter person, (as indeed he esteemed every one fitter than himself,) and when the Duke of Orléans came for the first time to the Oratory to prepare for the approaching festival of Whitsuntide, not having received any positive instructions on the subject, de Condren left his rooms, and was not to be found anywhere. In vain the Superior caused search to be made, while the young Prince, unaccustomed to be kept waiting, fidgeted and grew impatient; it was some time before the good Father could be found. At last he was discovered in a quiet nook, absorbed in prayer, and the summons to go and confess the Prince was given. Then at once, feeling that it was God's Will, de Condren obeyed, and went to his unwelcome and difficult task, in which he succeeded,—if not in controlling the wild boy, whose turbulence and passionate nature were often made use of by political parties to the disturbance of family and national peace, at all events in winning Gaston d'Orléans' affection; and on more than one occasion he succeeded in reconciling him and his brother Louis XIII. when probably no one else would have been able to do so much.

Another notable person who, under God's Blessing, owed his wonderful progress in spiritual things to Père de Condren, was Gaston de Renty, of whom he himself spoke as a saint. De Donadieu, afterwards Bishop of Comminges, was another of his spiritual children, and under his guidance was led to leave the army and devote himself to God's special service. So also was Claude Bertraud, known in his day as "the poor priest," and venerated in France for his peculiar devotion to the service of sinners and criminals. It is told of this "Christian Diogenes," (as he has been called,) that being once pressed by Cardinal Richelieu to ask some favour for himself, he answered readily by a request that the cart which conveyed condemned criminals to execution might be mended, as at present its shattered condition distracted them from attending to his spiritual instructions by the fear of falling through.[1]

[1] "Monseigneur, je prie votre Eminence d'ordonner qu'on mette de meilleures planches à la charrette dans laquelle je conduis les condamnés au supplice, afin que la crainte de tomber dans la rue ne les détourne pas de recommander leur âmes à Dieu." S. V. de Paul, Maynard, i. 65.

Claude Bertraud's connexion with de Condren began under peculiar circumstances. He was arguing one day with a Huguenot, and fell into straits, for his adversary was cleverer than he, and though Bertraud escaped the difficulty at that moment by adroitly turning his opponent into ridicule, he remained inwardly discomfited, and the sting of the Huguenot's argument lingered in his mind. In his vexation Bertraud hastened to the Oratory, where he asked the porter to fetch the cleverest man in the house to him. The good lay Brother "was not gifted," as Bertraud says, "with discerning of spirits,"—so he was a good deal perplexed by the request, but like a wise man he went to the Superior, and the result was that de Condren came down to the impatient client. When however Bertraud saw a man whom he imagined to be one of the youngest members of the Congregation, he was vexed, and turning to the porter he exclaimed rudely that he wanted "the most capable man in the house." (" *C'est le plus capable de céans que je cherche !*") With his wonted humility de Condren bade the porter fetch some other Father, but meanwhile he entered into conversation with Bertraud, who was forthwith captivated by him, and speedily saw that the porter was not so far wrong as he had thought.

"I soon saw," he says, "that this was the man for me. I told my tale, and asked the solution of my difficulty. After he had explained this, and armed me with the proper answers to my opponent, he began to speak about the things of God with such light and such power, that all my energies were turned in upon myself; my conscience was roused, I saw my own life in its true light, and felt that I must forsake the irregularities in which it abounded—in a word, a great change came over my whole mind. Père de Condren was used to such things, and soon seeing how it was, he recommended certain devotions and considerations to me for a few days, and then left me to God. I had scarcely left him before I longed to return, and my mind was now filled with a very different anxiety to that which first led me to him. All my jesting was replaced by deep meditation; my mental vision travelled backwards over my past life, and unable to bear with myself, I returned to the good Father and entreated him to hear my general confession, which he did, and after directing me himself for some time, he finally put me into the hands of a Jesuit Father."[1]

Another man whose spiritual life was formed by Père de Condren was Pierre Bertaud, who, after devoting himself in a most remarkable way to reclaiming fallen women from their evil lives, died amid an unusual outpour of heavenly consolations.

Père de Condren's Oratorian biographers tell at

[1] Vie, Pin, p. 204.

some length the history of a certain lady named de la Roche, who, in spite of a devout life and earnest piety, was beset with spiritual troubles, from which none of the holy men whose assistance she sought were able to set her free. Madlle. de la Roche's chief trial lay in a peculiar scruple as to her sins. She felt unable to express the real depths of her faults in words when coming to confession, neither could she excite any sufficient contrition in herself, so that she was tormented by a belief that her confessions were invalid. Even when her confessors were altogether satisfied, she was not satisfied herself, and she still maintained that she was unable to speak the truth, and therefore unworthy of absolution. Several good men gave up the attempt to quiet this scrupulous conscience, when fortunately for her, she fell into Père de Condren's hands, and he at once saw how to deal with her scruples. In reply to her assertion that she had not made, and could not make a proper confession of her sins, he answered, "It is quite true that you have not expressed yourself well, but the fact is that it is impossible for us to see all the real hideousness of sin in this life; we shall never know its real horror till we see it in God's own Light. Here it is only by the light of faith that we look upon our faults, and that, while it convinces us of sin, fails to shew us all its true loathsomeness. God gives you a hidden impression of the exceeding enormity of sin, but He will not give you a full view of it, or the power of expressing it, until the Day of Judgment. It is the same with all matters of faith. God gives us a certain consciousness of their greatness and depth, but He gives us no more than our ordinary language wherein to express them. So while your faith gives you a profound consciousness of your sins, you must be content to express them in such poor words as you can command. It is enough that both you and I clearly understand that they entirely exceed anything that you can tell me. In faith I judge of them as they seem in God's Sight, and thus your self-accusation is right in our Dear Lord's Eyes, and my judgment of them is true."

This quieted the penitent's fears, but she still thought herself unworthy to receive absolution. "It is true," Père de Condren answered, "that your confession in itself cannot make you worthy of absolution, and after we have done all that lies in our power, Absolution is still purely the result of His Divine Mercy, not anything that we can require of His Justice. But just as we cannot escape His severity if we are disobedient, so neither does it beseem us to prescribe limits to His Goodness when He vouchsafes to extend it to us. You have confessed your sins according to the rule given you by our Lord

Jesus Christ, and now, however unworthy you may be of His grace, it is not fitting that you should pretend to be wiser than He, nor to hinder Him from imparting it to you. Keep the conviction of your own unworthiness, but do not meddle with God's Sovereign Power. Of a truth, if you look only at yourself, you cannot hope for mercy; but turn your eyes on Him, and whatever you may be, submit yourself entirely to His Will."[1]

The needed cure was wrought after this fashion, and Madlle. de la Roche, freed from scruples, served God fervently for the remainder of her life. In her last illness, Père de Condren, who had continued to guide her soul, was questioning her as to its condition, and she replied, "I feel that God is very rigorous." He then led her to dwell upon the Holiness of God, and His hatred of that corruption of the flesh which besets us in this life. The dying woman answered, "I adore God in all that He is;" and after a pause she added, "I leave the Being which is present to me, and I take refuge in the Unknown Being of God;" saying which words she breathed her last. Père de Condren was so struck with these words that he wished to have them engraved on her tomb.[2]

[1] Vie, Pin, p. 156.
[2] "J'adore tout ce que Dieu est. . . Je me sépare de l'Etre présent, et me retire dans l'Etre inconnu de Dieu."

There was another spiritual case which came into Père de Condren's hands, of a very different character, a poor servant woman in Picardy, who had always led a saintly life, and whose power of realising the Presence of God, mingled with an intense humility, seemed to ensure that which we all so earnestly long for—final perseverance. But none may reckon in their own strength on such perseverance, and Barbe (her surname is not recorded) fell back, her earnestness slackened, she became less careful in prayer, and her spiritual light grew dim. Aroused from this danger by God's Grace, and thereafter having undergone various spiritual trials, the result of which was a more than ordinarily clear perception of the things of God, Barbe became almost overwhelmed with a sense of the weight of sin around her, and both she and her confessor, the Père Marin, felt convinced that God had some special designs for her. About this time Barbe was taken to Paris by her employers, and one day, while praying in the church of Saint Magloire, an interior voice as from God told her, that if she asked for the holiest and most spiritually-minded of the Oratorians, he would help and comfort her. She told the lay brother who kept the door what she wanted, and he immediately suggested Père de Condren. But that Father was absent, and when the Superior-General was fetched, Barbe had an instinct that, in spite of all his sanctity and his goodness to her, he was not the man. Père de Bérulle saw this too, and he sent her away, promising that she should soon have the help of a Father " who was infinitely beyond himself in the knowledge of God, and who would assuredly be able to relieve her spiritual wants."

Accordingly, soon after she saw Père de Condren, and immediately felt that his was the guidance God had promised her. He seemed to comprehend her mental position at once, and one of the first means he took for removing her troubles and strengthening her soul was to give her the privilege of daily communion. When Barbe returned to Compiègne, Père de Condren wrote to P. Marin concerning his charge as follows:—

"Dear Reverend Father,—May the peace of our Lord Jesus Christ be with you always.

"I thank Him humbly for granting me the privilege of your letters, and of your prayers, as promised me through this worthy soul, who has been trained up by you.

"I feel incapable of really judging the state either of this soul or any other. All I can do is to be the channel of God's Grace and of His Holy Spirit to her, so far as may be. But it seems to me that she has been given by God to her Crucified Lord, in order that she may suffer and be crucified in spirit with Him, and enter deeply into the Sacrifice which

He offered on the Cross to His Father. All I should desire, if I may presume to express a wish where God is working, would be that it might please Him to sustain her more under her sufferings, so that she might yield less beneath her infirmities, and that her painful condition might be more hidden under the Strength of Jesus Christ, Who bore a whole world of sorrows and an inconceivable weight of sufferings, without ceasing for one moment to fulfil every claim of God or man. I think it would be well for Barbe to communicate once every month in honour of the Strength and of the Holiness of our Suffering Lord. By His Strength He endured His grievous pangs without yielding to them and without any weak demonstration. By His Holiness, He cleaved so wholly to God, with such perfect detachment from all things, from Himself and His Own Sufferings, that they could not in the smallest degree mar the perfect union of His Manhood with God. I trust it may please God to grant Barbe this grace—at all events she should ask it, out of obedience, to the end that her sufferings may be more hidden, and that she may do her work in spite of them, foregoing neither her rightful employment nor that interior Cross which she is constrained to bear. Our Dear Lord in His Childhood and Infancy both served and suffered in His parents' house; for He bore His Cross even then by anticipation. Treading in His Steps, Barbe should love both her cross and the duties to which her condition as a servant bind her; and she ought to ask God, if such be His Will, that she may lose nothing of either the one or the other. If it be otherwise, however, she must not fret, but accept willingly the greater or less degree of grace which it may please Him to give her.

"Moreover, I hope it may please our Dear Lord to purge out through His Holy Spirit all that remains of self-love and self-complacency in her, so that she may receive His graces in a less earthly spirit. At present it seems to me that her natural mind and her senses are too much concerned. . . . We rarely receive God's gifts altogether in the same spirit with which He gives them—nature is too apt to claim her part, and to sully that which came in the first instance pure from God. She should pray that God would burn up whatever yet lingers in her of the old Adam, of self and natural impurity; and she should desire above all things to have all and do all for God's Sake Only.

"We ought to be ready to lose all things, so that we may find ourselves in God—to be nought ourselves, that He may be All—to die to all, even those things which He has been pleased to give us, so that He only may live in us through His Own gifts—to possess nothing of ourselves, that He may possess

F

all things. We must accept a living death, if it be His Will, or the most utter inward desolation and suffering. We ought even to pray Him to keep us in such a state of death, if thereby He lives in us; of inward poverty and privation wherein He possesses us wholly, and wherein the creature ceases to have any part in us, leaving God to be our sole Possessor. The whole spirit of the Cross of Jesus lies in poverty and suffering, and its only rightful limit is when by death the Christian makes his final sacrifice to God, Who is his End and his Perfection. We may truly say that souls which God has consecrated to Christ Crucified must dwell in an atmosphere of poverty and suffering, must perpetually die to self; must aspire only to sacrifice themselves to God, and to find their consummation in Him Who is the Fulness of their longing and their love—a longing which makes them desire that He may be all in all to them —*omnia in omnibus*, the Apostle says; and consequently they themselves are nothing." [1]

The earliest biographer of Père de Condren, Père Amelote, himself an Oratorian, heard all this woman's history from the Father, and from her own confessor, Père Marin, and he says that she obtained all these graces to the full, and that de Condren said he had never known any one so deeply versed in Christ

[1] Lettres, x.

Crucified as she was. He used to go year by year to Compiègne to see Barbe as long as she lived, and watched over the work she was doing by her prayers and example. On one occasion he foretold to Père Marin that this would be his last visit, and that Barbe would not live much longer. The prediction was fulfilled. She had done the work appointed by her Heavenly Master, and she departed from this life bearing great sufferings with a marvellous patience, and receiving equally abundant consolations.

Some of Père de Condren's spiritual letters are very striking in their uncompromising clearness and depth, if a certain lack of warmth of expression makes them seem rather chilling to ardent temperaments. Thus, to one who asked him for some instructions concerning the rule of life already given by another director, he says:—

"This rule appears to me very well framed, and I can neither add to it or take anything away; all I can do is to make some few suggestions as to the way you should seek the needful grace to observe it. This good Father has given you a law, as Moses of old gave to the world, but you must needs seek from Jesus Christ the spirit and grace which God will give you in order that you may fulfil it. For although you do not suppose yourself capable of so doing, and though you are convinced that every good thing comes from the Father of Light, as S. James says, nevertheless you are not sufficiently confirmed in the full knowledge of your own bondage to the law of sin, of your uselessness, your incapacity, your unworthiness to serve God, your utter insufficiency and poverty, your urgent need of Jesus Christ and His Grace. Your soul does not yearn enough after its Redeemer; you do not lean sufficiently on His Merits, or look enough to His Grace.

"God has permitted you to work hard in trying to observe your rule, without making much progress toward the perfection at which you aim, in order that by experience you may see things as they are, and that your own faults may teach you to seek elsewhere than in yourself for power to serve God and overcome sin. It was not God's Will to send His Son into the world, until He had been waited for during four thousand years—until the world had tried for two thousand years and found by experience its own powerlessness to keep the Law, or to free itself from sin, as likewise the need it had of a stronger Spirit to resist evil and seek good. And thereby He teaches us that, in order to receive His Grace, we must fully acknowledge our own wretchedness. I pray Him that He would give you a vivid perception that you are a child of Adam, conceived and born in sin, a slave of Satan, incapable of all supernatural good, or of shunning natural evil;

and that there is no way of salvation save by renouncing Adam and all that we inherit from him, renouncing self and self-reliance, giving ourselves wholly to the Son of God, and receiving the Spirit of His Grace.

"Apply your heart with full and firm faith to the study of Our Dear Lord's words, which tell you that you cannot be free, except 'the Son shall make you free' (S. John viii. 36). And again, 'without Him ye can do nothing' (xv. 5). And S. Paul says that 'we are not sufficient to think anything as of ourselves, but our sufficiency is of God' (2 Cor. iii. 5). Nor does this merely arise because of the nothingness of the creature, but from that subjection to sin which comes through Adam, and which hinders the life-spring within us. He was a slave, and therefore his children could not be free, neither could he restore to them the grace and friendship of God, of which sin had despoiled him. By God's just judgment we bear 'the yoke of iniquity,' which in Holy Scripture is also called 'the reign of death,' which keeps us from those free good works and perfection suitable to God's children, and sullies all our deeds, making them incapable of deserving Eternal Life.

"Remembering all this, you should at least once every day confess your wretchedness to God as seen with His Eyes, and renounce the works of Adam and of self. Renounce your own self-will, and whatever you may imagine is in your own power. By nature you have nought save incapacity for any real supernatural good thing, and if you think otherwise you are mistaken —it is a mere presumptuous illusion, the result of self-conceit. If we would have any real power to do right, we must seek it by putting self aside, and by living in the Spirit and the Strength of Jesus Christ.

"After this renunciation, adore Jesus Christ, give yourself unreservedly to Him, ask Him to accept you wholly. Resolve to make over to Him whatever you fancy is your own, come out of yourself, and cast your whole being upon Him, offer up your will, your intentions and inclinations, seek to lose them all in His. Ask Him of His great Mercy to draw you from out yourself. Strive to be lost in His Goodness, His Life, His Tenderness, His Love, and that not for your own selfish sake, but for His Glory. Ask nothing but that His Strength may be made perfect in your weakness.

"Do not be disturbed by the idea that I mean to impose all these prayers upon you daily in the precise form that I have set before you. You should rather be guided by the way in which it may please the Lord to draw you, from day to day. . . . As to the resolutions you are wont to form in meditation, henceforth join to them an act of self-abandonment to the Son of God for their accomplishment. Thus, if you are making a resolution to be humble, say, 'I give myself to Thee, O Lord Jesus Christ, in order that I may enter into the spirit of Thy Humility, that it may lower my pride. I offer to Thee whatever occasions for humility may present themselves; I renounce whatever of self may hinder me from entering into the Grace of Thy Humility.' You can do the like with all the other graces or good intentions which you seek to offer to God, and thus they will have their foundation laid in Our Lord Jesus Christ, and be confirmed through God's Grace and Mercy, instead of depending on that hollow reed, yourself. When we offer our good intentions to God, it ought to be with a firm conviction that we are both incapable and unworthy of offering any service to His Majesty, realising that, if we had our deserts, He would not allow us to pretend to offer anything to Him. We must be convinced that it is only through His Goodness, and the Precious Blood of His Son, that He endures us. How great is our unworthiness, which needed that Blood to purchase for us even a desire to serve His Father, or the right of offering ourselves to Him!

"We ought not to marvel, when we fail in our good resolutions, for we are sinners, and God does not owe us His Grace. 'I know,' says S. Paul, 'that in me dwelleth no good thing, for to will is present with me, but how to perform that which is good I find not' (Rom. vii. 18). Our weakness is so great that it is not enough that God inspire us with the thought of what is right, He must needs supply the will and resolution to do it; and even then, unless He vouchsafes us grace to fulfil that will, nothing will come of it. Further yet, He must uphold us to the end, and grant us final perseverance.

"We must desire and ask His Grace, but we must be content with what He gives, and adore His All-Wise Judgment. When we fall, we must not be discouraged, but humbling ourselves, we must persevere more resolutely, and thank Him for bearing with us, and for giving us the wish to serve Him. If after much toil and labour God vouchsafes us one good thought only, we ought to acknowledge that it is more than we deserve, and accept it as more than sufficient compensation for all our efforts."[1]

To a person living in the world, Père de Condren writes,—

" I pray Jesus Christ to give you His Grace, His Blessing and Peace.

"Although I am backward in writing, I do not fail to offer the needs of your soul to God, or to pray that He would rekindle and cause to live anew in you the graces of your calling.

[1] Lettres, lxii.

"Give yourself up to Jesus Christ and His Holy Will in a faithful spirit, without any clinging to your own thoughts and feelings, and without dwelling on what goes on within you. There is all the more need for us not to make any capital of the qualities we imagine ourselves to possess, inasmuch as often when we are pleasantly conscious of having very humble thoughts, we find them promptly followed by very vain actions; and in like manner mere thoughts of our love to God are apt to be followed by acts of very decided self-love.

"If we give way to a ready belief in what we see or feel in ourselves, we shall easily fancy ourselves filled with God's Grace, when really we are only full of ourselves, and of our own lights. We cannot see or understand the mystery of our natural, animal life, and dare we presume to fancy that we can see or understand the spiritual, supernatural life by which God's Grace dwells in our souls! Let us beware of such foolish presumption, and never pretend to investigate the secret motions of grace within our souls. Remember S. Paul's words, 'Happy is he that condemneth not himself in that thing which he alloweth' (Rom. xiv. 22).

"Our aim must be to live the simple life of faith, ruling our conduct by our duties, not by our feelings. If these are bad, God forbids us to dwell upon them in any way; and if they are good, we should use them as so many means for leading us to God, not dwelling upon them save in a spirit of humility. The real necessity for us in the spiritual life is that we should be busy in *doing*, not in looking about to see whether we are doing or not. And above all things we must walk before God in truth, with a single mind. To you in your present state, this is of the utmost importance, so that you may faithfully follow the grace of your vocation, simply and heartily obeying that which is laid upon you as from God, without stumbling at what seems to you suitable or the reverse. This is the only way by which you will attain perfectly to a spirit of obedience, which is so far beyond your natural thoughts and feelings.

"Neglect no opportunities of drawing nearer to God which your calling may afford, and remember that the most trifling incidents of life affect our salvation; the smallest actions done for God tend to our sanctification. The Son of God tells us that it is so, when He tells us that God numbers the very hairs of our heads, and that without Him not one of them shall perish. How great is His Love, which so largely rewards the little we do after all, and that little only through His Grace! He lays a loving obligation on us to have confident recourse to Him every day and every hour of our lives, wheresoever we may be, and in truth it would be faithless not to believe in His continual Will to do us good. But we must not forget that the good He wills to work for us is in keeping with His Own Greatness and Worth, not moulded upon our self-love and our petty imaginations.

"I pray our Lord Jesus Christ to give you grace to enter into the spirit of these things, and that you may be as humble and obedient as in my prayers I am constrained to ask that you may be. In His love I remain,"[1] &c.

To another person Père de Condren writes:—

"As to the first of your questions, you must strive to maintain a spirit of love for God's Will, and of fear lest you do your own will. For although we may be unworthy to do His Will, or to know it perfectly, nevertheless it is always well to renounce our own will for love of Him: and thus if we may not presume to think that we are following His Will, at least we have the comfort of feeling that we are not following our own will. The first step towards fulfilling His Will is to be free from clinging to our own, and if we can get so far as to hate or even to fear our own will, we shall not be very far from that of God.

"It is a holy practice, while waiting to know what is God's Will, to subject ourselves to that of others for love of Him, and to seek that light and guidance from

[1] Lettres, lxiii.

another which we have not in ourselves. This is a matter on which I cannot fully explain myself in writing—I hope to have the opportunity of speaking with you concerning it.

"With reference to your second question, my answer is, you must persevere in your resolutions when once made, unless you have plain proof that you are bound to do otherwise. You should try to do what you have undertaken to God's Glory, and in the Spirit of Jesus Christ, without any further discussion, and without admitting any thoughts of vacillation. You have every reason to hope that when you were seeking to know God's Will as to your conduct, He gave you sufficient light for your right guidance, and these afterthoughts only tend to make you weak and vacillating in His Service, and therefore you must reject them as temptations.

"As to the third point, concerning your prayer, you know that God's Light often shines amid darkness. There is a great difference between that Divine Light which is invisible and incomprehensible to us, and which, inasmuch as it is Divine, is rather acceptable to God than the cause of conscious satisfaction to one's self, and the natural light which is satisfactory to self—a satisfaction which might only tend to foster self-conceit, and so still further estrange us from God's Light. We had better be without such a treacherous light as this latter, and wait with closed eyes till it pleases God to give us His Own Light—wait in patience, in pure faith and simple love. In short, we ought neither to wish for darkness or light, but for God Only, and we must seek Him in His Own Way, as He opens it to us, without self-pleasing or impatience."[1]

A penitent had written in trouble about her meditation, which was so dry that she felt as though it were time wasted, and she was tempted to give up trying.

"Do not give up meditation, however difficult you may find it," Père de Condren replies. "If it pleases God to make it a penance to you, you will not be losing time. Moreover, surely He deserves that we should take some trouble in seeking intercourse with Him, if indeed it can be wearisome to pass a short time in His Presence. The ordinary courtesies of life constrain you often to give up your time to society which is not agreeable, and will you grudge that to God which you give freely to people who are indifferent or displeasing to you, merely out of compliance with what custom exacts?

"The difficulties which you experience in prayer come from three principal causes:—first, because God is seeking to draw you by the spirit of faith, and to wean you from your own selfish thoughts and feel-

[1] Lettres, lxxii.

ings; the result of which is that, losing your voluntary action, you imagine all to be lost, even God Himself. Then is the time for you to feel that you must worship God after His Own Mind, and not after yours; what are our thoughts and our mind before the Majesty of His Presence! Every earthly creature is thrown into the shade before His Infinite Greatness, and we must lose ourselves to find Him, we must be willing to leave the world of thought we know in order to enter into the unknown realms of His Spirit.

"The second cause of your difficulty lies in the activity and restlessness of your nature, which is too much disposed to fight against what troubles it. Do not attempt so much; abide rather in humble adoration, realizing that it is a great thing for God to endure you in His Presence, that you are only too happy to be able to lose time if it be so, for His Service, that you can offer that part of your day as a sacrifice to Him. It is no small thing to be able even to give up your time to God in His Presence.

" Your third difficulty arises because God wills that you should, so to say, do penance before Him and in His Presence. You must unite your will with His, and the more you do this, and the more you enter into His Plans, the less you will feel disturbed by your troubles—the love of penitence, and a reverent submission to God's appointments, will make you not merely bear them, but accept them willingly. Consider what you are, and what God is; reflect upon the shortness of this life and the Eternity of that which is to come; the little that you have hitherto done, the uselessness of that little, and of all that Jesus Christ has done for you, and thus kindle your heart to greater love of God. It is only during this life that you can in any sense dispose of yourself. Render to God the time He grants you now, and He will give you a blessed Eternity."[1]

On the same subject, Meditation, Père de Condren writes: "I should advise you once in every week to take the Most Holy Trinity as the subject of your meditation, adoring that Holiness, compared with which none can be accounted holy. Adore the Power, the Goodness, the Justice, the Mercy, the Eternity, the Immensity, the Infinity, and the other boundless Perfections of the Blessed Trinity, pausing on whichever God may most draw you to consider. Give yourself unreservedly to the Most Holy Trinity, ask that God's Name may be hallowed, His Kingdom come, His Will be done, and ask Him to help you to do it.

"Secondly, Consider how the Three Divine Persons

[1] Lettres, lxxix.

are one in thought, in will, in love, in life, in Being; ever One though Three, in perpetual and perfect union, in perfect rest and fruition. Neither man nor angels can in any way be compared to this. Kindle your heart to love and adore this Divine Fellowship; ask grace to honour It duly. Seek a blessing on yourself and on the Church.

"Thirdly, Adore the Blessed Trinity as having created all things, as having given you the power to use your own faculties and the things around you. Make a most humble thanksgiving, and entreat grace to use all as He would have you do. Give yourself up to follow any holy aspirations God may grant you.

"Once in the week too, I advise you to meditate on the Second Coming of the Son of God, once on the Passion, and once on the life of the Blessed Virgin. You will also find it very helpful to meditate once a week on Death, Judgment, Heaven and Hell. I need not suggest the considerations which these subjects will supply. You can also take such subjects as the services for the week bring before you, or such as your personal circumstances or inclinations may suggest.

"Further, and indeed above all things, do not let yourself grow disheartened, or be cast down, by depression or scruples. Keep to your rule as concerns confession, and make it, without shewing your confessor how difficult it is to you, or shew it as little as may be. Give yourself up to God in your confession; tell what you remember of your faults in a spirit of humility and contrition, and if you grow confused, and do not know how to go on, stop at once, mentioning some of your ordinary faults of infirmity —for instance, 'I accuse myself of my want of true penitence, of the time I have frittered and wasted, of my lack of humility,' and the like. When you feel unable to make a beginning, accuse yourself of your misspent time, your want of resignation and of energy and courage in obeying God, and of your many unperceived faults, and then go on with what you remember. It is enough that you go to confession once a week, though you communicate three times. If you feel any special need to disburden your mind you might go again in the week, but never more, and not that habitually. I do not think it would be well under your present circumstances for you to communicate through whole Octaves, it would attract too much attention, but you might add one or two communions at such seasons.

"As to your inward troubles and fears, do not be disturbed. They are a trial in which you must trust in God, and abide faithful to Him. Though you may fancy that your will has yielded, it is not so, and amid the weariness of the contest, you are no judge. Consequently you must be very constant to the rule given you, namely—unless you are so sure that you could swear to having yielded freely for five minutes to an evil thought, you are not to make it a subject of confession, but rest satisfied with heartily renouncing it before our Lord in heart and word, or by some external act, such as kissing the ground, or making the sign of the Cross; and you are not to abstain from Communion. You ought to abide quietly and contentedly in this prescribed rule;—while you obey it you are right with God and with your conscience, and it is not your business to sit in judgment on your own soul, so long as you strive to serve God humbly according to the instructions you receive in His Name.

"Let your Communions be very humble. Make them not for yourself but for God's Glory, for His Honour on earth, for the good of the Church and the souls He loves. You are one in the Body of our Dear Lord, of His Mother, of all the Saints, and as such you must work with them. You must strive to enter into their mind, and seek to live their life. Cast off self to do this, and by degrees you will do it more readily. Let it be done cheerfully, and with a full dedication to God."[1]

Writing to one who complained of his inward perplexities, Père de Condren says:

[1] Lettres, lxxx.

"May our Lord Jesus Christ be ever with you, and vouchsafe you the strength and support which you need in His service. Give yourself to Him confidently, and rest assured that all the little cares which trouble you will turn to your salvation. If you can help it, try not to heed them; accustoming yourself to perform every action in that measure of grace and strength which God wills to give you, rather than dwelling upon the hindrances with which you are tempted, and which will vanish as soon as you cease to need them. We are nothing and can do nothing of ourselves, and consequently it is a favour from God when He permits you to realise your own powerlessness and your absolute need of His Help in your most ordinary actions. You should thank Him for so doing, and rejoice that you are constrained by your own poverty to do all things through the abundance of His riches.

"Be quite sure that since God permits the temptation, He will also supply help, and as it is His Will that you stand in special need of Him, He is sure not to fail you. His Word is true, and it tells us that He is ever with His children in the hour of trial, and will not suffer them to be tempted above that they are able; that we can do all things to which we are called, in the strength of His Spirit. Therefore it behoves you to give yourself up to Him in perfect confidence, and so to fulfil all your duties, whether towards God or man, towards the public as an official, or towards your own family, as freely and fully as if you had the most vivid consciousness of that upholding Grace; and that because faith gives us so much more certain assurance than even our own sense and experience can give. I would far rather know by God's own Promise that His Help is ever present, and that He wills me to live by His Holy Spirit, and be led by His Grace, than merely to feel it to be so, and realise His Guiding Hand by my own consciousness. My own feeling and experience might be deceived, and might mislead me, but God is Infallible, and where He speaks, our reason and senses have no further claim to be heard. The purer His Grace, the less it becomes mingled with our senses; the more Divine, the more incomprehensible—it should suffice us to believe, and to act in that strength without aiming at an earthly appreciation thereof.

"As to your Communions, do not fail to communicate on Festivals, Sundays, and Thursdays, and from time to time, when no festival occurs during the week, on Saturday. Under your present inconvenient circumstances, if your communions have to be diminished, accept the privation in union with the many privations borne in this world by the Son of God and His blessed Mother; borne, as these chiefly were, because they would not rise beyond the ordinary level of those around them. In the same spirit of reverence for that state of privation, you might sometimes profitably deprive yourself of something, but it must be done in complete secrecy, and without being known to the world, or God would not have His part therein.

"I am very glad that you are satisfied with M. A.,[1] and to hear of her goodness and her usefulness among the poor. If you had not told me what she does, I should have known nothing about it, for she does not tell me when she writes. Still, if there should be any threat of plague or other epidemic, you must forbid her to go into it at once. But so far as the wounded and ordinary sick are concerned, it is a good work to minister to them, and God will reward both her for doing it, and you for allowing her to do so, and for taking pleasure in her good works.

"I am most affectionately and always yours."[2] . . .

The same lesson—of preferring faith to feeling—is continually pressed home in his letters. It is forcibly expressed again as follows to a friend :—

"May our Lord Jesus Christ be your Life, your Guide, and your Strength, in all your ways, and in all the works He may be pleased to commit to you. Never pause to dwell on whatever you feel in yourself

---

[1] His wife.   [2] Lettres, No. lxxxi.

of weakness or of strength, of light or of darkness, but live on in that simple faith, of which the apostle speaks when he says, 'the just shall live by faith,' without squandering your energies in analyzing feelings and the like. Do not imagine yourself to be weak because you feel weak, or strong because you feel strong. S. Peter believed himself to be strong, but was weak when the Son of God warned him that 'the spirit is ready but the flesh is weak;' and S. Paul believed himself to be weak, though he was strong when he said, 'when I am weak then am I strong' (2 Cor. xii. 10).

"God sees and judges us truly, but as to our feelings and judgments concerning ourselves, the only thing we can be sure of in them is, that we ought not to trust to them. However weak we may feel, we ought firmly to believe that His Divine Grace will suffice us for life and holiness, and remembering this we should go boldly at whatsoever He sets before us or calls us to do, and in like manner, however vigorous or fervent we may feel, we must remember S. Peter's words, '*nolite peregrinari in fervore*,'[1] but walk in that faith which promises us that we can do all things in Him Who strengtheneth us. Amid his manifold tribula-

---

[1] 1 S. Peter iv. 12. The English does not convey quite the same meaning as the words quoted by de Condren from the Vulgate.

tions S. Paul appealed to God, and the answer he received was that we have nought in us save death; we live under its sentence; of ourselves we have only condemnation, helplessness, inutility, in order that all our trust may be in Him Which raiseth the dead. 'We had the sentence of death in ourselves, that we should not trust in ourselves, but in God Which raiseth the dead, Who delivered us from so great a death, and doth deliver, in Whom we trust that He will yet deliver us' (2 Cor. i. 9, 10). Study the whole of this passage; it will comfort you. Give yourself up to Him Which raiseth the dead, so that through His Divine Grace you may be able to fulfil all your duties, both those which come upon you from without, and those which God's Providence has laid upon you within your family and yourself. Pray for me."[1]

Again, to one suffering under temptation, he writes,—

"I have read your letter very carefully. Of a truth it kindles my pity, not so much because of the magnitude of your trouble, as because you find it so difficult to use a remedy, which in itself is most easy and acceptable. For what can be more desirable than to live in our Lord; what more to be wished than that you might be drawn from these vexing thoughts of temptation, to be engrossed with so holy and attractive

[1] Lettres, No. lxxxiii.

an object? And what can be more annoying than to be distracted from peaceful happy thoughts of our Dear Lord, and find ourselves plunged in troubles and worries which disperse such slender devotional powers as we may possess, and make our service of God so difficult? You know so well by experience that nothing relieves you so much as opening your heart to some one who loves you;—why? except that in so doing you cease to dwell and brood over yourself and that which hinders you? But most assuredly no one loves your soul half so much as our Lord Jesus Christ. He is All-Powerful to help you. No one else can help you, save through Him, but He can help you alone; and be quite sure that if you pour out your heart and commune with Him, you will find wonderful relief. I can quite believe that at first you will find some difficulty, and that your mind will relapse into the train of thought which is most habitual to it—you have acquired a habit, your mind has got a warp which cannot be overcome all at once, but by degrees you will succeed with God's Grace. He will not fail to bear the heaviest weight of your trouble, and to draw you gently to Him. Let Him do His Will; let yourself be drawn;—and when you feel that you have fallen into your old troubles, make a vigorous effort to rouse yourself by fixing your mind on some good thought. Picture Him as stretching out His

Arms to you, offering you His Help, calling you to hold converse with Him; and longing, far beyond anything you can imagine, that you should dwell in Him and He in you. You have a thousand individual reasons for believing all this as concerns yourself, independently of what He has done for the whole world by His Incarnation, His Labour, His Passion. I want you rather to dwell on what you have seen and felt yourself. You have often confessed to me— and indeed we may both say the same,—that our Lord has done more for you in certain ways than you would wish; that He has given you greater grace and power to mortify your natural self, than you would have chosen if left to yourself. Surely here is a proof that our Dear Lord cares more for your welfare than you do yourself. I realise this in myself too well not to be sure that it is so with you and many others. Besides, how many mercies He has dealt to you, which you little recked of! All the evil we do not commit, all the temptations to which we do not consent, or which never visit us;—all our holy thoughts and good intentions, all our longings after that which is right, are so many witnesses of His Loving Kindness towards us;—for faith teaches us that without Him we can do nothing. How could He help you thus unless He cared for you? Surely all this not merely proves, but must press home to your heart, that our Lord cares for you, and that He cares for you more than you care for yourself. If sometimes thoughts of an opposite kind beset you, drive them away as presumptuous, unreal, and harmful. They are but some of the lies which tempt those who give heed to them;—they generally come before the mind when it is troubled by some temptation, just as dazzling sparks flit before a man's eyes under the influence of a stunning blow. Judge any such misgivings as you would judge of such lights, arising from a mere accident, and deceitful accordingly.

"Remember how often you make mistakes as to your fellow-men, and how many unfair hasty judgments you make concerning them. Well then, be sure that it is not concerning your neighbours only that we come to hasty conclusions—we do the same with respect to God Himself, and that not unfrequently, because we do not sufficiently submit our minds to His direction. So too we make mistakes with respect to ourselves, one while judging ourselves as better, another time as worse than we really are, owing to the very scanty knowledge which we really possess of ourselves and of God's Grace working in us. But indeed, our faulty judgment is too recognised a fact to need more words. Only bear in mind how often it has misled you, and beware of it. Open the eyes of your mind, and be sure that unless our Lord cared for you,

He would not sustain your life, He would not preserve you from the Evil One; He would not have given me the power or the will to help you. There is no love save that which comes from the Son of God; if then you believe that your relations, your friends, your confessors—that I myself care for you, you must own that He has taught us to do so, and therefore that He cares for you, and cares far more than I or the best of friends or relations can do. I know that you believe all this, and I am not urging it in order to make you believe, but rather because I want you to bring it to bear upon your mistaken feelings, and so measure their deceptive character fairly.

"I had almost forgotten to answer you concerning the austerities you have a mind to practise. But I should reckon the thought to be a delusion of the Evil One, if by austerities you mean fasting, or anything calculated to diminish your bodily strength, which is already very insufficient; indeed, your temptations arise partly from physical weakness, and to add to that would be a sure way of increasing those temptations. In imposing very little of penance upon you, I had in view that your ailments would partly supply what was lacking, and an exact obedience to your rules do the rest. If I could have given you strength of body and mind instead of any penance, I would gladly have done so, for knowing how feebly you observe the obligations which already bind you, I do not think it well to lay anything fresh upon you. As you think your malady so serious, you certainly ought not to seek any further penitential practices, especially what might make you worse, and lessen your power of bearing it, and of keeping your rule. Believe me, your penance henceforth is to bear your malady in patience, offering it to our Lord in penitence, and as an atonement for your faults.

"By your malady, I mean *all* that you suffer, especially your temptations and your spiritual difficulties. Pray, then, get rid of this injudicious desire for austerities, and devote yourself to the Humanity of our Lord, as I said before. Use Da Ponte as a foundation for your meditations on that Sacred Humanity, and keep the results in mind all through the day, above all when any temptation tries you. Take one subject every morning, and think it over as often as you are able through the day. This does not require any lengthy meditation. I mean you to keep your mind filled with a loving remembrance of the Divine Manhood, as seen in whatever mystery you have chosen for consideration. This is the way to overcome temptation, humbling yourself in His Holy Presence, and confessing that in Him lies all your strength; but I would never have you argue with your temptations. Indeed, I desire you never even to listen to them, under any pretext, but rather turn aside in acts of adoration, humiliation, love, or what you will, towards our Lord. This I believe to be what is necessary for you. Make continuous efforts always to represent our Saviour to yourself as Loving, full of compassion, bearing your cross and beckoning you to Him. Never dwell on the thought of Him as your Judge, or under any severe aspect; so long as we live and can repent, He is our Advocate. Do not torture yourself needlessly. Avoid terrifying subjects of meditation; let your soul feed upon your Dear Lord, in Whom Alone you will find the true remedy for all your temptations, the thought of His Love for you. Shun dwelling upon yourself and your own offences as you would shun hell. Nobody should ever dwell on these save in humiliation, and in love to the Lord, Who has refrained from their immediate chastisement and has waited for the culprit's repentance. Look upon yourself certainly as a sinner—of a truth there are many Saints now in Heaven who have been sinners. That should be enough for you."

On the same subject :—

"The temptations which you are bearing are not intended to overwhelm you, but to humble you, to teach you patience, and to constrain you to seek God, more than hitherto. These are the three uses to which you should turn your trials, instead of the discouragement and depression to which you seem to be giving way. I recommend you, in order to gather more strength under your troubles from the Lord, to ask leave to spend a quarter of an hour daily before the Blessed Sacrament, in honour of His Forty Days in the wilderness, when He vouchsafed to be tempted for our sake. If your health will not admit of this extra devotion, you can take it out of your usual time of meditation. Try therein to adore the Son of God, and intreat Him to take charge of your soul when under temptation, claim His All-powerful Help, confessing your own helplessness, and then give yourself up wholly to Him, for what can hell itself do against His Grace? Be at peace under the shelter of His Wings. The Apostle tells the Romans that there is no condemnation for them that are in Christ Jesus (Rom. viii. 1). Strive to be in Christ Jesus then, so that temptation and the power of sin may have no hold upon you. You will be in Him if you renounce yourself, sin and all else, in order to be solely His, giving yourself sincerely to Him. I beseech Him of His Grace to grant you this in the spirit of faith—it is your true remedy.

"In the next place, humble yourself as the greatest sinner in the world; the vilest not only in your house, but in all the earth; as deserving to be given up to your sins, as meriting nothing save the evil thoughts which beset you. For in truth, if God were strictly just both to you and me, we should have nothing better than such thoughts as those of the lost, among whom we deserve to be.

"Thirdly, accept from God's Hand all the distress which these temptations cause you as a punishment for your past sins, and in honour of the Sufferings of the Son of God in His Life and His Death, asking Him to enable you to do this sincerely. If your mind should be so disturbed that you cannot repress its temptations, make these acts aloud, or use some other vocal prayers to the same end. Be very careful in all your confessions, to offer the shame of your faults in honour of our Lord Jesus Christ, Who vouchsafed to bear the shame of sins which He had not committed on the Cross. I believe, indeed I am sure, that you think yourself faulty in many things without such being really the case—but till we meet, I can give you no better counsel than this. So do not be weary of bearing the reproach of sin with our Dear Lord, He on His Cross and you in confession, as far as your confessors allow—for the more you can humble yourself in confession, the greater will be your strength in temptation.

"Take delight in your work as far as obedience and your bodily strength permit of, but in beginning each action offer it, by some short mental aspiration, in honour of Christ Crucified. You should leave to Him the care of your salvation, while your part is to do or bear, for His Sake, whatever comes to hand ; so doing you may rest satisfied that He will not forsake you.

"I give you as large a share as I can of my prayers and devotions, and I ask our Dear Lord to give you more and more effectually than I can do. I ask to share in your spiritual troubles, a portion which I count as more precious than anything which I can give you. S. Paul says that it is a great thing to suffer for God's Sake—a dignity which the world knows not, because it is not of the world. May you receive its blessing on earth, and its crown in Heaven."[1]

The two following letters are singularly adapted to help that class of minds who are inclined to confuse temptation and sin, and to feel miserable and guilty because they are sorely tempted, though all the time they are earnestly resisting the temptations.

"I beseech our Lord Jesus Christ to be with you in the perfection of His Holy Love, and in that blessed union to work out His Own Glory and your salvation, as indeed I trust He will do of His Infinite Mercy.

"There are one or two things I would say to you.

[1] Lettres, No. xci.

And first, the state of temptation in which your mind is will not destroy your soul; I tell you so as a message from God. Therefore you must patiently bear with these thoughts of despair or reprobation, and not believe in them. God permits the lying spirit to torment you with such thoughts in order that you may 'sorrow to repentance and salvation,' as S. Paul says (2 Cor. vii. 10). Next, I want to say, you may ask God to deliver you from these troubles, if it is His Will, but you should not be too eager about obtaining deliverance or peace of mind, nor ask it too urgently. Rather resign yourself to God's Holy Will; cling to the Cross of Christ with a patient heart, entreat Him to uphold you in this path of sorrow and humiliation, and be content if He wills to keep you in it all your life.

"Lastly, as a rule, the sins of thought of which you believe yourself guilty are not sins;—they are rather the result of a wile of the Evil One, who disturbs your mind, and makes you imagine that you are entertaining thoughts, which in fact you are only enduring for His Sake Who bore our sins, without committing any of them or being touched by their guilt. Be sure that God, looking on you lovingly, as following in His Dear Son's Footsteps, is often pitying and blessing you when you condemn yourself most severely. Not that I would have you cease to know yourself to be sinful, or to humble and confess yourself. The hidden judgment of God to which I allude does not exempt you from the duties of penitence ;—it leaves the cross and burden of sin, without the malice thereof, through the Merits of the Son of God, Who bore our griefs and carried our sorrows, as the Prophet Isaiah and S. Paul tell us, only without spot or stain of sin. At the same time let your words in confession be few and simple ; diffuseness and dwelling on such things have an unfortunate tendency to renew their attacks. You say that you often cannot remember these temptations in confession—probably that is because God conceals them from your mind, which is inclined to dwell overmuch upon them. Be sincere and simple in confession, and when it is made do not begin tormenting yourself as to how it has been done."[1]

"There is no reason to be disheartened by the distressing state of mind you are in just now. It is rather a reason to have more earnest recourse to God, Who is the strength of the weak, and Who has promised His Help in every time of need. I am convinced that you are not guilty of the faults you imagine owing to your mental condition—so do not be troubled or give up your ordinary devotions, and keep to your rules as to confession. Thus, do not confess yourself guilty of consenting to these evil suggestions unless you are sure that you gave way to them deliber-

[1] Lettres, No. xcii.

ately for a quarter of an hour. While I am satisfied that even when you think you have consented to them you are rather under a delusion than really guilty, still I would rather counsel you to subject yourself to a considerable extent to the humiliation of confession—such humiliation is one of the fruits which God causes to grow from out temptation.

"Of course you should not justify yourself, but rather accuse yourself before God, and only make use of what I say in order to avoid being discouraged;—we must always humble ourselves before God. Still, as the tendency of these temptations is not so much to make you offend Him, as to harass yourself with scruples, and as you are disposed to give way to an unreasonable distress, it is better for you not to dwell upon your temptations or confess them, unless you have distinctly parleyed with them as before said. Neither would I have you tire yourself out with acts of resistance. One of the objects of the Enemy is to injure your health and weaken you so that you may be a still easier prey. You can see how incapable your increased headaches make you. Therefore, while your faith in God's Help grows stronger, it is not desirable that you add to your external acts of devotion towards Him. When temptation arises, offer yourself to your Lord and His Glory, by bearing whatsoever He will, with a firm faith that He will help you better than man or Angel, however loving, for God is Love itself; —and with full confidence that He is as well able to lead you through darkness as light, through temptation as through peace and tranquillity.

"We are apt to condemn ourselves at the very moment when most justified of God; and when we are best satisfied with ourselves perhaps He condemns us. You may not be able to find comfort in doing as I bid you, but nevertheless persevere. If one feels unable to make an interior act before God, it is well to make it verbally, and as I have often told you, to do that in a spirit of faith which we are not able to do as a matter of feeling. Besides, when you have fulfilled your duty to God, you ought to turn from your troubles, and put aside these excessive fears which cramp and weaken your spiritual life, rather giving yourself up to your Lord, Who Alone can save you. You know well enough that you cannot save yourself—all you can do is to weary yourself in vain, and make yourself ill."[1]

Many of Père de Condren's letters are eminently practical, and enter with minute detail into the spiritual life,—*e.g.* the following on self-examination:

"We ought to make three daily self-examinations, of which the chief is that in the evening, which should be made before the Son of God as a confession. Three things are to be attended to in this.

[1] Lettres, No. lxxxvi.

"First, that we adore the Son of God in His capacity of Judge, because He it is that will judge us, and we must not wait till death to meet Him as such. Love and faithfulness constrain us to do now what then we shall have to do as a necessity—therefore let us lay bare our conscience to Him now and await His Judgment.

"Secondly, we must adore Him as Priest—for He is not only our Judge, but our High Priest, to Whom we are bound to confess our sins and give account for the day past. To this end we must ask the aid of His Light, that we may see plainly wherein we have displeased Him during the day; for our own light is insufficient to shew us all the faults we have committed, above all, in the supernatural life. There are many reasons for earnestly asking this Light, one of the foremost being our blindness to our own faults, which faults our self-love conceals, our ignorance omits, and our weakness extenuates. Having asked this light, the next thing is to make a general review of the day's actions, looking at our omissions rather from our Dear Lord's point of view than from our own. It is well to observe that, in making this review, we ought not to dwell specially upon our good works, even in thanksgiving. There are always blemishes in them, and we have no right to judge them to be wholly good—for the

Church herself has no commission to make any such individual judgments before the Second Coming of the Son of God. At the same time, in order to avoid ingratitude, we should thank God for His Infinite Grace and Goodness as given to each one of us.

"Next, we should make an act of contrition, or sorrow for sin, because it is displeasing to God. Then give ourselves absolutely to Jesus Christ, for the coming night especially, and for the morrow and our whole life, that He may fulfil all His Holy Will in us, and do with us what He pleases, so that we may be tools in His Hand to obey and serve Him perfectly. If, during such self-examination, we feel perplexed after having done all that lies in our power, it is well to ask our Guardian Angel to adore the Son of God as our Judge, and to be our accuser before Him, so that nothing may be left unsaid or unforgiven.

"The morning examination should be no less carefully made than this at night, since while one helps to correct our past faults, the other warns and forearms us against those into which we are liable to fall. God has given us memory to deal with the past, and foresight for the future. To us it appertains to use both rightly; our memory to give God Glory, and strive to destroy the work of sin in us; foresight to consider how we can spend the day now beginning better than its predecessors, so that each day may tend to raise the whole tone of our life.

"In this examination we must again adore our Lord as the very Principle of our life and actions, since without Him we can do nothing that is good or acceptable to God. In this capacity there are three points to be considered:—

"I. His dominion and right over whatever we do. Everything is His, our days, our minutes, and all our powers, our body and all its members, our actions and labours; for we have nothing save through His Favour; and, 'Ye are not your own,' S. Paul says.

"II. The light, guidance and direction He will give us. Since all our actions are His, He will guide us to fulfil His intention and desire. And

"III. The grace, strength and power, with which He will enable us to do all perfectly through Himself. 'I can do all things through Christ which strengtheneth me,' S. Paul says.

"Now, in order to do all this faithfully, we must begin by giving ourselves to our Dear Lord, and dedicate all our most trifling duties to Him; we must renounce all self-guidance for His only; we must ask grace and strength from Him to fulfil His Will. Then we must glance over the duties of the day, with a view to fulfilling them better and more earnestly, and it is well to do the same with respect to our devotional exercises. It is well, too, briefly to foresee such occasions of falling as may be likely to arise, so as to prepare ourselves to meet them, and be armed with remedies, beseeching our Lord that we fall not.

"The mid-day examination differs from that made at night, wherein we come before our Lord as Judge; for in this we honour Him as the Head of Which we are members, as our Life-Giver, the Ruling Spirit of all we do. In the evening examination we should go into our sins against God's Law; in this at mid-day examining what faults we have committed in that inner life, and in our Christian vocation, which calls for so great watchfulness. We must see whether all our actions have been done in a right spirit, whether they have been guided by His Holy Will, whether we have acted up to the inspirations God has given us, specially in the particular points which we feel that He sets before us in our way, as also what have been our shortcomings in those respects. It is well to take some two or three points week by week, such as self-abnegation and renunciation, and dependence on God's Holy Spirit—going on the next week to what we most need in order to meditate well, and so on.

"In all this consider the misuse we make of those tendencies to good which Jesus Christ has given us, how we reject His inspirations and fail to second His impulses. Again, our misuse of His mysteries, not honouring Him in them as we ought, although we need diligently to study them with a view to obtain special graces, and to imitate His Virtues. And thirdly, our negligence in not making a worthy and sufficient use of our Dear Lord; we ought to live in and by Him, a life altogether above our nature and our natural powers; —nothing ought to seem hard or impossible to be done for Him, inasmuch as He gives us His Grace and His Holy Spirit so abundantly to help us in whatever we do. Let all these points of misused grace be duly considered in your self-examination."[1]

On the subject of Holy Communion, Père de Condren writes:—

"We must come to it, first, in order that Jesus Christ may be All in us that He should be, and that we may cease to be all that we are, losing ourselves in Him. Secondly, we must come to it in order that He may destroy whatever in us is contrary to God the Father—the old Adam and his sorrowful heritage, the reign of sin and Satan, and the cruel tyranny of self-love; and so coming we must ask of the Divine Humanity to put forth the Right Hand of His Justice, to crucify the old man in us and to confirm the Kingdom of the Adorable Trinity. Our imperfections should lead us to seek Communion, as the one sovereign remedy for their healing.

[1] Lettres, No. lxxxiii.

"Thirdly, the very gifts and graces which it has pleased our Lord to give us should urge us to Communion, so that we should not imagine them to be our own, or use them according to our own blind self-love, but leave Him absolute control over them, and let Him use them after His Own good pleasure.

"We ought to come to Holy Communion, in obedience to our Dear Lord's Will that we should dwell in Him and He in us; in order to root out our natural life and will, and to become what He is,—*i.e.* life, truth, love and holiness to God. Moreover we ought to come to it out of obedience to His desire that we should be His members, in whom He may dwell to the honour and glory of His Father in Heaven.

"While our own spiritual usefulness may rightly be a motive for frequent Communion, it ought not to be our foremost intention, since it is neither the best, the most urgent, or the most imperative. First of all we owe obedience to our Lord's desire to receive and to possess us—for Holy Communion not only gives Jesus Christ to us, it also gives us to Him, even as He Himself says, whoso receiveth Him abideth in Him. Now this desire of His to receive us is as wide as His Love;—as the rights which His Merits and His Mercy give Him over us. Therefore it becomes a grievous want of faithfulness to disappoint His gracious desires, when we have no necessary hindrance from Holy Communion.

"S. Paul tells us that we are the Fulness of Jesus Christ, Who takes us into Himself and grows in us as the members of His Body. This may be illustrated by the soul of a child, which does not grow by any increase of substance, but by an ever-increasing accession of light which enlarges its horizon, its relative position towards others, and its own sphere of action, in proportion as the child's body is developed, and becomes capable of serving the operations of the soul. In like manner with Communion— Our Lord fills us therein with Himself, and develops His own Life in us, and we do Him wrong in abstaining from Communion, unless rightfully withheld from it, and for due cause.

"Then again, the Son of God is not content with being offered to His Father in one place only, He wills to be so offered in many, and although His Sacrifice is One and unchangeable in reality, He wills it to be continually renewed to His Father's Glory in a certain sense. And the soul which receives Him in Holy Communion is really an altar on which Jesus Christ lies and whereon He is continually offered to God, not only in will and intention, which may be done without receiving Him sacramentally, but in very truth and act. And be sure that it is more pleasing to Jesus Christ and more to God's Glory to be thus offered in the souls He loves than on all the Altars in Christendom.

"There are sundry other reasons why we should communicate for God's Sole Glory. . . . You cannot give yourself too often to Him; without Him we have no power to cast off the yoke of self, and the sin which dwelleth in us will yield to none save Himself, and therefore I cannot approve of your diminishing your Communions. Even if you can seek His Help without that Sacrament which He instituted on purpose to give Himself to you, you are infinitely more sure to find Him in the means which He has appointed for uniting Himself to you, and for working with you in that which you have to do for God. Surely we are bound to seek Him in the way wherein He wills to be found, and to unite ourselves to Him in order to serve God more faithfully and purely, for of a truth we are very weak without Him. So too, we must go to Him to be strengthened against the power of sin, and the inclinations of the old man in us, which can never be subdued without Him. We have only too great experience of our own weakness; we need truly to seek Jesus where He is, and to unite ourselves to Him in order to do that which without Him we cannot do; just as a man who has to move a weight beyond his strength goes to seek another to help him.

"So long as we come to Holy Communion with a full feeling of our own weakness, and with that insight which faith gives of our need of His Strength to fight against sin, self, the world, and whatever is contrary to God's Will, we cannot come too often. No indeed, he cannot come too often who is led by the sense of his own helplessness and weakness in serving God there to seek strength and grace in Jesus Christ to do better. Frequent Communion is only to be feared when one is secretly influenced in coming to it by a good opinion of one's-self, or by a lurking impression that one is better than others because one communicates more frequently. Then indeed hidden vanity and spiritual pride rule us and cause us to misuse the Blessed Sacrament. But if one is not seeking any mere self-satisfaction, if one communicates only to serve God, and to win strength against sin and selfishness,—with a view to praise and obey God better, not from any rest in one's own goodness, then one need not be afraid to approach Him very frequently in Holy Communion. May our Dear Lord guide you in this as in all else."[1]

To one who was overwhelmed with weariness and intolerance of self, Père de Condren writes:—

[1] Lettres, Nos. lxxvi. and lxxvii.

"Judging by your letters I think you are giving way overmuch to sadness, and that you are not using it rightly to God's Glory and the good of your own soul. So far from being a hindrance to your spiritual progress, it would be a means of giving God glory, if you gave yourself up to Him as you might do. When He created you, He knew perfectly that He had made you subject to this weakness—He did it in order to help you to turn away from and reject self, in order to constrain you to seek all your rest in Him, in order that this very inward trial should be borne for His Glory. Keep in mind that God will call you to account for the use you have made of it. Resolve then to give yourself to God and to bear it patiently and without fretting, so long as He pleases. One must learn to bear with one's-self before one is able to bear the Cross of Christ. He bore the prospective weight of all men, their sorrows, their sadness, their weariness; and He bore it so faithfully that He would not lay aside the smallest part thereof;—so perseveringly that He never gave Himself a moment's relief during His earthly Life. Do you in likewise be faithful and persevering in bearing that share of His Cross which is laid on you,—I mean your own wretchedness, and do not be disheartened, for it is one of the ways given you in which to serve and honour God on earth, and to bear your part in your

Saviour's Cross. Give yourself up to the power of His Grace, so that you may do it perfectly. It is only for this life that we have to suffer, and the reward of that suffering is eternal. Meanwhile do not neglect seeking such relief as will tend to distract your mind duly. Take care of your own health, and of your wife's; and oblige her to attend to it herself.

"Do not give way to depression,—but resign yourself to our Dear Lord with the object of bearing the discomforts and petty contradictions of this life bravely. It appertains to God's Holy Spirit to make you welcome them, whereas it is characteristic of self-love to be grievously depressed by them. We must not wish to have our own will carried out in this world, or to find our satisfaction therein, but rather we must be content to die to all our own ways and wishes,—to all that is of the old Adam. When any circumstances of our life tend that way—as for the most part all that is trying does—we ought to be glad at heart, and bless God for helping us by casting us down in the flesh that He may build us up in the Spirit. Remember what the Apostle S. James says—'My brethren, count it all joy when ye fall into divers temptations' (i. 2). Love and joy, according to the Spirit of God, always take the shape of the Cross and of suffering for God in this life; even as fleshly love and joy take that of the enjoyment of and rest in creatures. Do not seek a remedy for your depression in love of the world or satisfaction of the senses; the remedy would be worse than the disease,—but seek it in God, striving not merely to love and praise Him, but to love and praise Him with a real interior joy. Do not give up any of your religious practices, and remember me in your prayers."[1]

To a sick friend he writes:—

"May our Lord Jesus Christ ever live in you, in Heaven to His Glory, in earth to do His work! I beseech Him not merely to control the whole use you make of your life, but also that He would preserve and sustain it by His vivifying powers, so that it may be wholly His, wholly dependent upon Him;—that He may not merely be the principle of a supernatural life of grace in you, but likewise the principle of your natural life which He preserves. He will be the sole principle of our future life to all eternity, in virtue of that Resurrection to which He will call us. While here on earth our being is sin-soiled, and He can have no part in sin, but inasmuch as we belong primarily to God the Father as our Creator, His Beloved Son preserves and sustains our life, subject as it is to sin, in order that we may become more wholly His, and that He may acquire continually fresh claims upon us.

[1] Lettres, Nos. lxxxvii. lxxxviii.

Sometimes even He vouchsafes to renew that life, as in Lazarus, who owed his earthly life to the Son of God —deriving not merely his spiritual but his temporal existence from Him, and being thereby bound to our Dear Lord by a very special tie. I pray that you may be made to share in the mind with which Lazarus must have received this renewed life from the Son of God, and in which he must have spent the remainder of his days in close union and dependence on Him.

"It seems to me that one of the uses to which you should put your sickness, is the longing to be more entirely Christ's, and less your own. But do not neglect the means which God vouchsafes to use for our restoration to health, through His Dear Son's Blessing. We are bound to receive them with thanksgiving, even as S. Paul says we are bound to receive our daily food (1 Tim. iv. 3). Accept willingly the humiliation of having to take so much care of your body, and do not seek to be better thought of by any one than God chooses you to be. But do not occupy yourself with dwelling on your own condition, or the moral cause of your sufferings. Perhaps it is not as you think, or if it be, God if He wills can repair the ill effect of your faults. Accept humiliation freely, and do not desire anything of any one save from a supernatural point of view, and through the Merits of Jesus Christ; for to wish only that men may be to us whatever God would have them, will always be the true road to peace and happiness for those souls which cleave to God in humility and patience. They know that He holds the hearts alike of bad and good in His Hand; that He can equally work His Will by means of devils or angels; that He continually feeds His friends by means of His enemies—His lambs by the help of very wolves. And so they are at peace in His Hand. We too shall find peace of heart and mind, beyond all we can imagine, if we seek nothing save that His Holy Will be done in all things."[1]

Speaking of the ruling motives of the Christian's life, Père de Condren says:—

"The first point at which to aim in all our actions, that they may be really Christian, is self-renunciation, as S. Paul says, 'Ye are not your own, for ye are bought with a price' (1 Cor. vi. 19, 20); and again, 'He died for all, that they which live should not henceforth live unto themselves, but unto Him Which died for them and rose again' (2 Cor. v. 15). So we should die to self through grace and the virtue of Christ's Death. He must live in us, and our one object in the world should be to do His Work therein.

"The second point is a like renunciation of all that is of self or our own mind, in order to enter into the Mind of Christ and to do His work through His Spirit,

[1] Lettres, No. xi.

Which Alone can enable us to effect it. And this must be done very heartily, with a strong conviction that God will enable us to do it, and that Jesus Christ works continually with us, to vivify and renew us in it. Even when we may not be conscious that we are upheld by this supernatural strength, we need not question it, for being altogether divine, it is imperceptible to the senses, and can only be realised by faith.

"The third point is total renunciation of every aim in our work save God. Jesus Christ Himself, Whose members we are, and in Whose Spirit we seek to live, had none other. Not that this hinders us from regulating our actions by sundry rules having application to what may seem other objects. Thus obedience is regulated by the will of those set over us, but the end which we set before us is God. Bodily nourishment ought to be regulated according to our needs, but the end for which we take it should be God; so that when we sustain the body, it should not be for our own earthly sakes, but for the Glory of God, Who is our Fulness, our Satiety, our Eternal Food. So again with respect to conversation, which should be regulated by charity and Christian courtesy; but its end should be to honour God, and Jesus Christ communing with men. In short, God ought to be the Sole End of all we do, not self. Hence you will draw one deduction, *i.e.* that the rule on which all your life is to be framed must be that you give yourself wholly to Jesus Christ, to do and suffer whatsoever comes before you for and in Him, and to His Glory and that of His Father. May He cause you to share largely in the fulness of His life."[1]

To one who asked guidance as to the right use of time, Père de Condren replies:—

"Our whole life ought to be shaped according to the light and truth of faith, and the precepts of Christianity, so that it may be as God would have it. We see how men of the world conduct themselves according to their worldly experience, ruling their ways with a view to the customs and opinions of society;—how philosophers boast of ruling their life according to the light of reason;—and how the sensualist follows the leadings of the flesh and self-indulgence; —surely it befits the Christian to be ruled by his faith, which leads him to seek a far higher standard than mere reason or nature can ever do. From this point of view I would suggest three truths which shew how important it is that we should daily make a right and holy use of our time.

"First then, God is the Creator of all things, and therein of Time. We ought to accept time as His Gift, and use it to His Glory, for 'the Lord hath made all things for Himself' (Prov. xvi. 4), and He gives

[1] Lettres, No. lxii.

us time only that we may employ it in His Service. We all feel bound to use a gift according to the intention of the giver;—if some one gives me a hundred crowns for the poor, I cannot use that money otherwise than in alms. So God gives us time, not that we may fritter it away in useless pursuits, or misspend it in evil actions which offend Him; but that we may employ it in good works to promote His Glory. Let us always keep this intention in mind, and our time will be better and more carefully spent than it too often is at present.

"The second truth I would commend to your thoughts is that we have not a single moment of time which is not won for us by Jesus Christ, and by His Death.

"God had said, 'In the day thou eatest of it' (the forbidden fruit), 'thou shalt surely die' (Gen. ii. 17); and had He heeded nothing save strict justice, sinful man had died without any time for repentance. Such a sentence was carried out upon the offending angels—they died their spiritual death immediately after they had sinned; but God spared man in virtue of the Merits of His Son, Who should come on earth to suffer and die for him. Therefore every hour which we have had hitherto, or are to have yet, we owe to Jesus Christ,—not one moment of time since Adam's fall but has been bought for man by the Redemption, at the price of our Saviour's Sufferings and Death. Consequently we owe Him that which He has bought for us at so great a price, and surely it behoves us to use the time He has won for us in a way worthy of His Labours, His Pains, His Cross, His Blood, and His Death. If we waste and misuse it, we are wasting that Precious Blood by which He gained it for us, and we shall have to give account for that time to God the Father. And therefore we ought to strive to use every moment of time as perfectly as we possibly can, remembering the price at which it has been bought. Think of the lost—how do you imagine they would use their time if God were to grant them again one single hour of all those they have misused,—and meanwhile we . . . ?

"The third truth I would have you ponder is that God's Holy Spirit was sent among men to help them to use time rightly. We cannot use it well without His Grace, we cannot lead a supernatural life apart from Him. In consequence of sin, we may use time to our eternal condemnation;—by nature we shall use it to earthly purposes, but we cannot use it according to the Will of Christ Jesus, save by the Holy Spirit of God. And therefore we ought continually and fervently to invoke that Holy Spirit, asking His Grace to use our time in union with His Intentions and Will. Continually through the day, we ought to refer to Him for guidance in the right use of our time; seeking to know how He would have us employ the actual hour now passing, and asking His aid not only to know, but to do His Will. . . . As members of Christ our standard should be a high one. . . . To this end, strive to unite your worship to the acts of devotion practised by the Son of God when on earth. Think what a condescension, what a humiliation this life of time, this subjection to hours and minutes, was to Him Who is Lord of Eternity;—to Him Who even then was Lord of that Glorious Eternity as much as He is now! Filled with this thought, let us adore Him in His voluntary subjection to our earthly bondage of time.

"The Fathers say that by vouchsafing to be baptized, Jesus Christ sanctified the waters of our Baptism; surely even so when He vouchsafed to be subject to our human laws of time, He sanctified it, and laid upon us the obligation to use it after a Christian fashion. Some brief devotion to His earthly life of time will help us in this—our best method of entering into the things of God is by adoration. . . . .

"Next, we must make God the End of all we do, and seek His Glory only. If Jesus Christ has won time for us, we must in return strive so to use it in all our actions after a manner worthy of His Cross and

Passion—and to do that we must have God ever before us in all our intentions. . . . When on earth, Jesus said, 'I can of mine own self do nothing. . . . I seek not mine own Will, but the Will of the Father which hath sent Me' (John v. 30), and we should strive to be of that mind throughout life, in whatever time brings us to do or bear. . . . . In Jesus Christ nothing is mean or vile—everything becomes great and noble, and so in His Church nothing done for Him can be contemptible or low; every action is refined and sanctified under the influence of the Holy Spirit, in the power of Whose Grace we ought to perform every action.

"But for the practical use of all these suggestions, one thing is indispensable as the groundwork; and that is total renunciation of self-seeking in our use of time, and in all we do. Otherwise while we think we are studying for God's Sake and His Glory, self-complacency or natural curiosity will intermingle, spoil the purity of our intention, and turn aside our aim. There is but one remedy—to give ourselves up absolutely to accept God's Hand ruling and guiding us."[1]

Tending to the same point, another letter says:—

"The principal occupation one created by God should have in this world is to glorify Him, and nothing should be allowed to divert us from this:—it

[1] Lettres, Nos. lxv. lxvi.

ought to be so absolutely our ruling thought that we may even turn the hindrances we meet with to the same end.

"Obviously our own anxieties tend to distract us, and therefore we ought to strive to make His Glory a more prominent object even than our own salvation. We ought to strive to be led solely by a spirit of faith, content with the light it gives, and always being more intent on *doing* than on stopping to see if we *are* doing.

"It is well, too, to give more heed to others than to one's-self, and to be content to serve God according to the instructions He gives through those He sets over us. You will do well to work for one hour daily in honour of the New Life of Jesus Christ raised from the dead. So, too, work for half an hour daily in honour of the Blessed Virgin, and of her hidden life in Christ—strive every day to fulfil some lowly task in honour of Jesus Christ making Himself the Servant of Man. Try to be less occupied with yourself and your own sufferings, and to bear them all in Him for God. You can pray something to this effect: 'I put aside all that I am—I cleave to all that God is—I will bear all that troubles me for His Glory,'" &c.[1]

Père de Condren's asceticism was by no means indiscriminating, as the following advice, volunteered to

[1] Lettres, No. lxxiii.

one whom he thought likely to observe Lent after a somewhat self-willed fashion, proves:—

"As Lent approaches, and hearing from you that you are not well, I feel obliged to write and urge you to submit to the advice given you about your food while you are weak. I have written to M. M—— to ask him to give you his advice, which you must conscientiously follow, and be scrupulously particular in doing so. The Evil One deadens the conscience of many who are quite able to observe this public penance (of Lent) which God has laid upon His Church from the earliest times, and leads them to neglect it; but on the other hand he tempts others who are incapable of a strict observance thereof, and causes them to injure their health, which is altogether contrary to the intention of God and His Church. We are just as much bound to submit to God when He requires us to deal charitably with ourselves as when He requires anything else of us.

"I think I have before now warned you that you are liable to an habitual temptation to injure yourself. I have noticed the consequences several times, and it seems to me that you are not sufficiently docile to the advice which has been given you on this score. One plain proof of this is the evident secret annoyance you feel when anything is said which interferes with your own views on the matter. Everybody has some special trial in this life; no one is free from struggle, and the holiest people are sometimes the most sorely tempted. It seems to me that by God's Mercy you are not tempted to sin against Him or against your neighbour, whose interests you are generally more disposed to serve than your own. God has been pleased to shield you from these attacks of the Enemy, so he turns them all on you yourself, and the repugnance you shew to the needful remedy almost makes me fear that he might succeed in his object, if it were not that I have still stronger hope in the help God's Mercy will send you. But you must mistrust his snares, for indeed it seems to me that you have a decided difficulty to face in all that concerns yourself, and that you are too much disposed to give way both in what concerns your temporal affairs and your health. Be on your guard, and strive to banish the malicious enemy, who after getting a hold upon you in matters of health and general affairs of life, will go on to what is more dangerous, and more directly affecting your salvation. The enemy does everything with a view to our final perdition, which is his real object.

"I am going on a long journey, and may not be in Paris again before the summer, and I feel it my duty to give you this warning before I go. Offer yourself to our Lord; ask His Grace to follow His Guidance in all things, and that you may yield in nothing to His enemies. Let yourself have full part in His Charity, as well as others. This is all the more necessary for you that you are under the influence of a distinct temptation to neglect your health, and that it is disagreeable to you to have to overcome it. Look back over your past conduct in all sincerity, and I hope you will perceive somewhat of this; but even if you do not, you cannot be wrong in deferring to the advice of your friends. I shall not cease to offer you diligently to God, indeed the further I am from you the more carefully I shall do so. I commend myself to your prayers."[1]

He could comfort the afflicted too, if not with the overflowing tenderness which characterises S. Francis de Sales' letters of consolation, yet with no cold apprehension of their needs:—

"May the Grace, the Blessing, and the Peace of our Lord Jesus Christ be granted you always. I pray Him, at this holy season wherein He deigned to rise to a new Life, that He would grant you renewed life and strength, not only to the mind, but to your body also, so that you may be the better able to minister to those souls He has committed to your care.

"I have often felt great compassion for what I have heard of your sufferings; my consolation is in the thought that the same Lord Who vouchsafed to be

[1] Lettres, No. cvii.

crucified out of love for you, is leading you on to His Glory, and chooses to fit you for His Bosom by the way of the Cross; as also, that the Spirit of God, Whose perfect work, the Apostle tells us, is patience, is perfecting you more and more. The Son of God would not stay His Sorrows or His Patience by consolation, or by anything short of that Sacrifice which put an end at once to His earthly Life and His Cross, and gave Him to the Father. So He wills that God should be the end of every Christian's cross and patience, and we ought not to desire to be free from pain and suffering in this life by putting aside sorrow or crosses, but by the putting aside of self, by leaving all else to cleave to Him. I doubt not but that God is in this manner the end of your Cross, and that as He has upheld you by His Spirit of patience, He will receive you in His own right time. I pray you, remember me in your prayers."[1]

To a mother who had just lost her child he writes:

"If I could leave town at the present moment I would have come to you, not that I could be of any use to your little one, but to comfort you, and help you to bear his loss without grieving overmuch. It is better that God's Will be wrought for the child than ours; it is more profitable for him. Life were far more perilous to him than death;—for death is to

[1] Lettres, No. xc.

your boy an entrance into Paradise and life eternal, whereas a longer sojourn upon earth might have perilled his salvation. Of a truth I love the dear little fellow, but I love him in God ;—I would choose rather his welfare than our satisfaction,—God's good pleasure before our wishes."[1]

And to a father who had lost two sons he writes :

"God is shewing you that when He committed these two children to you, it was not so much that you might bring them up in His Fear, as that you might offer them as two innocent hostages to His Glory. In so doing, He has given them perfect happiness ; they have known God before they knew anything of the world, or of themselves. You would have had the responsibility of their education, and now, calling them to reign with Him, God has given them the power of guiding and raising you, and they will be as two guardian Angels who, watching over all your life, with the help of God and His Holy Spirit, will lead you to Himself. The saints help us on our way not merely by their prayers, but likewise by their influence and inspirations, and by a silent supernatural communication to our souls of their own light and love of God. They have a mighty power with God. Our Dear Lord told S. John that they who overcome should sit with Him on His Throne and eat of the

[1] Lettres, No. xciv.

tree of life in the midst of the Paradise of God. It should be a great consolation, a great honour to you to have two children so blessed. Faith should overcome earthly sorrow, and change your father's tears into joy at the thought of their glory, and of the blessing they may be to you and yours."[1]

One touching note we find, written on the occasion of the death of an Oratorian, Père de Lorme, to his father :—

"If it had pleased God to grant the prayers of our Congregation, and to restore your son's health," (he says,) "I might have written to rejoice with you, but now I write to give account of him whom you trusted to us. . . . With all submission to God, Who has willed it thus, we are sorely grieved; for while we may not refuse God anything, there are some sacrifices which we cannot make without sharp pain, and wherein our tears are acceptable to Him. We are constrained to be willing that He should take your son from our love to His Own, and that having moulded Him awhile by His Grace, and brought him to that spiritual perfection which He required, He should call him to eternal joy in His Bosom.

"Your son's illness has been a long one, and it has called forth all the more his graces, and set a rare example before the Congregation, for he bore it all

[1] Lettres, No. xcv.

so well that it was as the crown to his edifying life.

"'Let patience have her perfect work,' says the Apostle S. James. Patience brings about perfection. Your son was carefully tended during his illness, and the doctors have testified their affection for your name by their assiduous care of him. But God has not willed to prosper their remedies, because He saw well rather to satisfy His own Love and His desire to take your son to Himself. The most skilled science could not withstand God's intentions, nor human help suffice to delay him in this world of sadness, when the Lord called him to eternal happiness. In the ordinary course of nature he would have ministered to you, and offered you to God, but since it has pleased God that he who was your child in this life should become as your elder brother in the life of glory, you must lay aside the father's feeling, and conceive a new kind of love, which looks upon him who was your son as now your protector—as a new guardian angel watching over your family. His death was so saintly, that we can have no other thought."[1]

A few short lines addressed to one dying will serve to shew his mind concerning death:—

"If I looked upon this life as a great good, or on

[1] Lettres, No. xcvi.

death as a great evil, I should be inconsolable at hearing of your state. But inasmuch as life is but a very dangerous journey which we are thankful to see end in a safe arrival with God; as death is the end of sin, the perfecting of a Christian's life, the accomplishment of his sacrifice, the beginning of his triumph, his entrance into glory, the hour when God takes him down from his cross to live in His Bosom for ever blessed; remembering all this, I cannot pity you, and all my sorrow turns into the one prayer which I am moved to make continually, that God will be ever with you. He will fill you with holier thoughts than anything I can suggest, and now that your whole mind must be fixed on God Who is so very near to you, I do not suppose you will care very much for my letters. Nevertheless, in compliance with M. N.'s letter, I will suggest to your mind three considerations concerning our Lord Jesus Christ, Who is the model of all perfection in life and death. First, He readily left all to go to His Father, all His works being done in Him. Next, He bore all the exceeding bitterness of His Cup willingly for His Father's Glory. And last, far from murmuring or being absorbed in His sufferings, He offered Himself with His whole Will to God. And it is our duty to strive to enter into all His ways and to abide therein with Him. May He give you grace to do so. I ask it with my whole heart."[1]

Concerning the sacrament of marriage, Père de Condren writes:—

"It is less understood, more profaned, and more hard to be perfectly observed than any other. But as every Christian is bound to aim at perfection in his own calling, it is important to know wherein that of marriage lies; its special dignity arising from the end to which it was instituted. Now this end is to set before us the union of Jesus Christ with His Bride the Church, the most perfect of all unions on earth, of which this sacrament is the type.

"Perfection of the marriage state, then, consists in setting forth as clearly as is possible to men this sacred union; so that by their intentions, actions, and use of marriage, the husband and wife may prove their intention of fulfilling our Lord Jesus Christ's objects in this Sacrament, which are spiritual, not earthly. To this end, they should ponder the extreme purity of Christ's union with His Church, and inasmuch as to equal that is beyond the power of mere mortals, they should adore it humbly, and pray that our Dear Lord would grant them His Holy Spirit, so that they may be able to attain a part in the holy objects and intentions which He sets before them in this Sacrament. It were

[1] Lettres, No. lxvii.

well, before approaching it, to read attentively and devoutly meditate both the office and ritual which the Church appoints to be used, so as to realize what is promised and undertaken. It is a pious practice to bid our Dear Lord and His Mother to the wedding, in memory of their presence at Cana of Galilee; as also S. Joseph, bearing in mind the reverence and decorum which is incumbent on all the guests. Too often the holiness of this Sacrament is violated by what passes on these occasions; by a license which savours more of paganism than Christianity, and which must avert the blessing God would impart to greater purity and reverence. You must not fail to offer to God the children He may please to give you, with a full resolution of devoting them to be faithful subjects of His Kingdom; and it would be a very suitable devotion at such a time to dedicate yourself specially to serve Christ and His Church, in honour of that blessed union between Him and His Bride of which this Sacrament is the type. Above all, ask of Him that you may enter upon the state of matrimony with no other intention than that of pleasing Him, remembering that in Baptism you renounced the flesh and became a new creature; that therein you put on Christ Jesus; you died to the old Adam; you came forth to live with Christ Risen, you were made a member of Christ Glorified, Who sitteth on the

Father's Right Hand. Let husband and wife dwell together, therefore, as Christians should, and let Jesus Christ, Who gave His Blood and His Life for His Church, be the model of your married life."[1]

One letter of Père de Condren, addressed to a religious who was disturbed at having to change his convent, expresses what was his own practice as well as precept in obeying all and any of God's calls:—

"It matters little," he says, "where we are, for God is everywhere, and His Dear Son sends His Holy Spirit and His Church into every part of the world; and as everywhere we have free access to Heaven, so too our Lord and His Saints can and will help us whithersoever we may be. But it does matter very considerably that we be wheresoever God wills us to be. Before the Incarnation, God's people received His messages by means of angels, who told them where God would have them dwell; but now, since God vouchsafed to become Man, He has appointed men to be the ministers of His Will towards their fellow-men; and we are bound to receive God's Orders from their lips with even greater reverence than the Patriarchs of old from those of His angels, because God, Who took upon Him the form not of an angel but of man, wills that His message be spoken to us not by angels but by men.

[1] Lettres, No. civ.

"I write thus with reference to your new abode, in order to induce you, out of reverence for the Mystery of the Incarnation, the Source of all your grace, to accept it willingly, as also to change it again for any other which your superiors may appoint. We have no right to any dwelling-place whatever on earth, save through our Lord Jesus Christ, Who has given us possession, or, more strictly speaking, the use of that which He won for us by His Blood; and this because sin, without His Redeeming Grace, would cast us forthwith into hell as our only abode. This truth ought to make us very faithful in accepting whatever abode He may allot to us, inasmuch as we owe any habitation whatsoever which we possess solely to Him and His Merits. I am writing on S. Paul's Day, which reminds me how he, who was carried up into Paradise, yet came back, in submission to God's Will, to preach, labour, and at last die in this world; leaving God, so to say, for God; after a fashion imitating our Lord, Who came forth from the Bosom of the Father into the world, as He Himself says. Now you quit neither God nor Paradise, but you come from the Convent of the Incarnation, and that very Mystery should strengthen you to do it in a spirit of adoration of Him Who left the Bosom of the Father to bear His Cross on earth. Each time that you communicate, He is sent to you by the Father, the Holy Spirit brings Him to you, and He gives Himself to you, and comes to dwell in a very poor and worthless dwelling, unworthy to be compared to that which He leaves. Nevertheless in His Mercy He chooses to come and abide with you. Apply this thought to your change of abode, and accept it in honour thereof. I think it will be profitable to you, for God ever returns a hundredfold whatsoever we give up for Him.

"It may seem to you that you are losing your wonted spiritual help in quitting Paris, but God will not suffer you to be deprived of it. Our Lord was more helpful to His Apostles through His Absence than through His Presence, as He had told them would be the case. I hope by His Grace that you will receive more spiritual aid from your House in Paris in your absence than you would by being there, since you leave it for God's Sake. You are with the Prioress, if no longer in the same town, yet in the Same Lord, if you are faithful to Him. You are with her in the same Holy Spirit, in whose Heart and Love our Lord has placed His Church; and you are with her in the Same God, in Whose Bosom dwell the Blessed Virgin and all the Saints—all, in short, who are born of Him. In that Home you dwell as a Christian, elsewhere you have nought save what is of sin, which must sooner or later be taken from you, and which therefore you should wish yourself to leave.

As the child of Adam you are in banishment in this world, and just now Dieppe is the place of your exile, whither God has driven you, as of old He drove your father Adam forth from Paradise. But as the child of God, Jerusalem is your home, and therein you are only separated from your Sisters in Paris by that which you are bound to despise and reject, by that which has not yet put on the new man, by that which 'waits for the adoption, to wit, the redemption of our body,' as S. Paul says (Rom. viii. 23). I think this ought to be a great consolation to you. You and your Sisters in Paris were the children of God, but the children of Adam likewise; now you have left that part of the union which belonged to Adam, but you are still united with them inasmuch as you both belong to God. So your mission to Dieppe has only separated you in that which it was well to quit, leaving whole and intact that which both you and they would wish to keep in this world and in the next, even more earnestly than your very life itself. . . . God is everywhere—He sends forth His Holy Spirit in all lands. There is no place from whence we may not have access to Him through His Son, and wheresoever we may be, Jesus Christ and His Saints help and succour us. God's commands, formerly transmitted to men through the Angels, have now a no less claim to our reverence when they come through our fellow-men, because the Word has vouchsafed to unite Himself to man, and to make the members of His Body channels and interpreters of His Will to their brethren. We have no right to any dwelling-place save through His Mercy, and therefore whatever place He may assign us ought to be thankfully accepted by us. If God's Own Son did not refuse to leave the Father and come into the world, surely there is no home we should hesitate to leave in honour of His Incarnation and of His Sojourn in Judæa. Think too how He comes to us in the Holy Sacrament in order to prove His Love for us, and remembering that, how can we hesitate to go wherever we are called out of love for Him? Whatever loss we think to find by a change of abode will be more than compensated, if we offer it as a freewill sacrifice; and the Unity of Jesus Christ, which cannot be broken or hindered by any distance, will prevent our being really deprived of the spiritual blessings we seem to leave. Doubtless removals involve a separation from friends, but it is only a separation which concerns the flesh, to which as Christians we ought to be dead. In the Spirit, we are one with them in the Spiritual Jerusalem, which extends over the whole earth—nay more, we are so welded and bound together, that we are but one body in Jesus Christ."[1]

[1] Lettres, Nos. xcvii. xcviii.

There is one letter of de Condren's on a subject of considerable importance, which nevertheless is not often treated of in spiritual correspondence, namely, the disposition of property; and at the risk of too extended quotation from the Oratorian's writings, this letter to a friend concerning his will and its importance must be given.

"The best way, as it seems to me, of making one's last will and testament," he says, "is to spend an hour in meditation before God, giving account to Him of ourselves, and of those external and internal gifts with which He has endowed us; humbly pondering what use we have made of them, and how far it has been in conformity with His Holy Will, and with the perfect disposition of life and all earthly things of our Dear Lord. I forgot to say that it is very profitable to begin such a meditation, as though one had but another day to live, so as to press home the importance of not delaying to fulfil all our last duties towards God; for fear lest time should fail, and we find ourselves deficient before Him, when it is too late to remedy the neglect. This consideration would oblige us to take suitable time for examining what God's Will is as to the final disposition of ourselves and our possessions, for surrendering them heartily to Him, and for realising those ultimate objects and intentions for His Glory, which we ought to have with respect to the good things we owe solely to His liberality.

"Next, we should give God thanks for these His gifts, rejoicing in the Goodness which has sent them to us, sorrowing over the misuse we have made of them, and willing absolutely to restore them to Him. It is well to linger somewhat over these acts of gratitude, joining our spirit of thanksgiving to that of angels and archangels, and desiring Eternity more for His Glory than our own blessedness. We may well desire that our spirit of thankfulness should not end with this earthly life, or be buried in our coffin, and, therefore, we may well try to express it in acts of lasting gratitude which will survive us." (Père de Condren then suggests certain pious bequests, observing that these had better be as free as possible, and without a view to personal exaltation, going on to say,) " It is well to be content to be forgotten ourselves, so that God Alone may dwell in men's hearts. We are apt to be too much engrossed with self, and to want to fill that share of interest and consideration in the minds of others which appertains to God Only. But it is good to seek rather that in this as in all else they 'be filled with the Fulness of God' Alone. (Eph. iii. 19.) Souls are temples which ought to be filled with His Sole Majesty, and hearts dedicated to Him should know no rival, lest that rival become an idol. . . . Let us be content to hide ourselves in God, until at our Lord Jesus Christ's Last Coming all things are revealed. Let us freely give Him this world and all that is in it, if He will but give us Heaven. The day will come when He will shew that those who have been most prominently seen in His works have not always done the most; and sometimes they who are least worthy receive most credit in this life, because in His Wisdom He does not choose that His faithful servants should run the risk of having their reward here.

"At the hour of death it behoves us to have a spirit of death, not of life : and as to our memory among our brethren, since our bodies must of necessity be humbly laid beneath the feet of men, it does not beseem us to strive to erect statues to our memory in their hearts; knowing as we do, that if they knew all our faults they would rather abhor us, and only think of us in pity, and for the sake of the humiliations and sufferings of Jesus Christ.

"I have dwelt somewhat lengthily on the temptation to create a lasting memory and reputation for one's-self by means of a will, because a man's will is really only a preparation for death, and an act which ought to be done in a spirit of humility and repentance; consequently to turn it into mere vainglory is really wrong. A man should make his will in the same spirit in which he wishes to die; that is, in a spirit of detachment from the world, of humble penitence, and of self-oblation to God. One's will is a sort of conclusion to one's life, the final disposition of that over which we have control, and consequently it ought to be a perfecting of one's life, after which nothing remains to be done save to die well. A man would do well to remember when making his will that death is a penalty involving all he is and all he possesses; he should think of Jesus Christ giving up Himself before His Passion as a perpetual Sacrifice to His Father, and so strive to sanctify whatever God has given him for God. Our bodies must return to the dust whence they came forth—our souls must be left to God, but while we have the power of offering them voluntarily to Him, we should do so; and as to our property, let us adore Him Who gave it, and Who, while calling us to enter upon a better inheritance, will require due account as to how we have used what He has given us. . . . Therefore see what you can do to minister to the wants of the Church, the Bride and Heiress of Christ. . . ."[1]

[1] Lettres, No. lxxxv.

CHAPTER IV.

THE ORATORY AND ITS SYSTEM.

WHILE de Condren was absorbed in what more specially concerned the inner life, study, the direction of souls, and the daily intensifying of his own personal advance in the Unitive way, de Bérulle was following the latter object by a different path. Political labours and negotiations thickened round him, royal favours were heaped upon him—public opinion pointed him out as the rival of Cardinal Richelieu, whose enmity was speedily kindled in consequence. But de Bérulle did not aim at the position of a world-famed statesman, nor even when appointed Counsellor of State and President of the Council of Regency (as he was in the year 1628), did these worldly honours turn his thoughts aside from that which had always been his one first thought. Nor were the scarcely less fascinating lures of science more successful. Prominently concerned in all that was stirring in the world of intellect,—the patron of and first to discover Descartes' genius as well as that of other scientific men—none of these things really filled his mind. Perfectly aware that his health was breaking, the Cardinal continued to toil wearily and painfully at his public duties, both political and those which concerned the Congregation, but meanwhile he was preparing to lay them all aside, and give in his last account to God. As early as April 1629, he made a general confession to Père de Condren in preparation for death, and he was repeatedly heard to express an earnest desire, if it might be, to die while actually celebrating the Blessed Sacrifice of the Eucharist.

Towards the end of September he went to Fontainebleau, where the King required his presence concerning a mission to Gaston d'Orléans, who, as usual, was in trouble. On the 27th the Cardinal returned to Paris so ill that he was unable to get to the Mother House, and remained that night at Saint Magloire. A day or two of rapidly increasing weakness followed, during which de Bérulle could not be induced to give up any part of his office; but on October 2nd, while celebrating with much effort, he fainted away at the end of the Gospel. Directly that he came round, however, he insisted on continuing the service, and broke down finally just before the Consecration, while saying the words "*Hanc igitur oblationem.*" The Oratorian Fathers placed their

General in an arm-chair, and gave him the Viaticum and Extreme Unction; during the few minutes of needful preparation he was heard to cry out, "Where is He? Let me see Him! Let me adore Him! Let me receive Him!" Almost directly after receiving the last Sacraments de Bérulle passed from this life, at the age of fifty-four.

Although up to the time of his death Cardinal de Bérulle had not framed Constitutions for the Congregation, or provided for many external details,[1] he had done much towards the development of its internal life, and to enable it to meet the needs of the day. From first to last his leading idea was "the close connexion of the new Congregation with the Priesthood; its special union with the Incarnate Word above all in His Divine Priesthood, wherein He is chiefly seen as adoring the Father, and mediating between God and man."[2] The various existing Religious Orders, he said, were founded by men, and have some special evangelic counsel as their main object—the Franciscans poverty, the Carthusians solitude, the Jesuits obedience; but the Priesthood owns no Founder save Our Lord Jesus Christ, and therefore it is pledged to seek all evangelic perfection, not to select and pursue one point alone. Too often the priests of God have forgotten and lowered

[1] L'Oratoire, Père Perraud, p. 164.   [2] *Ibid.* p. 81.

this their high standard, and Cardinal de Bérulle's object in founding the Oratory was to bring them back as far as possible to it. "The aim of the Congregation is to strive after the perfection of the Priesthood." Doubtless, he said, this should be the aim of each several priest, but united action is ever more powerful than the best-intentioned efforts of individuals can be, and the advantages of a Community life to those who are seeking to attain a high standard is very great.

"A common social life," de Bérulle says, "is most essential to the perfection of the ecclesiastical state of life, for solitude is injurious not merely to the weak, but also to those who need many things to promote their work which a Community affords, such as participation of labour, readiness to be found at all times by the people, constant co-operation alike in their functions in the Church and in those works of charity which claim their care.

"In addition to all this assistance given by a common life to the external work of the sacred ministry, it is a great help to those whom God calls to Christian perfection to subject themselves to the guidance of a Congregation, which shelters them from many hindrances, and assists them by example, by conferences, and many like means which are unattainable to individuals."[1]

[1] Règlements de l'Oratoire, Preface.

De Bérulle held that the priesthood is no less bound to seek after the highest perfection than those who have formally taken the Religious vows, and therefore he would not have his priests bound by more than their Ordination Vows; they were to aim at the Counsels of Perfection in virtue of that total self-dedication, which he looked upon as the very essence of sacerdotal life. "His intense love for the Church," says Bossuet, "kindled in him the desire of forming a Company which he would inspire with no other mind than that of the Church; to which he would give no rules save her Canons, no superiors save her Bishops, no possessions save her Charity, no vows save those of Baptism and Holy Orders. Therein holy liberty becomes a holy bondage; men obey without being dependent; they govern without commanding; authority finds all its strength in gentleness, and respect needs not to be upheld by fear. Love, banishing fear, works miracles, and without any further yoke than its own sweet self, knows not only how to subject, but to annihilate self-will. Here, in order to form true priests, they are led to the Source of all Truth;—they have the Holy Scriptures in their hand, perpetually seeking its letter in study, its spirit in prayer, its depth in retreat, its efficacy in practice, its end in charity—the true end of all, '*Christiani nominis thesaurus'*—the one treasure of Christianity, as says Tertullian."[1]

Père de Bérulle enlarges on his idea of the perfection set before the Priesthood in the following terms:—

"Inasmuch as all the members of this Congregation are bound by their calling to seek this perfection, their life should be perfect, submissive, regulated, social, edifying, and laborious.

"*Perfect* in intention—seeking God, not self, Heaven, not earth, desiring nothing save to possess Jesus, and to serve Him and His blessed Mother, putting aside all other claims as though they were not:

"*Submissive* in practice and functions, acting according to the will of others:

"*Regulated* in exact observance, obeying rules for the love of God and not constrainedly:

"*Social* in humility and gentleness, and in kindly forbearance towards one another, '*alter alterius onera portate. . . . Non quæ sua sunt singuli considerantes:*'

"*Edifying* others by modesty, by a humble spirit and holy conversation:

"*Laborious* externally, through constant occupation and work, and internally through a hidden life ever seeking God."

De Bérulle goes on to press the fact that these

[1] Oraison Funèbre du Père Bourgoing, Bossuet, Œuvres, edit. Lachat, vol. xii. p. 646.

obligations depend, not upon religious vows, but upon sacerdotal consecration :—

"To which manner of life priests are called by the Life of the Son of God, which they are bound to set forth in their own, inasmuch as our part is to live and move in Jesus, through Whom Alone we are called.

"The *perfect* life contemplates and adores His Divine Life :

"The life of *submission* has reference to His subjection to the abjection of our human nature in every stage from infancy to death :

"The life of *rule* has reference to the way in which His Life was subjected not only to the Father's Will, but to the ordinary course of natural things :

"*Social* life to His Life among the Apostles, with the Blessed Virgin and S. Joseph, etc. :

"The life of *edification and labour* to His Labours on earth and His Cross.

"The real link which binds this Congregation is Charity, and the aim of those who form it is to seek after evangelical perfection thereby, not by any solemn vows. Consequently their life, which ought to be specially interior, is in externals ordinary; and their attention is rather fixed on practical holiness, on Jesus Christ and His Church, on their duties, their responsibilities towards souls, than on ceremonies and external observances, which however are not to be neglected, but shaped according to the external life of the Community."[1]

Thus while other Orders devoted themselves specially to preaching, education, or contemplation, the Oratory contemplated the organisation of the secular priest's life, whatever might be his individual vocation.

"If you are capable of study," wrote Père Amelote (the friend and biographer of de Condren), "the Oratory will provide you with quiet, with books, and with pulpits from whence to teach. If you seek retirement, it offers you solitude as well as more busy positions; if you yearn after a life of penitence, you will find men among us as ascetic as the Carthusians themselves; or if you are consumed by zeal for God's service, our Society offers you a choice of missions and cures. Do you delight in music and splendid ritual? You can follow such. In a word, the Oratory charitably moulds herself to every Community without becoming identical with any, inasmuch as it is not separated from the Bishops, and is bound to all natural superiors."[2]

The Constitutions of the Oratory were not finally framed till Père de Condren's Generalship, but they may as well be referred to here, for their spirit

[1] Règlements, quoted by Père Perraud, p. 90.
[2] Vie de Condren, ii. p. c. viii.

was altogether that of Cardinal de Bérulle, and his successor's great aim was to act in all things according to his mind.

The Congregation was to be itself the source of and to exercise all authority, an authority the ministration of which it delegated to the Superior and certain assistants, but with the right reserved of questioning and examining their government by means of a General Assembly held every three years.

A living Oratorian makes some interesting comments on this Government, as being pre-eminently constitutional.

"It is curious," Père Adolphe Perraud says, "to study its mechanism by the light of the period in which it was framed and carried out. It was in that early part of the seventeenth century, when on all sides power was becoming more centralised, the exercise of authority more direct, the share of government to which inferiors were admitted smaller;— when Richelieu's system was paving the way for that of Louis XIV.,—on the eve of the day when France was so dazzled with glory as to forgive the 'Grand Roi' for presuming to say, '*l'Etat, c'est moi.*' It was at the beginning of that long period of a hundred and seventy-five years during which the national representation of the *Etats généraux* was to be altogether suspended, and when, from 1614 to 1789, France was never to be permitted by her rulers to make herself heard, to protest against the fatal wars into which she was dragged, to complain of the taxes which crushed, or to control by means of her representatives the financial ruin which was being wrought for her. It was in such times as these that the founders of the Oratory developed a Constitution in which the rights of all were so carefully guarded, which obliged superiors to consider the opinions of their inferiors, which called upon authority to render a periodical account of its acts, and to be set aside in due course before a higher power, namely, that of the Congregation itself as represented by its deputies.

"One might marvel less at this ample liberty were we contemplating one of those Religious Orders which were founded in the Middle Ages, contemporary with a condition of things in which the modern system of administrative centralisation was unknown. In those days the system of assemblies and elections was found in full vigour in conventual life, both among men and women, long before it was dreamt of in civil society,[1] and the modern declaimers who think to

[1] After analysing the Constitutions which S. Dominic gave to his Order of preachers, Lacordaire says: "Such were the Constitutions which a Christian man of the thirteenth century gave to other Christian men, and assuredly all modern charters have a strangely despotic savour compared with this. Thousands of men, scattered all over the face of the earth, lived during six

display their wisdom by denouncing the despotism and lack of liberty and progress of the Church, would be amazed, were they to read the Constitutions of Cîteaux, or S. Dominic, to find that these calumniated cloisters were so many small states governed by magistrates of their own choosing, and uniting practically the most heroic obedience with the noblest and most real liberty."[1]

The Oratory was governed by a triennial Assembly of deputies—one of whom represented every twelve members—such membership requiring a man to be in Priest's Orders, and to have been three years and three months in the Society. This Assembly elected all officers and reviewed all acts. The Superior General was to be re-elected every three years, according to S. Philip Neri, but during de Bérulle's life no measures were taken to rule this point in France, and the first Assembly under de Condren decided that the Superior should hold office for life "in honour of the Everlasting Priesthood of Jesus Christ."

The practical rule of life of Cardinal de Bérulle's Congregation was simple. The hours kept in the

hundred years under this régime, peaceful and united—the most industrious, the most obedient, the freest of men."—(Mémoire pour le Rétablissement des Frères Prêcheurs, c. ii.)

[1] L'Oratoire, p. 93.

seventeenth century were everywhere early, and the Oratorians adopted as implying no great austerity the same time for rising shortly after given by S. Vincent de Paul to his Sisters of Charity—4 A.M., nine o'clock P.M. being the hour of going to bed. The first act of the day was an hour's meditation. Those who were in their novitiate spent the rest of it in offices, study of Holy Scripture—a portion of which was to be learnt by heart daily—and of theology; due heed to exercise and recreation being taken. The Fathers who had completed their novitiate found no lack of employment in the exercise of their priestly functions, education, and the various intellectual works to which their respective capacities called them. There was no severe asceticism among them—the ordinary rules of the Church were supplemented by some few days of special observance, and silence was kept on the evenings of Friday and Saturday in memory of our Lord's Seasons of retirement even from the Blessed Virgin and His Apostles, as well as on all fast days, and when the Blessed Sacrament was exposed. More stress was laid by their pious Founder on the spirit than on the actual form of the Oratorian life. "The whole object and mind of this institution," he wrote,[1] "is special love and honour to Jesus Christ in His Eternal Priest-

[1] Esprit de l'Oratoire.

hood, the Founder of all priesthood; and to maintain this spirit duly we must recognise Jesus as the Founder and Ruler of our life. So too we must give Him all and more than the reverence and submission which religious Orders are wont to pay to their founders, recognising none other save Himself, but that without failing in obedience to such things as may be enjoined in His Name and His Authority by those who are His representatives."

This devotion to our Lord ought to imply :—

"A great union of our mind with the Mind of Jesus, which must rule us inwardly, and bear fruit externally:

"Great zeal for His Honour, as the object of our life:

"Renunciation of the world and of self, as the cross we are called on to bear for His Glory :

"Perfect imitation of His Life and Ways:

"Diligent co-operation with His intentions and works, ever remembering that the order of nature may subsist without our labour, but not so the order of grace which is committed to us:

"Great respect and devotion to His Church :

"Earnest efforts to advance His Kingdom upon earth.

"In short, so to live as to be filled with Him, seeking none save Him, despising all else, desiring that

He may even now be All in all to us through Grace, as hereafter He will be in Glory."

Every act was to be offered in this sense to our Lord. On first waking, the Oratorian was to adore His Incarnation; dressing, he was to remember how he had "put on Christ" in Baptism; his cassock was to remind him of the Lamb dumb before His shearers, and so forth. "Time," de Bérulle wrote, "is a possession bought for us by the Son of God, in order that by means of it we may acquire nothing less than God Himself. And Priests are more bound than other men to use it for this end, inasmuch as it is their part so to employ time, that they may win not only their own blessed eternity, but that of other men."

As near an approach to continual meditation on the High Priesthood of Christ as human imperfection admits of should be the source from whence His chosen servants must drink life and strength for their weighty office. From daily meditation upon the Life and Words of the Son of God there will inevitably result:

"Acts of *Adoration*, inasmuch as every action of the Son of God is Divine:

"Of *Self-dedication*, for Christ has bought us by His ever priceless act; and meditating on any of His words, acts, or thoughts, we should renew our gift of ourselves in thanksgiving for that special thing:

"Of *Thanksgiving*, for that He came on earth for us; His life and whatsoever He did being all for us:

"Of *Love*. All He did was Love for us, and we are bound to answer Him in love, renouncing all mere earthly love for His sake:

"Of *Zeal*, seeking that He may be known and loved of all men, that His Love may bear due fruit:

"Of *Petition*. His actions are the source of all Good Gifts, and we must ask all we need through them."

There is one very touching and beautiful admonition given by Cardinal de Bérulle to the members of his Congregation, namely, that their petitions should be, not personal and selfish, but general; that they ask, not that their own needs only may be supplied, but that whatever they pray for be for their neighbours, their community, the whole Church, seeking God's Glory in all. If you feel cold and languid in prayer, if routine chills your energies, and the spirit of devotion grows slack and formal within you, it will be rekindled by dwelling on the universality of the Love of Jesus Christ. You, as a Priest, will remind yourself that the salvation of a soul, the salvation of your flock, may hang upon the earnestness of your prayer; that with you it rests to rescue this soul from temptation or that other from despair; to cast down Satan's triumphs and stablish the Kingdom of Christ. Such thoughts as these will surely revive the slackening warmth of a man's heart, and enable him to cast himself with fresh fervour before that Loving Saviour Who has said, "Whatsoever ye shall ask in My Name, it shall be given unto you."

Cardinal de Bérulle also recommended the practice on which de Condren, as we have already seen, laid so much stress, the "*examen de prévoyance*," or forecasting the duties and probable temptations and trials of the coming day, so as to meet them forearmed, and strengthened by prayer and self-humiliation.

Needless to say how important a feature in each priestly life he esteemed the Blessed Sacrifice of the Altar. De Bérulle's death was but the final act of his life, through which the Holy Eucharist was ever his chief desire, his stay and consolation. "Those holy souls who endure life and long for death," he wrote,[1] "who count this world as an exile, find their consolation in the Eucharist, and that because they grow in the Love of God through the Divine virtue of that celestial manna, a privilege peculiar to this life; because their King and Saviour vouchsafes therein to be really present with them; and because by it He has given them the means of offering a worthy homage to His Heavenly Father. The Blessed Sacrament is the Manna of our desert, the Paschal Lamb of our exile, our

[1] Discours de l'Eucharistie.

Food till we reach the Mount Horeb, the Victim of propitiation to us, our praise-offering, our one perfect price by which we obtain all things from the Father."

With respect to all intellectual labour—(and the Oratorians have numbered no ordinary intellects among them)—their Founder still insisted on the precept already quoted from their original institution, that knowledge is not to be sought for itself alone, but that it may be used to set forward the Kingdom of Christ and the salvation of souls: "NON TAM CIRCA SCIENTIAM QUAM CIRCA USUM SCIENTIÆ."

Cardinal de Bérulle's instructions to his Congregation on the right use of intellectual study are founded on the words of Holy Scripture; "the Lord is a God of knowledge, and by Him actions are weighed" (1 Sam. 2, 3), or as it is in the Vulgate, "Deus scientiarum Dominus est, et ipsi præparantur cogitationes." He enjoins them to ponder well over these words, and not to defraud God of that which is His, by assuming any powers of mind or intellectual capacity to be their own gifts—nay, it is a very sacrilege for a man to attribute the beauty, or force, or depth of his conception and ideas to himself, all coming from Him Who breathed into man's nostrils the breath of life, Who is "the Father of Spirits" (Heb. xii. 9), and "the Father of lights" (James i. 17). "How," the

Cardinal asks, "shall we glory in our petty knowledge of such small earthly things, and not rather lose ourselves in the contemplation and hope of the glorious things which await us? What are we? What do we know? A handful of dust, knowing somewhat of earthly science and human language, and even that but imperfectly and uncertainly. But supposing such knowledge to be carried to the greatest perfection, what is it in comparison with the speech and the knowledge of angels, still more with that of God? We are called to greater things; we are called to know not this world, but the Author of the world, to live an endless life in Him. Surely it is no small dignity to live in God, to share His Eternal happiness! yet that is our life, and for ever—let us never rest satisfied in anything short of that."

De Bérulle warns his Congregation against the perils which beset the studious and intellectual;—presumption, arrogance, vanity; quoting S. Bernard's saying, that "some men learn in order to know, and that is curiosity: others to be known, and that is vanity: while others learn in order to edification, and that is charity." "*Alii sciunt ut sciant, et est curiositas; alii sciunt ut sciantur, et est vanitas; alii sciunt ut ædificent, et est caritas*" (In Cant. 36).

Recreation times were to be watchfully used; a few moments' prayer were to precede them, and the ejaculation, "The Word was made Flesh and dwelt among us," in order that His Mind and Conversation among men might be remembered as the model of that of His servants, a habit which de Bérulle said would cause their intercourse to be after S. Paul's precept, and "whatsoever things are true, whatsoever things are honest, whatsoever things are just, whatsoever things are pure, whatsoever things are lovely, whatsoever things are of good report" (Phil. iv. 8), would be the groundwork of their intercourse.

In treating of the special duties of superiors, Père de Bérulle says, "Our work is to become holy even as He is Holy, and through His Holy Spirit to learn how to promote the sanctification of others by our example and by our labours. All are bound to work for this end perseveringly and faithfully, giving all our best efforts, our longings and prayers, in a word, using every gift of nature and of grace which we may possess thereto. Each one of us is bound to do this, though after divers manners—each according to his power and according to the work assigned him—some in prayer, others in labour; some in ruling prudently, others in accepting direction meekly, for to rule well and be ruled well is a special gift from God, Who gives wisdom to some and docility to others—to the one authority, and to the other obedience—imparting His Grace alike to various conditions, giving sometimes indeed a more abundant grace to those who are ruled than to those who rule. Thus His secret counsels should mould us all in humility and mutual respect—superiors revering the hidden grace in those who are subject to them, and these again deferring to God's Authority as represented by their superiors—all the while being bound together in the unity of the One Spirit, Which worketh amid the 'diversities of gifts.'"

Superiors are warned to consider their duties under five heads :—

I. What they owe to God :

II. What they owe to themselves :

III. What they owe to their neighbour :

IV. What they owe to those under them :

V. What they owe to our Lord Jesus Christ, "Whose Blood we apply, Whose Spirit we impart, in Whose Power we act, for Whose Glory we work."

The Superior will continually lift up his heart to God as the Father of Light, and will study to preserve a ceaseless dependence upon that Power Which is the source and strength of all human power. He will strive to act solely as God's Instrument. With respect to himself, he will be diligent "in abnegation of earthly things, in seeking after Heavenly things ; in patience towards that which concerns others, in enduring his responsibilities rather as a cross to be borne than with any delight or satisfaction in them, watching that he himself and those under him be ruled by the Apostle's precept, "If we live in the Spirit, let us also walk in the Spirit" (Gal. v. 25). As regards his neighbour, the Superior is to be all charity, patience, kindness, solicitude, edification. Once a week he is to read over passages from S. Paul, which he is to recall and practise many times a day: "Charity suffereth long, and is kind, . . . vaunteth not itself—seeketh not her own—is not easily provoked, . . . beareth all things, . . . hopeth all things, endureth all things" (1 Cor. xiii. 4-7). "We are unto God a sweet savour of Christ" (2 Cor. ii. 15). And with respect to his responsibilities, the Superior is rather to maintain them as God's Will than to shrink under the burden. All his functions must be performed with authority and charity duly blended: he will give but few commands, and will rather lead those subject to him to do their duty by the force of example, of love, and of prayer; continually keeping in mind that he holds his authority not for the sake of authority, but for love's sake, and that inasmuch as all his authority comes from One Who is both Lord of all and Lamb of God, it had need be guided more by gentleness and humility than by power—more in patience than in strength. In the same spirit of humility the Superior was not to despise any details of his office, however small. "Moreover," as the Cardinal says, "everything that refers to God is great, and there is nothing little in God's House." Accordingly the Superior of the Oratorians was from time to time to superintend personally every household detail, however humble or distasteful.

With respect to the faults of those under him, de Bérulle says,—

"I. He will humble himself in other men's faults, bearing in mind that he would commit greater faults than theirs if God left him to himself.

"II. He will impute their faults to himself in God's Sight, inasmuch as his lack of wisdom, of charity, or of good example may have led to them.

"III. He will bear in mind that God seeks to train and perfect him through the shortcomings of others.

"IV. He will strive to foresee and avert faults by his prudence in preventing occasions of falling ;—he will bear them with patience, restrain them by example, amend them by love, correct them, but 'in the spirit of love,' not that of rule; and he will beware of the false zeal which is a temptation to some superiors, rather cultivating the utmost gentleness and patience in honour and imitation of the Son of God, Who bore so tenderly and patiently with the roughness and ignorance of His Apostles."

But who is sufficient for these things? Surely nothing short of a very continual recollection and sense of God's Presence can enable a man so to "lose himself, that he may find himself in God"? So thought Cardinal de Bérulle, for he goes on to say,—" The works of God must be done in the Spirit of God; the works of light in the Spirit of Light; the works of Grace by the help of Grace, and not by the mere darkness of nature and our earthly mind. When God created the world, He made the light first, and in that light all His other works, and He 'saw' or examined everything that He had made by it; according to which example we should view and review our actions, not to encourage self-satisfaction, but to rule them more and more after the counsels of perfection and our Dear Lord's intentions. We need to recollect ourselves, hour by hour, so as to acquire a holy habit of always living and acting as in God's Presence. It is well, in addition to our ordinary religious exercises, that the Superior should daily give a short time to self-examination as regards his office, studying wherein he can do more to promote both his own perfection and that of others."

The Superior's motto was to be, "Thy Kingdom come. Even so come, Lord Jesus!"

Such being the requirements for the General of the Oratorians, it was not unnatural that the Congregation, immediately after Cardinal de Bérulle's death, should have fixed upon de Condren as his worthiest successor. At that moment the latter was at Nancy, acting as mediator between Louis XIII. and his troublesome brother, Gaston d'Orléans. The Queen Mother had opposed the Duke of Orléans' marriage with a daughter of the Duke de Nevers, and the spoiled boy had plunged into every kind of wild excess in his disappointment. After a while he took refuge with the Duke of Lorraine, whence it was important to Richelieu's policy to recall him, and Père de Condren, who had more influence over the wayward prince than any one else, was sent upon the ungrateful embassy. He succeeded first in persuading the Duke to leave Lorraine and return to his own country, and after a time, in spite of Richelieu—who rather fomented than appeased the personal difference between the King and the Duke—de Condren brought about a reconciliation and a meeting between the royal brothers. It was however during the earlier stage of these negotiations that the Oratorians in Paris, fearing some intervention from the high hand of Cardinal Richelieu, hastened to elect their General without summoning deputies from their provincial houses. De Condren wrote from Nancy, earnestly deprecating this proceeding as informal and dangerous, but before his letter arrived the Congregation assembled and he himself was elected. On receiving due intimation of this election, de Condren wrote as follows :—

"Very dear and reverend Fathers,—May the grace of our Lord Jesus Christ be ever with you. Were I to consider nought save what I owe to you, I should reproach myself for my delay in answering your letter. But considering the importance of the subject, I hope you will not blame me for having taken a few days for turning to God, and seeking His Guidance in coming to a determination.

"I have had to struggle against my reason before I could resign myself to your election. Experience of my own incapacity and infirmity, the great drawing to retirement which God has given me, specially since the death of our reverend Father, my intention of spending the remainder of my days at the Feet of our Dear Lord, and the very love I bear in my soul towards the Congregation, all led me to wish that it should have some other Superior. In all sincerity, this last difficulty has been the greatest. I knew that the late Cardinal de Bérulle, our beloved Father and Founder, always hoped that when he was gone God would look mercifully upon the Congregation, and lead it on to higher degrees of grace, and this we must all desire. . . . Since his death I have felt much fear, many longings. . . . I have prayed for God's Mercy, and that He would give us a Superior after His Own

Heart; that He would guide your thoughts and acts by His Holy Spirit of counsel."

After dwelling at some length on the excellences of the late Cardinal, and regretting that the Congregation had not profited to a greater extent by his teaching and example, de Condren continues:—

"I was praying that my own unworthiness might not be any hindrance to God's Grace among us, when the tidings of your election came greatly to my surprise and dismay; and now my prayer is that I be no hindrance to the Congregation. . . . There are many things which make me fear, but I will not doubt God's Aid. I will glory in my infirmities, so that His Grace alone may abound in me. My joy shall be that I am nothing,—Jesus Christ All in all to you. I resign myself to His Power, in the hope that He Who has begun the work will fulfil it, inasmuch as I feel bound to yield to your choice. I do this the more readily that practically the Generalship of the Congregation implies a general servitude, and that I am thereby obliged to serve you all, and to belong more to each one of you than to myself. It is an administration which constrains me to be all things to all men within our Company; to share the duties of each, to bear the cross of all, to take my part in their troubles, since it is God's Will that every one should bear His Cross. I pray Him to give me grace to carry mine, even such as He lays upon me, and that I may willingly accept my share in that of others. It will always be a great joy to me to bear anything for any among you. 'Yea, and if I be offered upon the sacrifice and service of your faith, I joy, and do rejoice with you all' (Phil. ii. 17).

"I give myself unreservedly to God for you, and to you for God. Let this letter abide in witness against me if I ever fail, even as Moses caused the Book of the Law to be put aside in the Ark of the Covenant as a witness between Joshua and the people of Israel. I am and shall be all my life and with my whole affection—so I ask of our Dear Lord and His holy Mother—the very humble, obedient and faithful servant of each one of you,

"CHARLES DE CONDREN,
"Pr. de l'Or. de Jésus.[1]

"NANCY, *November* 9, 1629."

Writing to a great personage, a devoted friend of the Order, in reply to congratulations on his appointment, the new General says :—

"I do not hold, sir, that the Generalship is an advantage, or a means of power, as the world thinks. If one looks at it from a Christian's point of view it is but a general bondage which constrains me to serve every member of the Congregation, to be more at

[1] *Lettres*, No. xxxv.

their disposal than at my own, and to bear their Cross. And the power seemingly committed to me is not meant to subject any one whatsoever to me, but to subject all those entrusted to me to God, His Guidance and His Kingdom. It means that I should subject myself to God in each one of them, and to them in Him, so that practically if before I had any liberty or right over myself, it is taken away by this Superiorship, and transferred to those to whom I am given and subjected by God."[1]

One of Père de Condren's first acts, August 1631, was to call a General Assembly of the Congregation, which now—twenty years after its foundation—numbered 71 houses; and as a deputy was elected for every ten priests, and fifty-five deputies attended the Assembly, the Congregation must have consisted of 550 members.

After passing various acts which established and confirmed the Society, Père de Condren took advantage of the opportunity to humble himself before the Assembly, asking forgiveness for the imperfections with which he had fulfilled his office as Superior, and requesting to be allowed to resign it, and that then and there another General should be chosen. As might be expected, the Assembly replied to this by "approving, confirming and ratifying" his election as

[1] Lettres, No. xxxvi.

positively as it was possible to do, and the official acts say that " this was accepted after some persistent refusal, at the urgent entreaty of the Assembly."

A letter written to one of the Fathers, who apparently shrank from a post of responsibility, gives so clear a picture of de Condren's own mind on this subject, that we may read his acquiescence in his appointment by its light.

" May our Lord Jesus Christ live ever in you by His Holy Spirit, according to His Heavenly Will.

" He will be your Strength and your Guide in the office which you bear with Him and for love of Him, and so far as He sees it to be for your soul's good He will also be your Consolation. With Him nothing should be difficult or disagreeable, for He is All-sufficient, and nothing is more in the spirit of true charity, or fulfils its aim more perfectly, than forgetfulness of our own interests and our personal inclinations in the work which our vocation sets before us for the Love of Jesus; as also nothing tends more to the perfecting of our faith than to turn a deaf ear to all thoughts concerning our own sufficiency or insufficiency. Supposing one to possess every possible human and angelic virtue, what could one do without Jesus Christ? Nothing, emphatically nothing. Without Him we cannot turn our own capabilities, or Angels' ministrations, or man's works, no, not even

God's Own Gifts, to any good account; for He has said, 'Without Me ye can do nothing.' And if we attempt to use any of these things without Him, the result will be self-love and wilfulness, which can only tend to our condemnation.

"But, on the other hand, whatever insufficiency we may feel in ourselves, through Jesus Christ we can do whatsoever God would ask of us: 'I can do all things through Him Which strengtheneth me.' No indeed, we can never be so incapable but that Jesus Christ will fulfil in us and with us all the duties of our vocation. S. Peter was less prepared to be chief of the Apostles when the Son of God called him than you are for your office: whence we see that an unlearned fisherman could become Head of the Church, the rock on which Christ's Church is built, that Church which was to enlighten the world and convert the greatest of human intellects, through Jesus Christ. I should be much more afraid of committing the guidance of our members to you, if you believed in your own capability: in that case I might with good reason fear that you would sink in helpless confusion. He does not love to see His servants presuming on their own strength. But inasmuch as you are conscious of your own insufficiency, I feel that I need only ask a more lively faith in His Sufficiency for you: only need say in S. Peter's words—'Grace and peace be multiplied unto you through the knowledge of God, and of Jesus our Lord, according as His divine power hath given unto us all things that pertain unto life and godliness, through the knowledge of Him that hath called us to glory and virtue; . . . you giving all diligence, add to your virtue faith' (2 Peter i. 2-5).

"It is great ignorance of Jesus Christ not to know that it is through Him that God's Grace is given to us, and that in that Grace, not any that is our own, we can carry on His work, nor would God have us lean on any other strength. Give yourself up then to Him in order that you may attain to that strength. Do not dwell on what power of your own you may think to possess; but rather fix your mind on what God requires of you. David was punished for reckoning up the people,—that is, for trusting to his own strength. We must think of nothing save what God requires of us.

"And when we feel as though we were ready for that, whatsoever it may be, we must not stop short in any good intention or disposition which we may feel in ourselves; rather we must give ourselves freely to the Son of God, purposing to do whatever our duty is, in Him, and through His Grace; firmly believing that without Him we can but misuse even that grace, whereas with Him we can do all things whatsoever

He may require of us. Look upon your obligations as the secret indications of His Will—there can be none better; and instead of taking measure of your own virtues, adore His Grace set forth in you. The soul which adores Jesus Christ working in itself will never sink down discouraged, because that soul will undertake every duty in His Power and Strength, and will see the Lord in every chain and tie. So, too, the soul which does not pause to dwell upon its own sufficiency or insufficiency, but places itself wholly in His Hands to do whatsoever He may require, need never fear to go astray while doing His work; that soul's confidence is too deeply rooted. 'I will glory of the things which concern mine infirmities' (2 Cor. xi. 30).

"And I, for my part, will glory in that you cannot fulfil the duties of your office without Jesus Christ. It is a guarantee to me, a glory to the Congregation, and an untold gain to the community under you, that Jesus Christ Alone is your Light, your Counsellor, your Strength. The less of self in what you do the more of His Grace there will be; the less you see cause for trusting in yourself the more entirely you will lean on Him, and the more simply you will do His work. Yes, be sure—if you are nothing, He will be everything; for He never fails us when we are 'about His business,' and all that is lacking on our side He supplies tenfold on His.

"Go on then in mistrust of yourself, but be strong in the faith and grace of Jesus Christ, and do not give us cause to say to you as our Lord said to S. Peter, 'O thou of little faith, wherefore didst thou doubt?' I hope soon to see you, and then we will take counsel together concerning your own doings and those of your community. I am most heartily yours," etc.

". . . . Give yourself up to Jesus Christ without self-contemplation, without heeding your own state of mind or condition, without wishing to be or to have anything whatsoever, without being disturbed by what goes on within you. Leave it to Him to work in you exactly as He may see fit. Do you cease to be anything, that He may be everything. Seek in such a spirit to obtain to that 'glorious liberty of the children of God' of which S. Paul speaks (Rom. viii. 21)."[1]

What he preached, Père de Condren practised, and for the next few years his labours were very abundant; his principle in all, after that so forcibly expressed above of dependence upon the Lord, being that of acting with and submitting to the Bishops. "Our Congregation," he said at this time,

[1] Lettres, Nos. xii. and xiii.

"is so entirely formed under the Bishops' hands, that it cannot work heartily or hope for God's Blessing without this union, which we hold to be the very source of our life and strength. Of a truth, the Bishops being the pastors whom God has set over His Church, . . . we are bound to see the Son of God in them, and to cleave to Him through them. And that all the more because our Society is specially founded in the love and grace of our Lord's Eternal Priesthood, and that we aim at the fullest attainment of the spirit thereof, seeking to love, honour and adhere to it as our chief object and source of inspiration."[1]

The Bishops of the Church of France accepted this loyalty in the same spirit with which it was offered, and there was a greater demand for the Oratorian Fathers on behalf of every kind of Church work than their numbers, though so considerable, could supply. Missions, schools, and above all training the Clergy themselves to a higher tone and practice, were Père de Condren's chief objects. Some few of his letters to the Fathers remain, which all set forth the same calm, trustful, unselfish spirit, which he pressed so earnestly on others. Thus, to the Superior of a provincial house, he writes,—

"Do not be disturbed because of some little diffi-

[1] Père Amelote, ii. p. 294.

culties with the members of your Community as regards yourself. Think rather that it is much to be wished that men should only be wanting towards us. If they find it hard to submit to God, and do not accept His Guidance without murmuring, how can we hope to make our rule more acceptable than His? It is a mistake to foster such a delusion. Nevertheless be assured that we are not indifferent to your difficulties, and we will do whatever lies in our power to make your charge bearable, but the existing state of the Congregation renders it impossible to satisfy you as fully as we should desire. The Church was in a far more harassed condition when the Son of God left it to His Apostles, but at the same time He left them His Spirit and a great love of the Cross. If our vocation met with no trials, no cross, no need for patience, we might well mistrust it, and fear lest we had no part in Jesus Christ Crucified.

"The Apostle says that we are called to be partakers of the Sufferings of Jesus Christ, but nevertheless, if we duly weigh our little griefs, we shall often find them to be rather the result of our own imperfections than a share in the Cross of the Son of God ; we shall realise too that they are so trivial that we may well be ashamed to call them crosses. My dear Father, we must imitate God and His Son, and rule lovingly those who resist government, not failing to take care of those who will not take care of themselves—I mean of their own souls. I pray you go on tending God's House in this spirit, and watch over souls. May He bless you. Give me a place in your prayers."[1]

What a gentle wise mind the following letter to a Father, who was unwilling to take the responsibility of a Community, shews:—

"We had thought to give you as Superior one whom our Good Master has just taken from us; and now we are asking Him to supply another after His own Heart. He can raise up children unto Abraham of the stones, which is what we cannot do of ourselves;—and so not having any Father to dispose of who is altogether fit for this office, we pray to Him, Who fits and moulds those whom He vouchsafes to use. To seek no further, He could make a good Superior of you yourself if He willed it, but He seems pleased rather to grant your prayers to the contrary than mine to that effect. For my own part, I give way to the wish with which He inspires you, and will not attempt to do it violence. Nevertheless, until such time as we can find him who is designed of God to be the Head of your House, I pray you to take charge of it—you may rely that it shall not be for long.

"Tell those members of your House who want

[1] Lettres, No. xxxviii.

more retirement, that we must not look upon the Congregation as a place of mere selfish retreat, where each man may seek his own personal satisfaction, but rather as a place for devotion, holiness, and work for Jesus Christ, in all of which we are bound to follow Him bearing His Cross:—the first rule of our Family is to be found in the words 'Deny thyself, take up thy Cross, and follow me,' and whosoever seeks anything else, is mistaken."[1]

Again, to a Father who was suffering from ill-health and consequent depression, Père de Condren writes:—

" . . . I see from your letter that your ailments are severe, and do not allow of your doing as much as another might be able to do; but they will never be greater than the indulgence of the Congregation. It will help you to bear with yourself—we shall duly prize your patience and goodness. I have always thought that those suffering members who edify the Congregation by their holiness, and who bear their trials patiently according to their Rules and the devout spirit which is therein inculcated, are more useful and ought to be dearer to us than those who preach, teach, or otherwise serve, without a like dutiful heed to their Rule, and that because the great treasure of the Congregation lies in the grace, the piety, the

[1] Lettres, No. xl.

modesty of her members, wherein truly they attain to the Mind of Christ. The most useful among us are those who help to preserve this treasure, while those who do otherwise are more hurtful than helpful, whatever outside show they may make to the contrary.

"If you can make up your mind to work in this spirit for the Congregation, your maladies will be profitable both to you and to us, and we will give special orders that all possible help be given you. I will make it my personal business to do so, and I feel sure that our Fathers will not fail to answer to the appeal. But if you find it too hard to do this, as your letter seems to imply, we will still do our very best for you with the most affectionate solicitude, in whatsoever position you may assume in the Congregation, or even out of it. Meanwhile we will pray our Dear Lord to guide you rightly. If you can make up your mind to patience and obedience, it will be far the best thing for you, but whatever you may do, I shall be always, yours heartily, P. DE CONDREN."[1]

A contest among certain members of the Congregation for priority of rank called forth the following words of moderate but firm rebuke :—

"The question raised among the three persons mentioned in your letter proves too plainly that they

[1] Lettres, No. xli.

have as yet made but little progress in the school of Jesus Christ. When the Disciples were guilty of disputing who should have the pre-eminence, they were still untaught in the lessons of His Humility, and had not fully received the outpourings of His Grace. But we who are so ready to speak of the Spirit of Jesus, and who are called by His Grace to His Church to spread abroad the sweet odour of His Humility among men—we are utterly without excuse if we foster any such unworthy feelings; we ought to blush at any symptom thereof.

"When our Assemblies appointed the due place of each among us, it was not with a view to any personal exultation, but only to that of the priesthood; neither was it with a view to pride and vanity, which we rather seek wholly to uproot: but the object was to regulate the zealous humility which would lead every one to seek the lowliest place, and which consequently might result in confusion and disorder. If these three men who are at issue, were striving who should humble himself most for the love of Jesus Christ in His Humiliation, I should say, in the spirit of our Assemblies, that nothing save the priesthood is to be considered among us. For save this dignity, which our Lord wills to maintain its honour and holiness, no gifts but are to be possessed in humility; and the most holy and most perfect gifts which can be attained through His Grace are only to humble us and keep us prostrate before Him, until He has judged them at the Last Great Day. If we judge them ourselves, or esteem them highly, or take to ourselves the glory thereof, we are guilty of an encroachment upon His Divine Judgment, which He will not overlook—we thereby forestall His Sentence, and become unworthy of His Favour, for which we ought to wait and hope humbly.

"In accordance with this principle, which is binding on all Christians, and which has been accepted by our Assembly, I can only, when called on to decide this difference, condemn all three partakers in it, as having offended against the mind and intention of our Congregation, which requires humility, not pride in her members. You say that I have certain powers to order matters of this kind, but my power is only intended to be used 'to edification, not to destruction' (2 Cor. xiii. 10); as indeed every power committed to us by God is for the advancement of grace, not of self-will. I am bound to use it to the uprooting, not the encouragement, of pride in His children. If any of our members seek to take the lowest place at the Gospel Feast,—we may fairly say to him in Christ's own words, 'Friend, come up higher,' if it seems expedient so to do, but it is otherwise with those who affect the pre-eminence. To such it were more fitly said 'Give place, and take the lowest room,' since they are so entirely wanting in the mind and disposition of our Society. All such we would send to learn of S. Paul what was 'the Mind which was in Christ Jesus, Who, being in the Form of God, made Himself of no reputation,' and 'thought it no robbery,' no indignity to His Godhead, to bear with, nay to seek out, all the humiliations of human life.

"If we are kindled by the same spirit we shall in due time be exalted with Him, but if not we have little right to claim an abundant share in His Glory. I beg those three persons who have had thoughts so opposed to the Christian, still more to the priestly mind, to repent heartily, and to spend a week in special devotion to the Humiliations of Jesus Christ, so that He may grant them a better mind. I would have them consider well that they are Christians and Priests, and that they ought to esteem these more highly than any other rank." [1]

To a Missionary the Superior writes the following brief words of encouragement :—

"I thank our Dear Saviour with all my soul for the blessing He is giving to your preaching in your mission. We are far from worthy of such grace, but we can adore and admire His Grandeur and Power,

[1] Lettres, No. xliii.

Which deign to carry out His Work by means of us unworthy sinners. The workman's glory is to succeed with frail tools. God's Word is holy even in a sinner's mouth, and it retains its efficacy therein; but it will produce still greater results when those who bear it to others lose all sight of themselves, and speak solely in Him and in His Holy Spirit. Let this be your aim. Woe to that Gospel preacher who seeks to be heard for his own sake! The crown and glory of Gospel truth is only for such as seek that Christ be listened to in their words, and who lose themselves in their message, like the ministering Angels, or the holy Apostles, who rejoiced to be despised of men, so long as they might see God Only, and that He was filling their hearts and minds."[1]

To a Priest of the Oratory who had yielded to the infirmities of temper, the Superior says:—

"I entreat you to live the most edifying life that you can in the House where you are. I am very sorry for what has happened;—you owe our Dear Lord much greater patience than this. Remember that you are a child of the Cross, and that were you even crucified, you ought to abide in silence and patience. I quite believe that you may have had reasons for what you did, but I cannot think that they were in accordance with Christ Crucified. I have

[1] Lettres, No. xlv.

not yet been fully informed as to what took place; but knowing you better than the others, I feel constrained to speak to you and entreat you to take up the Cross, and learn its patience. Our greatest gain in this world is to suffer; and our greatest loss is to cause suffering to others :—the first is the lot of God's children, and the last of the devil's children. May God shield both you and me from having any part in so terrible a lot. Be assured that all my life I shall be yours,"[1] &c.

Perhaps, in our busy days of perpetual over-work and over-strain, Père de Condren's words to one of his Mission Fathers, whose zeal abounded, may find their aim among ourselves :—

". . . I thank our Dear Lord," he says, "with all my heart, for the success He has given you in your Mission ;—it is a proof that He accepts your service in that kind of work. But nevertheless, my dear Father, do not forget that if our visiting and our outer work is to be really Christian it must not be continued. The Son of God frequently went apart Alone with His Father, one while amid the mountains, another time in the desert, and yet He had not the same need that we have to renew His inner life in the Spirit of God, or to repair the waste made by time and exterior work—a reparation essential to him

[1] Lettres, No. xlvii.

who would talk with God and live under His Guidance. He intended thereby to teach us what we ought to do; He is not only the Founder of all Evangelical Mission work, He is also the Rule and perfection of all its detail.

"He said, 'As the Father sendeth Me, even so send I you.' That charity which He left to us, and which ought to be the very life of all true Missions, has reference first of all to God rather than to the people, and passes on to them by means of the love we win from Him. And therefore, from time to time, we need to give ourselves up to Him Alone, He being our God, and requiring that our love be fixed on Him before and above all else; remembering that our chief homage is due to Him, that He is the Beginning and the End of all our spiritual work; that we must gather from Him that which we are going to give out again for His Glory; that we must return it to Him when the object is attained. It was thus that Jesus Christ ever did with respect to the Father. He never did anything on earth 'but what He saw the Father do' (John v. 19). He lived and acted in Him Only, referring all to Him, finally giving Himself up for the Kingdom and Glory of His Father. Such is our example, and so, dear Father, I would have you make it your rule, after having been at work, to reserve a suitable time for retreat and rest with God;—for He ought to be our Rest in this world as well as in the next. From the very creation He willed that man's rest should be consecrated to Himself, and He still wills it so."[1]

Père de Condren's letters to his Fathers engaged in Missions are full of minute details, which shew that nothing escaped his watchful vigilance: the trifling oppositions, the storms raised, "not fierce enough to be attributed to the Evil One;"[2] the coldness of those who ought to be fervent in God's work; the petty jealousies of others; the various individual prejudices which must inevitably come in the way of all such efforts for dealing with souls; the occasional failure even of a missionary himself, find their respective notice. Careful arrangements as to the places where Missions should be held, watching for the openings God may give, cautions to the Mission Fathers to carry on their own work "without entering into any party feelings; . . . following S. Paul's teaching, 'that there be no divisions among you, but that ye be perfectly joined together in the same mind and in the same judgment' (1 Cor. i. 10); shunning all that tends to a breach of Christian love and simplicity;" warnings to keep the Lord's Example ever before them, and so work on at their Father's business ' with few words, and giving little heed to the contra-

[1] Lettres, No. xlix.   [2] Ibid. No. liv.

dictions of men;" such are the chief substance of the General's correspondence. He specially charges his Fathers to be very careful how they proceed in fresh places, where hitherto their work has not been known. "New things are ever apt to give offence. Confidence only comes with knowledge and habit, and if you go too fast you will only bring down opposition upon your work. In a year's time you will meet with general commendation for the very things which at this moment would raise a perfect storm, if suggested. You see God wills that His Work should spread and wax strong in secret, in humility, ignored or misunderstood of men."

He was never weary of pressing upon those under him the importance of working without any view to an earthly reward, whether such comes through the applause of men, or even that of conscious satisfaction in the success of work well done.

"This family of the Son of God [the Oratory] needs good and faithful servants, who will ever bear in mind that their Head was Crucified because of His good works, and that while serving Him they must seek to offer themselves with Him a sacrifice to His Father; they must immolate themselves in His Spirit of patience on the altar of human contradiction and persecution, doing what is right without expecting any satisfaction or gratitude from men. Real

Christian work is too God-like to have its reward in this world, and those men who do not renounce self even in this respect have not attained to the true Spirit of God. If we were holier we should encounter still more opposition from the world, and if we lived according to the perfect holiness of Jesus Christ the men of our times would no more tolerate us than they tolerated Him—there would be nothing about us that would in any way meet and satisfy the views and spirit of the world. . . .

"For my own part, I must needs humble myself because I have hitherto had to suffer so little; in very truth I believe that had I been better, men would have looked less favourably on me. . . . Just now you are happier than I have been in this respect; I thank God on your behalf, and above all for that He gives you grace to profit by it.

"The wicked thief was lost though his cross was so close to Jesus Christ, and unless we cleave closely to Him, unless we are upheld by Grace and enabled to offer ourselves together with Him, the Cross will not save us—rather we shall deserve punishment because we have not used it rightly. Contradiction and affliction are common enough in this world, but a full and right use of them is more rare than one might be disposed to imagine; to receive and use them in a loving Christian spirit and in the Patience of Christ is altogether a gift of grace, which we may well crave earnestly, although it is for the most part little esteemed of men. . . . . Let us offer ourselves to Him in all the trifling contradictions we are called on to bear; let us see them with loving eyes, as a cup of blessing which our Father offers us to drink for His good pleasure. And if the flesh murmur, let us say with the Son of God, 'Get thee behind me, Satan ; the cup which my Father hath given me, shall I not drink it?' A common fault, but a very serious one among Christians, is that they reject the reality of that Cross which they are so ready to adore in painting and sculpture. But if we only love the Image, our love, be sure, is only imaginary too.

"If we are weak in our undertaking, Jesus Christ vouchsafes to be the Angel strengthening us. Worship the fulness of His love with all your might, and give yourself up wholly to the guidance of His Spirit. Herein, indeed, you are better off than He was, for whereas only an Angel was sent to comfort Him, He wills Himself to be your Strength. Gather yourself together then, and strive to prize the Cross aright, and then resolve fervently to bear it with Him in whatsoever shape He may offer it to you. Seek to attain a resolute will to bear it in well-doing, although all your good works seem crowned with thorns. Be content that God should reserve all their satisfaction, all their reward, all their glory, for Paradise; leave Him to hide them beneath the shadow of His Holy Spirit as long as He will, so long as you bear all things in the strength of the Saviour's Love even towards those who cause you most suffering; so long as you offer yourself to Him for their sake."[1]

In the same spirit of self-abnegation which enabled Père de Condren almost to rejoice in calumny, he answers a friend who had written in great indignation at the false reports spread concerning him and his work:—

"You dwell too much upon what is said concerning your friends. We have much more need to be troubled at the offences which are continually committed against God, than at anything which can be said or done with respect to ourselves; and when we are so sensitive to these, it is a sign that our love for Him is cold, and that we cling too closely to self and the things which so disturb us. We must strive to purify our hearts before God, and to transform every thought into love for Him, while we marvel that He suffers so many even to blaspheme Him, and that so many even among professing Christians murmur against His rule. Surely, if we dwell on this thought, we shall worship His Patience, and the

[1] Lettres, No. lxiv.

wondrous way in which He overlooks man's complaints, continuing to pour out His Love upon him. It were well if we strove rather to rest in His Divine Government, and so not to fret so much, or to set our hearts on converting those to us whom He does not convert to us, perhaps not even to Himself. We have much more real reason to fear lest we be too well off in this world; too much respected, too much praised. Hitherto we have not had any great share of our Lord's Cross to carry—perhaps we may be more favoured in future. We ought to count any prospect thereof as a great grace, and if we really believe the Gospel, we shall look upon persecution as one of the beatitudes. . . .

"When we have altogether rooted blasphemy from out the world, and restrained all men from speaking evil of God and His Son Jesus Christ;—when we have brought the whole world to fulfil their duty towards His Divine Majesty,—then there may be nothing left to do, but to restrain men from sinning against ourselves, and perhaps it will be time then to see about it. But meanwhile such efforts would be mistimed;—our whole care must be given now to prevent offences against God, and let us rejoice if men's malice be levelled rather at us than at God. One result thereof should be to make us look within and be more filled with humility, since how shall we presume to resent persecution, knowing as we do that if we are not guilty of that which is imputed to us, at all events we have committed many other faults? Jesus Christ Alone had a full and perfect right to justify Himself; and we must strive by penitence, by humility, by love, to purify our hearts of self-love, and to win as large a share as may be in the Innocence of Christ Crucified, rejoicing through love of His Cross to be persecuted, not blamelessly indeed, like Him, but according to our strength. Better so, than not at all. Let us spend this life in patience and humility, seeking only to love and serve God."[1]

One more letter must be quoted here, in which, writing to an Oratorian, Père de Condren dwells upon the "liberty of the children of God," in words which seem to be a summary of his own inner life :—

"First of all," he says, "I want to warn you, if need be to entreat you, to remember that it is your duty really and effectively to take care of your health; not merely to think or speak of doing so. . . . Be resigned to God in all things, and thus your soul will find rest. Shun all anxiety of mind, and all constraint in spiritual things. Just as we ought to seek to subject the flesh to the spirit, *i.e.* all that is not born of the Spirit of God (for 'that which is born of the flesh is flesh, and that which is born of the Spirit is spirit')

[1] Lettres, No. lxix.

(John iii. 6), even so ought we to seek that liberty of soul which S. Paul calls 'the glorious liberty of the children of God' (Rom. viii. 21). His children, so the Apostle teaches us, are not subject to the things of this world either through 'love' or fear—but willing only with their whole heart to do Him honour, whether by doing or suffering, their minds are always in perfect freedom towards Him and superior to every obstacle. They know how to turn their very hindrances into means of better serving and glorifying God;—accepting all such freely, and turning them to account by offering them up to Him. They know that the one thing most acceptable to God is the sacrifice of the will:—so they resign themselves wholly to Him, and are as ready to serve Him after one way as another. Their real desire is to leave all choice to God, accepting His choice with an absolute and loving submission; as ready to receive those hindrances which His Supreme Will permits as to work unhindered when He wills it, for what they believe to be His greater Glory. After all, His real Glory is, that we obey Him out of love. Oh! be sure that it is a great secret of Christian life to be wholly God's without clinging to any earthly thing, without choosing any way of our own for serving Him, but abiding in simple readiness always to use every circumstance and event which His Providence may send to His Glory. To do this the will must be resolutely set towards Him, and we must be fully persuaded that nothing can happen to us which is not destined to help us onward, if we cleave wholly to His Guiding Hand; nothing but what may be a means of honouring Him, in act, if it be something to do;—in suffering, if it be something to be borne;—in severance, if it be something to be given up;—in prosecuting, if it be something to be persevered in, as some holy thought or grace. May our Lord mould all our hearts to this, and may we let Him mould us as He will."[1]

Three years of experience served, as might be expected, to confirm the Congregation in the wisdom of the selection they had made of a Superior; but when another Assembly was held in 1634, they were thrown into great dismay at the prospect of losing him. Without making any allusion to his intentions, Père de Condren carried on the work of the Assembly till the last day of its session, when, without telling any one whatsoever where he was going, he borrowed a friend's horses and took a roundabout road to a very quiet house belonging to the Congregation, and concealed himself there, as he hoped effectually, until another Superior should be elected.

The Assembly, finding that their President did not

[1] Lettres, No. lxix.

appear, voted the Bishop of Saint Malo, who was present as Honorary Assessor, to the chair; and just as this was done, the secretary presented a letter directed in Père de Condren's handwriting to the Assembly. The first step the Assembly took was to decide by acclamation that this letter should not be opened, foreseeing, as every one did, its purport.

The letter was in fact a touchingly humble entreaty to be relieved of his office as General; "not," as he said, "to avoid the trouble, which is not great;—not that I do not love the Congregation, or that I have any complaint to make against any one—far from it, I ask pardon of all who have any complaint against me; nor that I am wanting in submission to your will —I would fain live in obedience all my life. But you know that he who in his innermost conscience feels himself unworthy and incapable of an ecclesiastical office ought not to yield when elected. And my only reason for departing is to give you time to decide on another Superior. I am going to one of our houses (I dare not say which), till such time as you shall have given to the Congregation and to me a Superior-General. Then I shall hasten to ask his blessing, and tender my obedience."[1] At the same time de Condren wrote privately to one of the Fathers,

[1] Lettres, No. xxxiii.

entreating his co-operation, and reiterating his conviction that it was for the good of the Congregation that he should retire.

The Assembly wrote an answer to the letter they had not read, purporting that let Père de Condren go where he would, their General he should be so long as he lived; and having signed this document unanimously, the Fathers separated. Three days were spent in seeking the fugitive, but at last he was found, and then his very humility prevented any further contest. De Condren read the Assembly's document, and observing that it was in real love to the Congregation he had wished to give it a better Head, he returned to Paris with his captors, and meekly resumed his office, though to the last he maintained that he was incapable and unworthy of it. Once more de Condren attempted to retire from office. This was when the Assembly of 1638 was held. But his design was frustrated on all sides. Hoping to gain help from Cardinal Richelieu, he appealed to him for support, and was thrust back with the assurance, that if he resigned his present office he should immediately be appointed to an Archbishopric! while his confessor, after hearing a general confession made with a view to his retirement, positively assured him that he would be acting against God's Will if he persisted, and even went so far as to threaten to refuse absolution unless de Condren gave up his intention.

The remainder, therefore, of his life—until January 7, 1641—Charles de Condren spent at the Head of his Congregation.

CHAPTER V.

S. VINCENT DE PAUL AND THE LAZARISTS.

THE Oratory had set a great stone rolling, and although, in the order of God's Providence, it came to pass that after a comparatively short time the great work of training and spiritualising the Clergy in France passed out of the hands of the Oratorian Fathers, the work begun by Cardinal de Bérulle was carried on in two great branches, both of which sprang from the parent vine of the Oratory. One man sows, and another reaps the increase;—so it ever has been, so probably it ever will be, in God's natural as well as His spiritual Kingdom, and who among His chosen servants but would ever be ready to cry out with David, "Not unto us, O Lord, not unto us, but unto Thy Name give the Glory!" or with S. John Baptist, "He must increase, but I must decrease"? And if, as we humbly venture to hope and believe, the life of Paradise will see a great ingathering of those who have loved and toiled together for Christ here, no fear lest there should be any rivalry, any grudging as to who has done the work, so long as He, the Dear Lord, the precious Master and Saviour of East and West, of Oratorian and Lazarist, of Philip Neri, Pierre de Bérulle, Vincent de Paul, Jean Jacques Olier, ay, and of many another saintly soul whose name may be scarce remembered, or even forgotten altogether of men—so long as He and His Holy Name are glorified.

Probably among the numbers who are familiar with the name of S. Vincent de Paul, and who justly look upon him as the great Apostle of his day, few know how close his connexion with the Oratory and de Bérulle was.

The two men were born within a year of one another, de Bérulle, as has been already said, February 4, 1575, and Vincent de Paul, April 24, 1576. There was little resemblance in their early history. S. Vincent was the son of peasant parents inhabiting the hamlet of Rauquines, near Dax, on the edge of the Landes. His childhood was spent, David-like, keeping the sheep, and the oak tree whose hollow trunk was his oratory and shelter, has for many years been an object of reverent interest to Western Christendom. His first simple education was given by the Cordeliers of Dax, and while teaching others in order to supply funds for his own maintenance, he continued to study at Toulouse, where he took his degree, being ordained priest, September 23, 1600, by the Bishop of Périgueux—the See of Dax being at that period vacant. The tale of Vincent de Paul's voyage to Narbonne—during which the vessel he was in was captured by a Turkish brigantine, and all on board carried to Tunis, where they were sold as slaves—is well known. From his personal experience of the fearful sufferings, mental and bodily, which all such Christian captives underwent, sprang one of S. Vincent's great works, the Mission to Barbary, in which he toiled unremittingly for the relief of the numerous slaves of every nation who were continually captured and brought into the markets of Tunis and Algiers.

Having been released, Vincent found his way to Rome, and thence he was sent on a political mission to Paris, where he had various conferences with the King, Henri IV. It was this visit to Paris which led to his first acquaintance with Cardinal de Bérulle, and its important consequences. Vincent's special errand accomplished, he remained in Paris, occupying a lodging in the Faubourg Saint-Germain, close to the hospital called la Charité, at that time the principal work of the kind in Paris, and which consequently drew around it most of those whose minds were working out the problem how best to relieve Christ's suffering poor. Here, as before mentioned, ministering both to the souls and bodies of the sick, Vincent found a congenial task, and it was here that he and de Bérulle came across one another. The latter heard various rumours concerning a humble priest who went about in the hospital doing the work of a good angel, and with pious curiosity seeking him out, he found Vincent de Paul. A close friendship between two such choice souls was the natural result, and when suffering under a prolonged season of spiritual trial and temptation, Vincent sought refuge in the Oratory, and laid open his whole heart to de Bérulle. His past life, his present fears, his hopes and aspirations for the future, were all submitted to the clear guidance of the Oratorian Superior, whose quick perceptions did not fail to perceive that God intended great things to be done by this holy man, and far from pressing him to join his own Congregation, de Bérulle told Vincent plainly that he was destined to found a new Congregation of his own, which should work with a similar object, though after a somewhat different plan.

During the two years thus spent in the Oratory, Vincent worked out in his own mind more and more the thought which travailed in him—of the fearful ignorance and neglected spiritual condition of the country people generally; and the desire to meet it with some special remedy grew stronger and stronger in his heart. It has been already said, how at de Bérulle's request, he took charge of the parish of Clichy, when François Bourgoing, the Curé thereof, joined the Oratorians; and it was again in compliance with his advice that Vincent left Clichy at the end of a year to fill the post of tutor in the noble house of Gondi, descendants of the celebrated Duc de Retz. At this time—1613—de Gondi was Archbishop of Paris (as indeed three of the family were in succession); and it was in the household of another son of the soldier of Moncontour, Philip Emanuel—who although a courtier and a warrior was also a deeply religious man, (ending his life indeed as a priest of the Oratory) —that Vincent spent the next twelve years of his life. Madame de Gondi—Marguerite de Silly—was one of those "*femmes fortes*" which that brilliant period of French society produced, and husband and wife agreeing in their anxiety to train up their children as good Christians, they applied to Cardinal de Bérulle for a suitable tutor from among his Oratorian Fathers; but he, having his own views concerning Vincent de Paul, sent him to fill the post. It seemed a strange way of promoting that work among the country people, towards which Vincent's special attraction lay, and he marvelled himself at the call, only complying out of obedience; but " it was God's doing" (*c'est Dieu qui a fait cela*), he used to say himself in after-life, and the result proved that de Bérulle's judgment was good. The veneration with which Madame de Gondi soon learned to regard Vincent, led to her placing herself under his direction, again at de Bérulle's desire—for the lowly priest held himself unworthy of the charge—and he found in her an active fellow-labourer in the work he already had begun to do among the country people on the large estates of the family. S. Vincent used to say that the first sermon of the Mission was preached on a certain Conversion of S. Paul at Folleville, in consequence of a seemingly trifling event which occurred there. He was summoned one day to hear the last confession of a dying man, a peasant, well to do, and reckoned as a good liver among his neighbours; but beneath the decent exterior there lay a festering sin, long concealed through false shame. Fulfilling his ministry as Vincent did, after no mere perfunctory fashion, he soon saw how matters stood, and led the penitent to make a general confession, to his own intense relief and thankfulness. The strong expressions of gratitude used by this man to Madame de Gondi, and his conviction that but for Vincent's wise handling his soul would have been lost, while to the world without he seemed all right, had so strong effect upon her, that she cried out in despair at the thought of the many souls whose spiritual state must be even worse than his, and implored Vincent to preach in the parish church on the subject of general confessions, and how to make them, which he did with most encouraging results. So great a movement and awakening followed among the people round about, that Vincent was obliged to call in the aid of two Jesuit Fathers from Amiens to supply their needs. Henceforth the Conversion of S. Paul has always been observed among his spiritual children as practically the birthday of the Mission.

It would take up too much space here to dwell upon S. Vincent's other works while in the de Gondi family. He attempted once to leave it in 1619, when he undertook the parish of Chatillon in the diocese of Lyons, again at Père de Bérulle's suggestion; but Madame de Gondi succeeded in persuading the latter to urge his return, not however before he had left his stamp on this new sphere of labour, in the first beginnings of the Confréries de la Charité—whence sprung at a later period the "Société de Saint Vincent de Paul," which has done so great a work in Modern Europe, and with which the name of Frédéric Ozanam is so closely connected.

Philip Emanuel de Gondi held the office of General of the Galleys, and Vincent soon learnt by personal experience what a miserably neglected condition the convicts who filled them were in. This he represented to the General in strong language, warning him that he would have to give account to God for it, and thence arose the work generally known as the "Œuvre des Galères." Both this and the missions to Barbary and Algiers, with their martyr heroes, Louis Guérin, the le Vachers, Noueli, Pierre Borguny, and Barreau, can only be alluded to here. While all other openings that presented themselves for promoting God's service were eagerly seized on by Vincent de Paul, he never lost sight of that work to which he believed himself to be specially called, *i.e.* mission work at home. The Congregation of Missionaries, of which the first seed was sown, as before said, on the Conversion of S. Paul, was to take more definite shape while Vincent was in the house of de Gondi. Those slender beginnings had stimulated Madame de Gondi's pious enthusiasm, and in the year 1617 she proposed giving 16,000 livres to some community on condition that they would hold missions every five years on the estates belonging to her family, and Vincent tried unsuccessfully to induce either the Jesuits or Oratorians to take it up. For seven years this went on, and then the de Gondis asked why Vincent himself should not found the work they craved for, and seconding their wishes, their brother the Archbishop offered the old College des Bons Enfants, now vacant, to the proposed new Society.

This was accepted, and in April 1624, the "Company, Congregation or Confraternity of Mission Fathers or Priests," and Antoine Portail, Vincent's first disciple, went to live at the Bons Enfants; he himself remaining with Madame de Gondi until her death, which followed in June 1625. Then, after doing his best to comfort the bereaved husband, he joined Portail; and so humble was the beginning of the since mighty Order of the Lazarists, that when Vincent and his colleague went forth on their earliest missions, they could not even afford to employ any one to keep the house, but were wont to lock the door and leave the keys with a neighbour! In September 1626 two more priests joined them, and the document incorporating himself and his three companions, signed by all four, is preserved among the archives of Saint Lazare, as the original act constituting the Congregation. It was so far only that Vincent de Paul's beloved friend and director saw the beginning of the work which de Bérulle's prophetic mind believed would develop into something far greater. He died in October 1629, and it was not till 1630 that the first steps were taken which led to the establishment of Vincent and his company in the ancient foundation known as the Léproserie de Saint Lazare.

This house was served in 1630 by eight regular

Canons of Saint Victor, under Adrien le Bon; but leprosy had ceased to be a prevalent disease in France,—there were scarcely any patients in the hospital, and le Bon was utterly dissatisfied, and most anxious to turn his house to better account. Having heard of "a company of Missionaries, who gave themselves up to the poor under one M. Vincent," he went to see them in company with M. Lestocq, the Curé of Saint Laurent, and convinced of the reality of their work, he at once offered the Priory of Saint Lazare to Vincent de Paul. Not unnaturally, he expected the offer to be received with eager satisfaction, but to le Bon's surprise and disappointment, the holy man at the Bons Enfants remained silent and as one overwhelmed, and on being pressed to reply, he answered that the proposal was too much above his aims. "We are but a few poor priests, leading the simplest of lives, and aiming at nothing greater than to minister among the country folk," he said, and so he declined the offer.

Le Bon was only made more anxious that Vincent should accept it, by this absence of all self-interest, and he insisted on waiting six months for an answer. But at the end of that time he still met with a persistent refusal. "We are too few," Vincent said, "we are but a new-born Community, and these humble quarters are sufficient for us. I dread the publicity and talk which would follow on such a step. We are unworthy of such promotion; leave us in the obscurity which suits us best." Le Bon continued to urge the greater service which might be done for God, and while he was pleading the dinner-bell rang, and he went into the refectory with the little Community. Their simplicity and devotion struck him more and more, and he determined to leave no stone unturned to effect his object. During the next six months he and the Curé of Saint Laurent perfectly besieged Vincent with their arguments, and the latter went so far as to tell him that he was resisting God's Holy Spirit, and would have to answer to Him for rejecting so favourable an opportunity of establishing a work destined to promote His Glory and the good of many souls. " I would fain have taken the good Father of the Missionaries on my back, and have carried him forcibly to Saint Lazare," the Abbé Lestocq said, in recounting the prolonged struggle; "hoping that the beauty of the spot and its many advantages might overcome him; but he was invulnerable to such charms, and during the whole eighteen months' discussion he never once went near the place."

At length, in despair, Le Bon entreated Vincent de Paul to refer the matter to some friend on whose judgment he could rely, and to his great satisfaction Vincent consented. André Duval, his director and ordinary confessor, was mentioned, and he promised to abide by this venerable Doctor's judgment. As might be expected, Duval sided entirely with Le Bon, and Vincent succumbed. After discussing and clearing away certain difficulties arising out of points of discipline and the like, a concordat was signed January 7, 1632, between Adrien Le Bon and the few remaining religious of Saint Lazare, and Vincent de Paul and his little company of priests. The former was to remain there during his life, and his brethren were to receive a certain annuity from the funds of Saint Lazare—guaranteed to them by Philip Emanuel de Gondi, the former General of Galleys, now a humble Oratorian Father. The Archbishop of Paris confirmed the arrangement, subject to certain conditions, among which were, that the Mission Fathers should continue to receive lepers if necessary, that they should carry out their Missionary work in all the villages and hamlets of his diocese, as also that they should receive his Candidates for Ordination for a fortnight's spiritual retreat at every Ember season ; indicating by this last stipulation how valuable he felt their teaching and example to be to the rising generation of the Priesthood. The King and the civil authorities of Paris likewise ratified the transfer, and on January 8, 1632, Vincent de Paul took possession of Saint Lazare, the Archbishop himself installing him.

The way was not yet altogether smooth. The Prior of Saint Victor questioned Le Bon's right to hand over the hospital to the Mission Father, and instituted a lawsuit against Vincent, concerning which the characteristic trait is recorded of him, that while his cause was pleading at the Palais de Justice, Vincent remained kneeling in the Sainte Chapelle hard by, asking not for success, but simply that God would do as seemed best to Him, and grant to His servant a contented heart whichever way the cause might be decided. There was no doubt as to the legal question, and this hindrance was soon cleared away. The Pope's sanction was also given, but Urban VIII. died before his Bull was promulgated, and the official approval of Rome was not given till twenty years later by Alexander VII., and not then without trouble, as Pope Urban's Bull accepted the Missionary Fathers as secular priests, whereas during the interval they had become a Regular Order, and considerable opposition was raised to them on this score.

During the last century a strong feeling against formal religious vows had sprung forth; and probably the line taken by the Oratorians, and their influence over the spiritual mind of their period, had tended to confirm this. M. Olier, the founder of Saint Sulpice—of whom more shortly—had followed the Oratorian view in this matter; S. Francis de

Sales' original intention, when founding the Visitation, had been that his daughters should only take the simple, as opposed to the formal Religious vows. Probably during his earlier years, while Vincent de Paul's mind was receiving its impression from his beloved friend and guide, de Bérulle, he imbibed this opinion; and at this period, although he was anxious that his Congregation should be subject to a formal Rule, instead of the "simple" vows, which at present they renewed every two or three years, at the same time he did not wish them to pass from the ranks of Secular Clergy. He always maintained that the works to which his Congregation were specially destined were incompatible with a technical "religious life;" and, above all, he held that the education of the Secular Clergy, which he considered its most important office, positively required instructors out of their own body, *similia similibus*.[1] With this object in view, he decided that his Missionaries should be called Monsieur, not Father;—that they should retain their family names, and wear the ordinary garb of secular priests,—in a word, that the only visible distinction between them and the Secular Clergy should be their more abundant zeal in the exercise of their Apostolic functions. Instead of a novitiate for those who wished to join the Congregation, he established

[1] Vie de S. V. de Paul, Maynard, vol. i. p. 391.

what he called an interior seminary (*séminaire interne*) as distinguished from the existing *externes* or diocesan seminaries.

Those who became members of the Congregation were required the first year to express their deliberate intention of remaining in it for life;[1] the second year they took a simple vow of "stability;" *i.e.* an engagement to work all their lives at the objects of the institution; and this was to be renewed at the end of eight or ten years, as the Superior might judge advisable. As to the three vows—poverty, obedience, and chastity,—for the present he was content with a solemn excommunication to be pronounced on such as should belie them, once every year in Chapter. The first Assembly General, small in number, was held October 13, 1642, when Vincent de Paul resigned the office of Superior, and hastened to a small chapel adjoining the Church of Saint Lazare, leaving his Congregation to elect a new Head. Deputies came to request his return,—but he only replied, "I am no longer Superior, choose another."

Thereupon the whole Assembly came to the rescue, and after some brief discussion, they solemnly and unanimously elected him for life. Vincent bowed to

[1] "Le bon propos de vivre et de mourir dans la Mission."
—Vie de S. V. Paul, Maynard, vol. i. p. 387.

the decision, saying, "Brothers, pray for me. It is the greatest act of obedience the Company can exact."

For some years the question of formulating vows continued a matter of discussion and perplexity, Vincent de Paul feeling that certain restraints were necessary for the Congregation, while yet he was reluctant to give up its position among the Secular Clergy. Ultimately a form was decided on, which was pronounced and subscribed by Vincent and his Company, January 25, 1656, to this effect:—" I, N——, an unworthy Priest of the Congregation of the Mission, in the presence of the B. Virgin and all the Company of Heaven, vow before God poverty, chastity, and obedience to our Superior and his successors, according to the rules and constitutions of our Institution. Further, I vow to labour all my life in the said Congregation for the salvation of the country poor, with the help of God's All-powerful Grace, which thereto I invoke."[1]

Thus another great work, destined to raise the tone of the Secular Clergy, had sprung forth from the

---

[1] "Ego, N——, indignus sacerdos Congregationis Missionis, coram beatissima Virgine et curia cœlesti universa, bono Deo paupertatem, castitatem, et superiori nostro ejusque successoribus obedientiam, juxta instituti nostri regulas seu constitutiones, Voveo me præterea pauperum rusticanorum saluti toto vitæ tempore in dicta Congregatione vacaturum, ejusdem Dei omnipotentis gratia adjuvante, quem ob hoc suppliciter invoco."

mustard seed originally sown by S. Philip Neri. Nor yet, although, as so often occurs in God's providential order—the branch waxed powerful, and overshadowed the parent stock—should the Church forget that she owes the development of S. Vincent de Paul's Missionary Company, and the blessed work of the Lazarist Fathers, spread as it has been over the whole face of the world, to the lowly House of the Petit Bourbon, and the spiritual counsels of its wise head, Cardinal de Bérulle.

Among the many points in which Vincent de Paul followed de Bérulle's mind, one cannot but be struck with the slowness both exhibited in framing permanent rules and constitutions, until time and experience shewed what would really work best for the objects of the new Company. We have seen how de Bérulle died, leaving the stamp of his mind, and his tradition indeed, in his rapidly increasing Congregation, but with its Constitution yet to be framed; and in the same way Vincent de Paul continued to be the living rule of his Company, until, at eighty-two years of age, he felt that it behoved him to leave a written record of their founder's mind, to his already numerous, and since then vastly increased family. He had been diligently pondering the matter through all those long years; he had consulted the ablest Canonists in Rome, the most profound theologians of la Sorbonne, the best lawyers, the most practical, and the most spiritual members of the Company; but, following the Example of his Master, he believed it wiser first "to do" and then "to teach." So that when at last the Company received its rules and regulations, there was nothing new, nothing which practice and experience had not already made familiar and acceptable.

They are written in Latin, and formularised in twelve chapters.

The first sets forth the triple object of the Congregation, *i.e.* (1) the spiritual perfection of the members; (2) evangelising the poor, specially the country poor; (3) training clergy in the knowledge and graces essential to their office. It consists of clergy and laity. The duties of the former—following the example of Jesus Christ and His Disciples—are, to go forth among the towns and hamlets, teaching and catechising, hearing general confessions, reconciling differences, restraining contentions; further, they are to establish the *Confrérie de la Charité* when able, to conduct Seminaries, and to afford Retreats and Conferences to the Clergy generally. The lay members are to assist their priestly brethren in their various functions, and to co-operate in prayer, penitence and good example. Both alike are to remember that they can only attain their object by "putting on the Spirit of the Lord Jesus Christ," which takes form in the evangelic precepts—in His poverty, purity, obedience—His compassion for the sick, His humility, in His daily instruction to His disciples, His intercourse with men, His habits of devotion, His mission and labours among the people.

The next ten chapters are an expansion of this summary. The Congregation is always to seek spiritual rather than temporal objects, the good of souls before that of the body, God's Glory before the praise of man; it is to accept poverty, infamy, torture and death itself, rather than "separate from the Love of Jesus Christ;"—it is always to seek God's Will, shunning all evil and seeking that which is good, voluntarily choosing that which is hardest in things indifferent, receiving joys and sufferings with a like gratitude from God's Hand, blending the harmlessness of a dove with the wisdom of the serpent, and exercising that Christlike gentleness which "possesses the earth," that humility which wins Heaven; and therein esteeming itself worthy of contempt, willing to be lightly esteemed, seeking to hide whatever it has of God, or at least referring all the praise to God; renouncing self-will, and private judgment, sensual indulgence, excessive family affection, attachment to office, place or person, and all individual peculiarities in manners or dress, way of teaching, preaching or directing, even in religious exercises;—loving all enemies and seeking to do them good. While obeying all the Evangelical precepts, the Congregation is specially to cultivate simplicity, humility, gentleness, mortification and zeal. These five graces are to be as the very soul of the Company, its chief motive power. Yet, at the same time, inasmuch as Jesus Christ overthrew Satan and established His Kingdom chiefly through poverty, chastity and obedience, the Congregation is diligently to imitate His Example: in poverty, possessing all property in common, no one disposing of anything as an individual; all their appliances, whether of furniture or food, are to be humble, nothing under lock and key, and this poverty is to influence even their wishes; and specially the members of the Congregation are to remember that it is perilous to desire ecclesiastical place or dignity. Purity is to be watchfully guarded, temperance and diligence practised as its mainstays, and S. Vincent's sons are to avoid all appearance of evil, remembering that even a suspicion hinders the work of their ministry. Obedience includes the precept to "ask nothing and accept all things." Those who visit the sick are to behold their Lord Himself in every sick man. The Missionaries are to be externally remarkable for nothing save their modest demeanour; among themselves they are to be friendly and even-tempered, avoiding special likings and aversions; their intercourse should chiefly be with respect to religious or literary matters suitable to their vocation, and they should avoid discussing politics or the like. As a wise speech is cultivated by silence, they are to be careful in obeying their rule of silence. With respect to the outer world they are to imitate their Great Example, Who was the Light of the world; as God's servants they are not to cumber themselves with worldly affairs, not even with extra good works, save by permission; they are not to bring strangers to the House, or to take meals without, except when authorised to do so.

Spiritual exercises are to be diligently practised—an hour's meditation daily, daily Celebration or assisting at Mass, daily reading of Holy Scripture and some spiritual book, self-examination twice every day, the Office said in common, a brief visit to the Blessed Sacrament on going out and coming in, an act of adoration on leaving the room and returning to it, reading aloud at meals, weekly confession and conference, spiritual direction and manifestation of conscience every three months, a special penitential exercise on Fridays and certain other days, an annual Retreat and review of past life: such rules comprise the simple spiritual system which has trained so many holy priests for their Master's Service.

The preference to Mission work before all else is to be an invariable principle with the Congregation, and even the training of Clergy is to be secondary to that. All the Missionaries are to strive to make God's Glory their one single aim, and to shun all that savours of mere self-satisfaction or love of praise, and they are all carefully to avoid the perils which beset them in the shape of languor and indolence on one side, and of indiscreet zeal on the other.[1] It was at one of the customary Friday evening conferences, May 17, 1658, that Vincent de Paul gave this rule, finally drawn up, to his Congregation, explaining in simple words how the various parts had gradually grown into shape, without deliberate framing, and rather as a matter of experience than of foresight. After his discourse, the venerable Founder gave a copy of the Rule to each member of the Community, beginning with Antoine Portail, his first colleague in the work. Each Missionary knelt to receive the book, kissing the beloved hand which gave it, and to each Vincent spoke some little word of special kindness, ending with "May God bless you." When this was done, Almeras asked his blessing in the name of the Company kneeling around. Vincent was so infirm that he needed to be supported on either side before

[1] This summary of S. Vincent's Rules is taken from the Abbé Maynard's Vie de S. V. de Paul, vol. i. p. 400.

he could kneel down himself, and then after a few words of fervent prayer, he pronounced the solemn Blessing in the Name of the Holy Trinity.

The end was not very far off. Rather more than another year was granted of the beloved Father's presence, but it was a season of great and varied suffering to himself, though also one of continued work. It was September 27, 1659, at 4 A.M., the hour at which for so many long years Vincent had daily begun his work for God's Service, that he passed to his rest; "faithful to his rule, only this time his devotions were to be entered on in God's Own Presence."

Before passing from S. Vincent's share in the great work of raising the Priesthood to a higher tone of life and doctrine, a few words more must be said on one part of his work which has been already alluded to, that of Retreats for those about to be ordained. One of the French Bishops on whose mind the demoralised condition of the Clergy preyed most heavily, was Mgr. Potier, Bishop of Beauvais. He was intimate with most of the men of his period who were feeling after better things, among others with the Abbé Bourdoise, also a disciple of de Bérulle, who had founded a small community with a view to promote the better education and higher tone of the Clergy, under the inspiration he himself had gained during a Retreat at the Oratory in 1611.

Discussing the subject with Bourdoise and Vincent de Paul, sometimes well-nigh with despair, they urged the importance of beginning at an earlier step: they pleaded that it was little short of impossible to materially alter the existing priesthood, and that a hardened priest is rarely converted, but they were prepared to seek a remedy amid the rising generation,— among the aspirants to the priesthood. "Admit none to Holy Orders," Vincent said, "save such as have the requisite knowledge, and give token of a real vocation; and let those who have such a vocation have the longest possible preparation, and be trained as far as may be for their sacred calling."

Mgr. Potier felt the wisdom of this advice, but how was it to be carried out? He pondered the matter continually, and at last one day he told Vincent de Paul that for the present all he saw possible was to collect all his own candidates for Holy Orders in his own house for a few days at least before their ordination, and to teach them as much as could be got into that space of time, hoping to rouse them to a sense of the weighty task upon which they were entering;—he went on to ask Vincent to draw up a plan for this retreat and a systematic course of instruction, and further asked him to spend a fortnight or three weeks at Beauvais before the next ordination, to carry it out. This was done—Duchesne and Messier, two doctors of the Faculté de Paris, were also present to assist;—the Bishop examined the Ordinands, and opened the Retreat himself, and the whole thing was conducted according to Vincent's plan, which proved so satisfactory that it continued to be the model of all future similar retreats. Vincent de Paul himself gave a series of meditations on the Commandments, which was so practical and awakening, that the whole body of listeners, including Duchesne, made their general confession in consequence to the conductor.

This led to a rule made by the Archbishop of Paris, that all Ordinands in his Diocese should prepare for the laying on of hands by a ten days' Retreat, and as has been already said, when confirming the grant of Saint Lazare to the Missionaries, Archbishop de Gondi made it a condition that they should thus receive and prepare his ordination candidates. The result of this plan was most satisfactory, and in the present day all Ordinands' retreats in France are moulded upon S. Vincent de Paul's first system.

The young men who came to the Bons Enfants or to Saint Lazare were cared for and ministered to by the good Missionaries themselves;—two instructions were given daily—those of the morning being devoted to moral theology, the higher administration of the Sacraments; the qualifications and preparation necessary for the priesthood as confessors and guides of souls, and the various kindred topics branching out from these great subjects. In the evening, instructions were given on meditation and mental prayer; on priestly vocation, its signs, and how to correspond thereto, on the obligations of God's ministers, and the details of their arduous and laborious life. Of course the time was too short to exhaust these weighty topics, but in order to make the best possible use of that time, after each instruction the Ordinands broke up into classes of twelve or thirteen, each under a Mission Priest, who examined them in its subject, promoted discussion thereof among themselves, and assisted each man to profit by it. The men were also instructed in the practical performance of the various sacred offices on which they were about to enter—the recitation of public services, and administration of ceremonies. They were further moved to close this season of solemn preparation with a general confession, and they were not dismissed till the day after their ordination, after a high Mass and a Thanksgiving Communion.

Vincent de Paul used to say that there could be no higher work possible than training good priests;—and he encouraged those whose hearts failed them before the difficulties and disappointments inevitable in such an undertaking, by the thought that our Lord Himself only trained twelve Apostles, and one out of those fell away. He was never weary of asking all good Christians—men and women, religious and secular—to pray for the Clergy, especially all those about to be ordained in the Ember Weeks. A humble man, going about his usual work, yet from time to time lifting up his heart in prayer, may do much to forward the Church's life, he said. Speaking of this one day in a Conference, S. Vincent began to quote the Psalm, "Desiderium pauperum exaudivit Dominus:" and not being able to continue the quotation he turned in his simple way to his listeners, saying, "Who will help me?" whereupon some one immediately finished the verse, "preparationem cordis eorum audivit auris tua."[1] "God bless you, sir!" Vincent replied (it was his usual way of expressing thanks); and he went on with his subject.

The example of humility and piety witnessed by those who were so happy as to make their Ordination Retreat at Saint Lazare, must have been almost as instructive as any words. It is recorded that on one occasion the venerable Founder himself was found cleaning the boots of a candidate who had been neglected by the servant whose proper work it was!

"What the eye sees goes more straightly to the

---

[1] Ps. ix. 17, Vulgate; x. 19, English version: "Lord, Thou hast heard the desire of the poor, Thou preparest their heart, and Thine Ear hearkeneth thereto."

heart than what the ear hears," S. Vincent wrote, "and we believe more unquestioningly therein. . . . There is a somewhat indescribable in the exterior of God's own servants, a something lowly, recollected, devout, which springs from their inward grace, and which reacts upon the souls of those who are brought in contact with them. *There are men among us so full of God that it is impossible to look at them without being touched by the sense of it.*"

Thank God that what S. Vincent said then, we can yet say among ourselves, and his words will bring tender loving thoughts to many a mind among us, of purity of life and exquisite holiness bearing its outward impress, so that all beholding have felt that him on whom they looked "had been with Jesus" (Acts iv. 13).

S. Vincent used to tell his priests that even if they had no visible gifts for teaching the Ordinands who came among them, they had a mighty power of indirect influence by their example, by their own diligent aim at perfection, which ever reflects itself on all around. And in the same spirit he used to exhort them to give great heed to the reverence with which they performed all offices and ceremonies, avoiding anything like unseemly hurry, inattention, or carelessness as they would avoid more overt sin. Among the numbers of men who passed through these Retreats there were of course some of considerable talent and intellectual attainment, who were not to be reached by any mere display of knowledge or eloquence. "You will not win them by saying fine things," Vincent used to tell his priests; "they know more than we do—nothing we can tell them that such men have not heard or read before: but it is what they see that will help their souls."

He always urged the conductors of the Retreats to give heed to simplicity in the outward expression, and purity in the inward intention of all they said:—to deal familiarly with subjects which need bringing home to the heart, and to enter into careful and close detail, avoiding mere generalities, always aiming at a clear definite impression to be left on the listener's mind in each instruction. These counsels he invariably gave to all who took part in this important work, and there were many besides the Missionaries;—Bishops and doctors—the most learned and eloquent that France could furnish, rejoiced in taking their share in the efforts made for the edification of their younger brethren. Among those who were so trained, many great names occur, of whom one at least must be singled out for mention—Bossuet. The future Bishop of Meaux made his Ordination Retreat at Saint Lazare in the Lent of 1652, and in 1659 and 1660 he conducted that retreat for his successors by which he had himself gained so much.[1]

There was still another step to be taken on behalf of the Clergy, and with a view to the higher tone and standard to be aimed at for them. The beneficial effects of the Ordinand's retreat were necessarily variable. Some men would be permanently impressed,—the whole future tenor of their lives would be influenced by those solemn seasons ; but this could hardly be anticipated of the mass,—the lack of a sufficiently fixed purpose, indolence, self-indulgence, evil example, and the snares of the world, would efface or weaken those impressions in many minds. Something must be done to keep up those pious influences, if any really permanent results were to be expected among the mass of Clergy. Vincent de Paul and his missionaries were accustomed to gather together the priests of that particular neighbourhood in which they were about to hold a mission, and to discuss with them various practical questions concerning the best way of teaching the children of their flocks, of hearing confessions, of preaching, and the like. But this was only a partial way of meeting the want. A more extended means thereto was soon suggested by a young ecclesiastic (his name is not on record) who had

---

[1] Bossuet also conducted Ordination Retreats at Saint Lazare in 1663 and 1666, after the Founder's death.

himself profited by his Ordination Retreat, and who was anxious, on his own account and that of others, to keep up the good work then begun. He proposed to Vincent to establish periodical gatherings at Saint Lazare of Clergy who were anxious to keep alive and increase the good impressions they had received, and who felt that mutual encouragement and conference concerning the duties of their calling would strengthen their hands and quicken their spiritual life. From this movement arose the "Conférences Ecclesiastiques" of the Lazarists. Vincent de Paul began by selecting a few of the young clergy who had continued under his direction after their Ordination, and proving them by intrusting a mission to the workmen employed in building the Church of the Visitation to their care. He watched over this Mission himself with a special object, and then, satisfied with his men, he proposed first to each separately, and then to them all collectively, to unite in a society with the view of strengthening and raising their spiritual life.

The system was soon organised. The Superior of the Mission was to be director of the Conférences—a prefect, two assistants, and a secretary completed the official staff. There was to be a conference every Tuesday at 2 p.m.; held during part of the year at Saint Lazare,—during the rest at the Bons Enfants. Later on there were conferences at both places.

Certain rules were drawn up. The applicants were to be formally admitted when satisfactory proof was given as to their conduct and doctrine, and after preparation by going through a retreat and making a general confession. All members had a simple rule of life to keep, a fixed hour for rising, at least half an hour's meditation, hearing or celebrating Mass, daily reading of the Holy Scriptures on their knees, more or less study, according to their circumstances, self-examination, and a yearly retreat;—rules which, without being burdensome, were likely to keep men in a habit of self-discipline, both outward and interior. All members who were not lawfully hindered (in which case they were to give notice of the same to the Prefect) were bound to attend the Tuesday meetings, to which all Bishops had a right of admission, but other clergy not members were seldom admitted. These meetings began with the *Veni Creator*, after which the subject appointed was discussed. These subjects were classed under certain heads,—the graces general to all Christians, the duties peculiar to the Clergy—administration of Sacraments, sacred services, ritual, etc., and the special duties of particular ecclesiastical offices, such as grand vicaire, dean, curé, etc. No one was to speak for more than a quarter of an hour. Any special subject, such as a mission about to be undertaken, a difficult case of conscience, or similar matters, on which any priest wished to consult his brethren, might be brought forward. Towards the close, the director or any Bishop present gave a brief exhortation, and after the subject proposed for the next conference had been announced, the members separated. Most of the leading men in Paris joined this union, and it proved the source of supply to many of the most important ecclesiastical appointments. The members undertook various spiritual works, missions to the different hospitals, missions in Paris itself, as well as in various large towns, which the Lazarists themselves did not undertake. Among these the mission of Metz was prominent, a place fearfully neglected during the disgraceful episcopate (if so it can be called) of Henri de Bourbon, natural son of Henri IV. and Madame de Verneuil, on whom the see was conferred when he was six years old, and who was never ordained! Bossuet was Archdeacon of Metz, and after a visit paid there by the Court in 1658, he succeeded in exciting an earnest desire in the heart of Anne of Austria to do something for the spiritual benefit of the place. Finding that the Lazarists did not undertake town missions, the Queen asked if the Conférence could not do the work, and accordingly at the next Tuesday meeting it was proposed, and the members decided on accepting it, and were warmly aided in every way by Bossuet, who succeeded in establishing a permanent foundation of Lazarists in Metz, to carry on the improvement of the priesthood,[1] and missionary action upon the surrounding country.

The Conferences lasted in their original form until the Great Revolution, and more or less they have been revived in France since that tide of evil rolled back.

There is one more of S. Vincent de Paul's works which must be mentioned here, although not exclusively confined to the Clergy; since unquestionably it was another useful engine in raising the tone of ecclesiastical life in France. This was a great undertaking, no less a matter than throwing open the gates of Saint Lazare to all, whatever might be their station or means, for spiritual retreat. Priests who could not join the Conferences, Clergy from all parts, laymen of every age and position, devoted Christians who sought to confirm their devout life, sinners touched with grace and anxious to turn to God—all were welcomed within the hospitable walls of Saint Lazare, to the enormous increase both of labour and expense to the missionaries. Hitherto retreats had been almost exclusively used among religious, or at most among ecclesiastics, but now whoever would might profit by

---

[1] "A l'avancement de l'état ecclésiastique."—Archives, Imp. M. M. 535-539.

this, one of the very most helpful practices of the spiritual life. Careful training was given to the priests, whose business it was to conduct the retreats and direct the *exercitants*, as they were called. Sometimes the retreat was given to a number of persons at once;—in other cases, individuals kept their solitary retreat at Saint Lazare. Vincent de Paul drew up a most minute directory for the guidance of his priests in this pious labour. They were to adapt themselves most carefully to the needs of each *exercitant*, putting aside all personal views and objects, never seeking to force their own opinions, never assuming a tone of authority or dictation. Patience and forbearance, encouragement, entreaty,—these were to be their method of treatment. There is a touching quaintness in the instructions to the conductor how he is to enter the *exercitant's* room,—"with modest cheerfulness and cheerful modesty," and the suggestions made of pleasant little speeches; how he is to explain the timetable to any one coming into retreat for the first time, and the meaning and object of its practices, helping the *exercitant* as to his meditations and spiritual reading, according to his needs as priest or layman, well read or ignorant;—and before leaving him for the first night, the director of his retreat is to make sure that nothing needful to the *exercitant's* material comfort is wanting, that he has pen, ink, and paper, books, light, even—S. Vincent specially notifies—coverings to his bed, and a nightcap!

It was in vain that the comptroller of the household represented from time to time his incapability of meeting the enormous additional expense of all these guests. "My dear brother, they want to save their souls," was usually the answer; and if the said official in his ire ventured to reply that a great many came who apparently did not succeed in this pious intention, the Superior would reply, "But surely it is a great thing if some few only are saved! And how are you to tell which is which?" One day, after being beset on all sides, from within and from without, with remonstrances as to his too free hospitality, S. Vincent declared that he would restrain it, and in order to be sure that this was properly done, he would himself be doorkeeper, and only admit such applicants as were unquestionably not to be rejected. Of course he refused nobody, and when night came there were more guests than usual! A brother came to tell the Superior that not a room remained free. "Very well, take mine then!" was the only answer he received.

Bishops established retreats in their dioceses on all sides, and it is recorded that priests who came to them reluctantly went forth to lead a new life, often exclaiming, "Had I known sooner what was required to undertake the office rightly, I should not have entered Holy Orders so carelessly as I did!"

The last work undertaken by Vincent de Paul for this great object of training a more spiritually-minded clergy was the establishment of his *Séminaire interne*, where young men were to be educated for the priesthood rather than specially trained as a novitiate for the Missionary Congregation. Perhaps it was in the natural order of things that S. Vincent should lay less stress on intellectual cultivation than de Bérulle or de Condren had done in training priests; but at the same time he was very far from despising science and learning, although he prized humility far above either. "The desire for knowledge is good," he wrote to a priest (July 18, 1659), "so long as it is in moderation. Remember S. Paul's warning words. Mediocrity will suffice, and that which goes beyond it is sometimes more to be feared than desired by Gospel labourers, because there is danger lest such should lead to a man being puffed up, inclined to shew off, to take credit to himself, and to neglect simple familiar duties, which all the while are the most useful. For this reason our Lord chose disciples who were no more than competent for such duties. If we labour to save souls in the Lord's own Spirit, He will give us the light and grace we need for success. If you are willing to know nothing save Jesus Christ Crucified, to live only in His Life, you need not doubt but that He Himself will give you wisdom and success." And he used to warn his younger brethren that no science could be really beneficial to mankind apart from piety. "I would crave for you all," he said, "the wisdom of Saint Thomas, but only on condition that with it you had the Angelic Doctor's humility. Pride causes wise men to fall, even as it made the Angels fall, and knowledge without humility has always been hurtful to the Church. . . . The pettiest little demon in hell knows more, probably, than the most subtle philosopher and the wisest theologian on earth. . . . Make good use of your youth to learn how best to serve your neighbour. Do not lose time, for the work is urgent and far exceeds the supply of labourers. Our countrypeople are being lost for want of teaching, and the greater part of the earth is still sunk in the darkness of unbelief. Study diligently then, strive to be learned, but without losing the grace of humility."

Gradually S. Vincent de Paul became more in favour of colleges, where young men nearly ready for Holy Orders might receive one or two years' definite preparation for their sacred calling, than of establishments intended for younger persons; and up to the time of the Revolution the Lazariste Fathers counted fifty-three *grands Séminaires*, and nine *petits Séminaires*, as the latter are called.

Thus the work of revival grew in France among her Clergy, men's hearts were turned to God, and if the great storm of Revolution was slowly gathering over the land, so too the strength with which the Church of Christ should meet that fearful storm was being gathered in also, and when the evil day came at last, the work of Oratorians and Lazarists was a very bulwark of the Faith. There was another great work besides, also springing forth from the same source, which has had no small share in maintaining Christ's Kingdom amid the terrible assaults which have been made upon it—that of Saint Sulpice.

CHAPTER VI.

ST. SULPICE AND JEAN JACQUES OLIER.

CLOSELY linked with the names of S. Vincent de Paul and Père de Condren, as God's instruments for the spiritual reformation of the Church and Clergy in France, is that of Jean Jacques Olier, the Founder of the Seminary of Saint Sulpice. He was the youngest son of Jacques Olier de Verneuil, Secretary and Maître des Requêtes to Henri IV., and was born Sept. 20, 1608, at which time his parents were living in Paris; but Henri IV. was murdered in 1610, and a few years later Louis XIII. appointed M. Olier to the post of Intendant, or Governor of Lyons, and here he and his family became intimate with S. Francis de Sales. They had always thought that Jean Jacques displayed a vocation for the priesthood, and though judging by after events Madame Olier thought at least as much of the worldly side of the matter, and of temporal dignities for her son, as of a higher aim, still they were disturbed by the very impetuous wilful nature of the lad, which from time to time roused serious doubts in their minds as to his fitness for the sacred calling. At last Madame Olier took an opportunity of laying her misgivings before the venerable Bishop of Geneva, and asking his opinion. He promised to weigh the matter well, and accordingly one Thursday after Mass had been said in the Chapel of the Visitation, when Madame Olier brought her children to S. Francis, "he received them with all fatherly kindness, kissed them, and as he spoke with the like goodness to all, the mother told that great prelate that Jean Jacques, the youngest, was not a good boy, but refractory, and so unruly in his ways that he often put her and his father very much out. Whereupon the Saint, to console this dolorous mother, answered, 'Hé! Madame, a little patience! Do not be afflicted, for God is training up a great servant of the Church in the person of this dear child;' and putting his hands on the boy's head, he kissed him tenderly, and gave him his blessing."[1]

S. Francis, moreover, promised to take her son, when, as he proposed, he should retire to his quiet hermitage on the Lake of Annecy, and train Jean himself for his sacred calling; but very soon after this the venerable Bishop was given a more perfect rest from the many cares of his busy diocese, and this promise could not be fulfilled. Young Olier grew up a vigor-

[1] Vie de M. Olier, pt. i. 8.

ous hearty schoolboy, yet with a deep-seated religious feeling; for he used to say himself in after life that if he had done anything really wrong he never could get on with his lessons, or remember what he had learnt by heart, until he had confessed it. His father being appointed Conseiller d'Etat, returned to Paris, and young Olier's education was carried on in the University of that city and at the Sorbonne. He distinguished himself, and his father looked forward to a brilliant worldly career for him, which according to the views of those days was not at all incompatible with the ecclesiastical profession. Accordingly he obtained the Priory of la Trinité de Clisson in the Diocese of Nantes, and the Abbey of Notre Dame de Pébrac in that of Saint Flour, for his son, and at eighteen the handsome schoolboy, for he was scarcely more, took possession of his Abbey, to which was shortly added the Priory of Bazainville in the Diocese of Chartres, and the title of Chanoine Comte in the Chapter of Saint Julien de Brioude!

With the same object in view, his parents were anxious that he should display his natural gifts of eloquence, and although not in Holy Orders, his title of Abbot was a qualification as preacher. So he was handed about, making a great display in sundry of the most famed Parisian pulpits, to the great delight of his mother, who drank in all the pretty things that were said about her son greedily. He says himself that she was highly pleased with him when she saw him prized and flattered by the world, preaching with *entrain* and *gentillesse*, fine fashionable sermons, full of vanity, bristling with eloquent and fanciful conceits, so long as he said nothing that could offend the world and its ways! All the more likely, as at the same time young Olier mingled freely with the said world and its pleasures; and his parents were in nowise reluctant to afford him the means of doing so. They gave him a liveried suite, two handsome carriages, and promoted his success in society to the utmost.

Nevertheless there came a day when the mother at least opened her eyes to the danger she had helped to gather round her son, and to desire his conversion earnestly. Such a manner of life was too common among the upper ranks of the Clergy at that period to excite any astonishment save among the few; but a few there were who shuddered at the frightful desecration of holy things which prevailed all around, and from

> . . . "Many a hidden dell,
> From many a rural nook, unthought of there,
> Arose for that proud world the saints' prevailing prayer."

Nor were such intercessions confined to the "rural nooks." A poor woman, by name Marie Rousseau, widow of a wine-seller, was constant in prayer for a revival of faith and holiness among the Clergy, and specially for those of the Faubourg Saint Germain, wherein she dwelt, and which (as S. Vincent de Paul's history and that of the Mission conducted there by the members of his Conférence shew) was one of the very worst parts of Paris. One day, meeting Jean Jacques Olier and some other young ecclesiastics whose lives were more fashionable than sacerdotal, Marie Rousseau addressed them, exclaiming that they cost her many a weary hour in praying for their conversion, but that she hoped some day God would grant her prayers! To this circumstance M. Olier attributed his first awakening to the perils of his present life. He broke away from his social bonds, but for the time being it was only a transfer of worldly eagerness to a different channel. A new ambition seized him to distinguish himself at the Sorbonne in Hebrew, and he hastened to Rome, where he expected to find greater opportunities of studying this language than in Paris. But an acute inflammation of the eyes, which for a time even threatened total loss of sight, put an end to his project, and this malady was followed by a severe fever which seized him while on a pilgrimage to Loretto. These shocks, and God's merciful deliverance from both, fairly roused J. J. Olier from his spiritual torpor; and he was seriously contemplating entering upon the religious life in some Italian convent, when his father died, and Madame Olier urgently recalled her son to France. In spite of her better self, Madame Olier was an intensely ambitious mother. She had succeeded in obtaining high office for her two lay sons, and she was anxious that her priestly son should not fare worse than his brothers. Accordingly she had obtained the promise of a Chaplaincy to the King for him, which she hoped would be the first-fruits of greater dignities, and she was eager, her son says, that he should be known in the world, and become conspicuous at Court. She wanted him to attract people to her house, and meant to shine in the reflected credit of her child. Accordingly, when Madame Olier found that he resolutely persevered in a perfectly different line, forsaking the Court and all worldly society, and giving himself up to the poor, the sick, and the ignorant, she was indignant, and looked upon him as a disgrace to the family. Her motherly affection seemed to be all gone, and she became positively unkind to him, so that sometimes he used in sadness of heart to turn into Notre Dame, and kneeling down before the statue of the Blessed Virgin, would cry out, "Be my Mother, since my own mother casts me out!"

Meanwhile, another saintly person was led by God to pray fervently for Jean Jacques Olier, though she had never seen him. This was the Prioress of the Dominican Convent at Langeac, not far from Pébrac. This holy woman, like most other really earnest people, felt that the only hope for reforming the laity lay in a reformed Clergy, and her prayers and intercessions were perpetual on behalf of the Church. One day, when the spiritual desolation of her country was weighing more heavily than usual on her heart, the Mère Agnes prayed, Elijah-like, that she might leave this sin-stricken, weary world; when within her soul the Lord Himself seemed to say, "I have need of thee yet to help a soul which is destined to set forward My Glory:" and not long after, in the same way, it was revealed to her that the Abbot of Pébrac was the person indicated.

She had then never heard his name, but for three years the Mère Agnes persevered in prayers and mortifications on his behalf without any further knowledge of the object of her intercessions. The Abbé Olier had an instinctive consciousness that powerful spiritual influences were drawing him, but he knew not whence they came, and he was meditating an entrance into the Carthusian Order, with a view of labouring for life for the salvation of souls, when a remarkable dream altogether altered his plans. His own account of it is as follows:—

"The Mère Agnes was praying for me without my knowing it, and I was very much troubled as to my vocation. I had no director then; I did not even feel my need of one, but I thought of becoming a Carthusian. I had cut myself off to the best of my ability from what was sinful in my life, and just then a worthy Curé, who had ministered to me for a time, was dying, and I went to see him. Knowing that there was nothing he cared for more sincerely than my salvation, I begged him, that the first thing he asked of God on entering into His more immediate Presence might be on my behalf,—namely, grace for me to know clearly in what way He would have me serve Him? Two nights running, soon after, it pleased God that in my sleep I saw Heaven's gates opened, and S. Gregory sitting on a throne, with S. Ambrose on another below. Lower still there was an empty cure, and lower still a number of Carthusian monks. Perhaps, I thought, this means that it is God's Will that I should serve in the ranks of the Clergy, wherein those two great men ministered, filling the post of parish priest, which may be a more necessary duty than that of a Carthusian; and I may be intended to work with an order of priests and curés whose mission is to help on and sanctify the Clergy."

From this time M. Olier felt a decided distaste to the idea of joining the Carthusians, though his respect for the Order, and his pleasure in joining their offices and striving to imbibe their spirit, was as strong as ever. He now determined on taking Holy Orders;

and so doing, he was one of the first set of candidates who made their Ordination Retreat at the Collége des Bons Enfants, under S. Vincent de Paul, whom he accepted thenceforth as his confessor and spiritual guide. After working as a missionary in the country for a year, under Vincent's orders, Olier returned to the Bons Enfants for his Priest's Orders, but here he was so overwhelmed by a sense of the awful responsibility of the Priesthood, and of his own insufficiency for it, that but for Vincent de Paul's authority he would have shrunk back from being ordained. He spent three months in a preparatory Retreat, and on March 21, 1633, the future founder of Saint Sulpice was admitted to Priest's Orders. He was one of the young priests who first gathered round S. Vincent as the nucleus of the *Conférences de Saint Lazare*, and before long he went with several other members to evangelize the parishes belonging to his own Abbey of Pébrac. During a ten days' Retreat which he made in preparation for this Mission, Jean Jacques Olier twice saw, while praying, the figure of a Dominicaness, who said, "I weep for thee." He told his director of the vision, but neither of them knew at all who the nun could be; and he proceeded into Auvergne on his mission. During this mission, Olier often heard mention made of the exceeding saintliness of the Prioress of Langeac, and as soon as his missionary labours allowed time, he went to see her; but it was only after several fruitless attempts that he succeeded in obtaining an interview with the Mère Agnes, when he at once beheld in her the nun of his visions, and she recognised the object of her persevering prayers. From that time one of those close spiritual friendships which it sometimes pleases God to call forth between two souls, and to bless with such wondrous fruit, arose, and lasted during the Prioress's brief life. Well versed in the Religious life, she counselled him in the reform of his own Abbey, which M. Olier undertook at once, but in the teeth of violent opposition—fostered by his own mother, who saw that her son was thereby throwing away, what were in her eyes, the good things of this world! And while the Mère Agnes helped M. Olier not a little by her devotion and her deep insight into the hidden life, he led her on into a clearer, brighter, more cheerful perception of the things of God than she had hitherto enjoyed.

It was not for long. Those members of the Community of Pébrac who did not wish to be reformed attacked their Abbot vehemently, and he was summoned to appear before Cardinal de la Rochefoucauld on the matter. Père de Condren, General of the Oratorians, wrote to urge his immediate presence in Paris, and the two friends who had been so touchingly drawn together parted, never to meet again in this world. At their last interview Mère Agnes gave M. Olier her own crucifix, taking a final leave of him, and almost immediately afterwards fell ill and died; writing just before her death to the Père de Condren, whom she knew intimately, to commend M. Olier to his special spiritual affection and guidance.

M. Olier was hearing confessions in the Church of Saint Paul on All Saints' Day 1634, when the tidings of Mère Agnes's death reached him. "Much touched," he says, "I knelt at once before the Blessed Sacrament, to pour out my sorrow to our Dear Lord, Who had taken away this great help to my soul ; . . . and soon my tears were stayed, and I felt unable to grieve any longer : for indeed at that time I was still foolish enough to believe that one must grieve at such losses, and that it was a token of respect and affection to those who were gone—a very worldly notion forsooth, as if the saints who go hence were not infinitely gainers by their departure !"

This was a new stage in M. Olier's spiritual life. Hitherto Vincent de Paul, doubtless with good reasons, had advised him to retain his carriage and horses, and a certain amount of retinue and conventional habits. But Mère Agnes's love of poverty overruled this, and M. Olier gave up everything except the services of one servant, who was only retained by S. Vincent's express command.

The important business for which Père de Condren urged M. Olier's presence in Paris was a proposal to raise him to the episcopate, a Bishop who had become aware of his great zeal and earnestness having applied to the King for Olier's appointment as his coadjutor and successor. He was not adverse to the idea, and S. Vincent de Paul would at once have encouraged him to accept it, but it was not God's Will—He had other work in store for His servant.

The matter was decided in this wise. Nothing particular had come of Mère Agnes's dying request to Père de Condren, of which M. Olier probably knew nothing, and for some months he continued as before under Vincent de Paul's guidance; but he was unsettled and disturbed in his mind. He felt that God had special designs for him, but he could not read them; and apparently Vincent himself felt that there was something he knew not how to deal with in his penitent's mind, for he failed to quiet or comfort him. Then Olier went into Retreat, hoping therein, face to face with God, to find the rest he needed; and even so it was. While struggling with the fear of having committed a grievous sin (he does not say what it was), suddenly an irresistible voice whispered within him, "Père de Condren would give you peace:" and from that moment he was at rest. Most assuredly, that most humble of saintly men, S. Vincent de Paul, would be the last to feel injured or grieved at one of his penitents finding more help from another than himself, and he gladly assented to Olier's seeking the same source whence he had himself derived so much strength at an earlier period—within the Oratory.

Apparently it pleased God to give Père de Condren plainer light as to His designs for Olier, as from the first he resolutely opposed the idea of a bishopric, whereas S. Vincent de Paul encouraged it. "God has other intentions for you," de Condren said; "they are not so brilliant or so conspicuous as the episcopate, but they will make you more useful to the Church." From this time Olier put himself entirely under Père de Condren's spiritual direction, without ceasing to maintain the warmest friendship and most constant intercourse with Vincent de Paul; and although that holy man was never again his director, M. Olier did not cease to consult him in all the important questions which arose during his life: and when the younger priest died, at the comparatively early age of forty-eight, the venerable Saint stood beside his dying bed, and ministered to him to the last.

Meanwhile Père de Condren used every effort to prepare the young priest, whom he believed destined to a great work for the Church, rightly to fulfil that destiny. An ever-increasing knowledge of the importance, the responsibilities, and the duties of the priesthood, was what both set before them; and Olier's admiration for the saintly life of his teacher made him an apt pupil. He writes of Père de Condren as fulfilling more than any one he ever knew the Apostle's description of holiness—Christ living in the man, so that it was no longer himself, but Christ in him that served on earth.

The Oratorian's chief aim now was so to train his disciples to the highest views of the priesthood as to make them capable of training others, and for the present he counselled M. Olier to persevere in mission work. A Retreat which he made under de Condren before returning for this purpose to Auvergne, had a lasting influence upon him. "My second director," he writes, "began by giving me up more to the Spirit of God than the first had done. He left me very much to myself in my Retreat, not even giving me subjects for the four meditations of an hour each which I made daily, and only coming to see me once; his occupations hindering him from coming into the country often. And now I began consciously to realise the guidance of God's Holy Spirit, and the wonderful care He took of me. I remember how I learnt then for the first time, and to my great astonishment, that Jesus Christ is really Present to our souls. When my director came to me I was glad to be taught and enlightened concerning this truth. 'It is even so,' he said, 'Our Lord is really Present to our souls. *Christum habitare per fidem in cordibus vestris. Per fidem*, that is, faith is the foundation of His Indwelling, and it is formed by His Holy Spirit, *donec formetur Christus in vobis.*' And he said further to me, 'Now henceforth you must perform all your works in union with the Son of God, either by feeling, intention, or faith. If you have a conscious feeling of His Presence, unite yourself to Him through feeling. If you have none of that, unite yourself to Him in intention, that is to say, try to work with the same mind and intention as He had; and if you cannot do this, then unite yourself to Him in faith, that is to say, make a spiritual offering of all you do in union with His works, thus offering those as well as your own to God.'"

This teaching henceforth became the foundation of M. Olier's own spiritual life, and the key-stone of all his efforts to lead others to the perfection of the priesthood at Saint Sulpice.[1]

At this time M. Olier was firmly persuaded that he had not physical strength for mission work; indeed, his

---

[1] M. Olier gave the Saint Sulpiciens a short prayer which Père de Condren had given him, and which has continued in daily use, night and morning, among them: "Venez, Seigneur Jésus, et vivez en votre serviteur dans la plénitude de votre force, dans la perfection de vos voies, dans la sainteté de votre Esprit, et dominez sur toute puissance ennemie dans la vertu de votre Esprit, et la gloire de votre Père."

doctors had said as much. But his health grew visibly stronger, and, like other obstacles, he triumphed over this, in spite of most exhausting toil, and a hardness and roughness of life which must have been more trying to a man nurtured so long in luxury than to many a fellow-labourer. Whatever time was not filled up by the arduous toils of the Mission (one of his coadjutors says) was spent in prayer, and when interrupted by a summons to meals, M. Olier might be heard ejaculating "*Amor meus crucifixus est*" ("Jesus, my love is crucified!") in a tone which penetrated all hearts.

In a letter written during this Mission to Vincent de Paul and the priests of the Conférence, pleading for more workers, M. Olier says: "Do not refuse such help to Jesus: it is too great an honour to work under Him, to set forward the salvation of souls, and His Glory therein, which will last for all eternity. . . . Go on in this blessed work—there is nothing like it on earth. O Paris! Paris! you and your trifling distract men who might convert several worlds!" In another letter, describing a subsequent mission in Auvergne, M. Olier says that though they were but a body of six priests, they had heard more than two thousand general confessions. The country-people from long distances brought provisions for two or three days, and slept as they might in barns and sheds, where they might be heard talking over what they had heard, and singing the hymns they had been taught. He made great efforts to induce the local clergy to rouse themselves and assist the Missioners, and that most successfully; for many cathedral dignitaries and priors of convents joined them, and went about helping to preach and catechise. M. Olier says that he could not help attributing this in a great measure to the persevering prayers of the Mère Agnes; and he adds that Père de Condren used often to say that he believed the whole results of a sermon or instruction were often owing to prayer,—it might be the prayers of some poor, unlearned woman in the congregation.

Eighteen months of such work, however, proved too much for the Missioner's strength. His own account of his illness is too touching to pass over. "I had been saying to one of my friends that I wanted nothing but a fortnight's illness to be sure that God had accepted our work; and so it fell out, that on the very last day of our last Mission—that of De la Motte-Canillac—as I was returning home, I felt in a very unwonted state of peace, free from all cares, although hitherto I had been surrounded with anxieties. It seemed as if crosses were a very strength and stay to my soul, without which I was weak; and now I felt quite overwhelmed at their apparent absence. It was not to be for long; for just as I arrived at Langeac, and was entering the church of the monastery where the blessed Sister Agnes had lived and died—she who had foretold so many crosses to me—I was seized with a most violent headache, which was the beginning of a severe illness. Directly that I was seized with the pain, I felt inwardly drawn to make a vow to Mgr. de Genève for restoration to health, and I felt somehow sure of it at once. I remember that, although half unconscious, I felt as though some voice within had blessed me and assured me that I should not die; and I called my dear friend M. de Foix and said, 'I shall not die; go and fetch the Blessed Sacrament from the convent church.' We were then in the Aumonier's room, and as it was two o'clock in the night, he could not have procured that Blessing for me elsewhere. Meanwhile the pain became so intense that the doctors gave me up, and exhausting all their remedies, they tried one which threw me into a sort of apoplexy. During this time they tried to confess me, but I could only give broken answers, and soon lost all power of speech. The doctors struck their lancets deep into my shoulders without my seeming to feel anything, and believing that my last hour was come, they administered the Extreme Unction. I just remember then that although I had lost speech and hearing, I answered at the Name of Jesus, as also to that of the Blessed

Virgin, whom I called my *maman* like a child, for I had no command of my reason then....

"This illness was a proof to me of the Saviour's Promise that He will give a hundredfold to those who have forsaken or sacrificed anything for Him. Being thus *in extremis*, in a lonely place far away from my family, God willed to succour me with His Providence, and to give me every possible earthly assistance. It so happened that that very day, two first-rate physicians came to Langeac, as if on purpose for me, one without any summons from a place two hundred miles off, the other had been sent for to see the little daughter of the *seigneur de la ville*. The impossibility of getting to my own abbey was a fresh sign of God's Providence, because I remained close to these good doctors; and instead of the mother, sister, and two brothers whom I had left, I found numberless people who shewed more than mother's and brothers' love for me—all they did was done out of such pure, disinterested charity, that it seemed as though God only were ministering to me. My own family were far off, but I had the family of God my Father round, and they provided for all my wants with such abundance and profusion, that our Lord not only fulfilled in my favour the prophecy, that they who forsake flesh and blood for His Sake shall receive a hundredfold, but in exchange for those I had left, He gave me far holier ties—people who were able to do far more for me than my own relations—especially my friends,[1] who ministered continually to me, and were more than brothers to me. . . .

"During this time my sister, who was in Paris, and who was greatly opposed, like the rest of my relations, to my work, died in the midst of her family without being assisted by any one, forsaken of all her friends. Surely this might be a proof to all my family that there is no profit in serving the world, which forsakes one in extremity, while on the other hand there is everything to gain in serving God, Who uses even men of the world in spite of themselves for the service of His children.

"I had gone to those wild parts against the will of my relations, but now God sent my mother and my youngest brother to me. On hearing of my illness, my mother set out, meaning to take me back to Paris in her carriage; for in my great weakness I could not have sat a horse. But she found me cured, and in order to shew her Who had watched over me while I was serving Him, I let her see some three or four hundred poor people, who followed me out of the town; and then she saw how they loved me, and how their prayers and entreaties had won my cure. Poor

---

[1] His brother Missioners, M. de Foix, M. Meyster, and M. de Perrochel.

things, in their astonishment at my recovery, they all kept saying, 'He was gone to Paradise, but he has come back!' Not all the wealth and position of my family could have obtained my cure, as the prayers of these poor people did. Thanks be to God, Who never fails to preserve them that are His, however weak and needy—of a truth we never lose anything by serving Him!"[1]

On his return to Paris, M. Olier was warmly received by the religious world generally, as well as by Vincent de Paul, who embracing him, said, "I do not know what you do to bring it about, but assuredly God's Blessing follows you wherever you go." He continued working thus, reforming several large convents, and giving everywhere the rule of his own life—"*Plaire à Dieu*" ("to please God,")—as the watchword of a holy life.

Apparently it was at this time that M. Olier became intimate with the Père Bourdoise, already mentioned as working in the cause of ecclesiastical education and reform. He seems to have been very rough and uncomplimentary in his language, and somewhat exacting in his standard of ecclesiastical fitness; for he rebuked M. Olier and his companions de Foix and de Ferrier, as wanting in external clerical simplicity, and he is said to have taxed S. Vincent de Paul with

[1] Vie, pt. i. p. 86.

timidity and cowardice, so far as to have called him a *poule mouillée !*[1] Nevertheless his advice on various points connected with the subject which was so close to both their hearts proved very valuable to M. Olier, and he and his companions always looked upon the Père Bourdoise as their master in clerical life.

Again M. Olier was on the point of receiving the episcopate, and again Père de Condren interfered. The Bishop of Châlons, like all other true pastors, mourned over the deplorable condition of his diocese; and believing that nothing would tend so much to its reformation as a good Training College for the Clergy, he applied to Cardinal Richelieu for M. Olier as his coadjutor. Louis XIII. at once confirmed the appointment, and the *brevet* was actually sent to M. Olier; who however referred the question to Père de Condren, and was again told that God had other designs for him: whereupon he immediately declined the office.

Cardinal Richelieu pressed the appointment, and it was only after a personal interview with the Missioner that he could believe in an ecclesiastic of that day deliberately refusing such an office, which held out the additional attraction of making its holder a *pair de France*. The disappointment of Madame Olier on this occasion knew no bounds. However lightly her

[1] Vie de M. Olier, pt. i. p. 99.

son might esteem such worldly dignities, they had the highest possible attraction for her, and her mortification took vent in the most bitter reproaches and almost estrangement from her son. He was not living under her roof at this time. Guided by de Condren's advice, M. Olier and his friends were living at Saint-Maur-des-Fossés, near Paris, preparing for their great work, and leading a community life, with M. Amelote as their Superior. M. Olier was an object of general esteem and admiration—his personal advantages, his successful work, his resolute indifference to high worldly office, all tended to make him a great name, and he suffered acutely from the temptations of pride and vanity which beset him. He says that he felt himself entangled in a very network of self-conceit and human respect; and "when I came to that part of my confessions," he says naïvely, "I was in despair! Sometimes, walking alone in our garden after meals, I was so tormented by these ideas, that with tears I used to cry out, 'When shall I find the Divine Life, and live to God Only!'"

His earnest prayers to be made humble were answered—as God is wont to answer the sincere prayers of His children—in a way M. Olier did not look for, and through bitter suffering. A complete mental paralysis seemed to come upon him. He lost all powers of memory and apprehension; he could not understand what he heard, or express his own thoughts; sometimes when he tried to write, he did not succeed in producing two or three legible lines after some hours' work. Whatever he undertook failed—a thick cloud had passed over all his faculties, natural and supernatural. Of these last, he says (writing about that dark season) : " I had looked upon them (supernatural gifts) as personal acquisitions, and their withdrawal left me in a strange state of darkness and dryness— without any sense of God in me, full of ebullitions of pride and self-love, hedged in with human respect, sensitively anxious as to what the world would think of me. These notions gave me no rest, and were the greater cross that I seemed to yield to them. From the bottom of my soul I longed to do nothing save for God, but nevertheless I felt as if I did everything for myself. So, too, I had fancied that the blessings attendant on my ministry were personal, and God in His Goodness withdrew them, in order to make me realise what I was without His Help, and Whose were these gifts which I had fondly thought to be my own. Thus, when I had to speak or expound some passage of Holy Scripture, I did it so confusedly and badly, in such incorrect words, as to prove that there was no spark of heavenly fire in me.

" Hearing confessions, I knew not what to say to my penitents; I was as one forsaken of God. I felt so sorry for the people who came to me that I used to ejaculate mentally, 'Poor souls! you know not whom you seek! What a misfortune I am to you!' When I was called on to preach I had neither ideas or words at command; and though I continued stedfast in prayer, no ray of light gladdened me in it. I felt nought save darkness, dryness, impossibility of looking up to God; and so I thought all I had rejoiced in before was but an illusion, and my worst trouble of all was that I had no grounds to believe that God loved me. One day Père de Condren was assuring me that all this was but trial and temptation. 'Would to God,' I answered, 'that these were only trials, even if they lasted to all eternity; so long as I am not abhorred of God, I should not mind.' And my big tears fell fast."

Every kind of external humiliation was added to these severe inward trials—the whole world, relations, friends, attendants, great and small, every one seemed to despise and reject him. His refusal of the Bishopric of Châlons was turned against him as though he were deficient in intellect to lose such an office—the King, the Cardinal, the Chancellor, the Bishops, all his relations and friends, spoke contemptuously of him—stranger still, his fellow-labourers changed their high opinion of his merits, and began to look down upon him as foolish and devoid of God's guiding

Spirit. They restrained him from his ordinary work, forbade him to preach or teach, or to hear confessions save in case of absolute necessity; they attributed his extreme depression to regrets at having been hindered accepting the bishopric, and the Superior of their little community, Amelote, told him that he was good for nothing, and had better go away and hide himself!

Truly his prayer that the high esteem and perilous good opinion men had of him might be averted had received a bitter answer! Even Père de Condren, in whom poor M. Olier rested more than in any other human being, appeared to his troubled mind to forsake him, although evidently that saintly man, who had himself gone through spiritual trials and knew their signification, looked upon these which beset his spiritual son as only a part of God's training to make him fitter for the great work. De Condren's life was drawing to a close; and on the very last occasion that M. Olier visited him, after dwelling upon the Angel of the Apocalypse, and urging devotion to the Blessed Sacrament as that specially incumbent on the priesthood, he concluded by saying very earnestly, "Take the Infant Jesus for your Director"—words which impressed M. Olier all the more forcibly, that he had already given himself up to the special guidance of the Child Jesus,—feeling drawn above all else to the sweet helplessness and tender patience of the Saviour's

Infancy, in his own mental and physical weakness and incapacity.

They never met again. De Condren had by this time worked out his ideas concerning the education of the Clergy, and intended committing them to writing, a proceeding which he had delayed, not from indolence, but, as it would appear, from a desire to give prolonged thought and consideration to the matter. Now his illness advanced in rapid strides upon him, and when Marie Rousseau (that devout widow whose influence was so marked and peculiar among all these learned holy men) came to see him, and he spoke of beginning to write, she told him at once that it was too late. Père de Condren accepted her assertion calmly, and resolved to impart his thoughts verbally instead to M. du Ferrier, the disciple who was nearest at hand, and who was asking instruction on certain points. "We will leave these matters for the present," de Condren said; "I have other things to speak of, but it is late now: come to-morrow at eight o'clock."

Accordingly, the next morning, the venerable Father entered at length into his views, and set forth his belief that, however valuable missions might be, their value was comparatively lost if the impressions made therein were not followed up by competent handling of the people on the part of the local Clergy; expressing a strong opinion that if any real work of reformation was to be effected in the Church, it must be by deepening the religious life of the priesthood, and training the younger members thereof. M. du Ferrier alleged the many difficulties which were looked upon as well-nigh insurmountable, but the venerable Oratorian dismissed them all, only requiring that those received into the Seminaries he wished to see established should not be mere boys, but young men, with character so sufficiently formed that a short time might give evidence as to their vocation and the probable good result of training them.

De Condren was still talking earnestly when his attendant lay brother came to summon him to say Mass. He bade him wait. At eleven Frère Martin returned, and was rather urgent with his superior. Du Ferrier, knowing his master's usually exact habits, was surprised to hear him say, "Brother, if you knew what I am doing, you would not hurry me; this is even more important than what you want of me." And he went on talking till midday, when he broke off, saying, "Poor Frère Martin, he will be quite vexed—we will leave the rest till to-morrow morning." So saying, the General of the Oratory went to say Mass, and M. du Ferrier never saw him again. The next morning he was suffering from such acute inflammation of the lungs that he was unable to speak, and during the week for which his life was prolonged, anything like continued conversation was impossible. Du Ferrier of course communicated all that had passed between him and their venerated director to the other priests of the little Company; and foreseeing that there would be no farther opportunity of any verbal intercourse, he sent a little note on the evening of Epiphany (the last night of Père de Condren's life), entreating that if God called their Father to Himself, he would pray that his mind and lights concerning the most important subject might be inherited by some one amongst them.

Meanwhile Père de Condren's last hour drew near. In his intense humility he wished to make his last general confession before the whole community, and this being refused to him, he begged the Father who confessed him to make no secret of his sins, and earnestly entreated every one to forgive his shortcomings and failings. There was a great stir in the religious world when it was known that the General of the Oratorians lay dying, and his wayward penitent, Gaston, Duke of Orléans, came, in real sorrow of heart, to the bedside of his venerable director to hear some few parting words of earnest exhortation. Père de Condren accepted all remedies patiently, only sometimes he said, " It is a misfortune to be a Superior, if more is to be done for him than for others." " Pray that God will this day convert the greatest of sinners," he said of himself to the Father who was ministering to him. After receiving Extreme Unction, he gave his last blessing to the assembled community: "*Veni Domine Jesu, et vive in his famulis Tuis in plenitudine virtutis Tuæ, et dominare adversæ potestati, qui vivis et regnas in secula seculorum.*"

He was constantly making acts of contrition and hope, through the pains of death, which were severe. "*Manus Domini tetigit me!*"[1] he exclaimed shortly before the last. Just at the end, when sorely overwhelmed with a bitterness which those around likened to our Lord's last Agony on the Cross, he cried out, "*Domine, propitiaberis peccato meo, multum est enim!*"[2]

Père de Saint Pé, who stood by, said, "Father, give yourself up to God." Whereupon, with a clear strong voice, the dying man replied, "My God, I commit my soul into Thy Hands!" and so saying he expired, January 7, 1641.

Du Ferrier's little note had been received the night before, but no reply was sent, or indeed expected. The day after Père de Condren's burial, however, M. Meyster—one of the small band he was training for his great work—saw him in a vision, and received communications as to that work, which exactly fitted

---

[1] "The Hand of God hath touched me."—Job xix. 21.

[2] Vulgate, Psa. xxiv. 11, English version, xxv. 10: "For Thy Name's Sake, Lord, be merciful unto my sin; for it is great."

in with those already given to du Ferrier, beginning in fact where Père de Condren's spoken instructions had ended ; and M. Olier himself was likewise permitted to see his beloved spiritual Father in vision, who repeated our Lord's words, " *Confidite, ego vici mundum.*"

At the time of Père de Condren's death, M. Olier was still suffering under the spiritual trials already mentioned, and this fresh grief might have been expected to increase his misery, but he accepted it with the most absolute resignation, as may be seen from a letter written at this time to a nun in one of the communities he had reformed.

" Of a truth, my dear daughter," he says, " if we are to be overwhelmed at every change and chance, we should know but little peace in this world. I will tell you what has happened to me—my father and master has been taken from me by the Divine Will, which is our dearest Master, alike in giving and taking away, in dryness or in the sweetest joys. He was a man who helped me greatly in reaching towards God, which is what I crave and delight in most. He led me to try and be useful to you, and recommended your House to my care. He has taught me so many good and holy things ! Well, my Sister, but is not God's Will worth as much to me as even this holy man, who had nothing in himself save through that Holy Will?

Cannot He make up for all that He takes away? and cannot He do now above that which it pleased Him for a while to do through another? My very dear daughter, let us adore the Will of Jesus, let us adore our Dearest Master; He turns the thorniest paths to our sanctification."

It was not till late in that same year that M. Olier was gradually delivered from his spiritual trials; by which time the little Community had moved to Chartres, where they hoped to begin a Seminary for priests. But the plan entirely failed there, and the members were scattered about, and differences of opinion and plan—not as to the main object, but as to its execution—threatened to extinguish the whole concern. Just as they were in this doubtful position, one of the number, M. Picoté, went to Vaugirard, on the outskirts of Paris, to help a devout lady, a former spiritual child of Francis de Sales, who had established a Community for the object of educating the peasant children around. Madame de Villeneuve, like other pious people, longed for better things among the Clergy, and had prayed for years that God would prosper the work of Seminaries; and when M. Picoté told her of the failure at Chartres, she suggested that perhaps God would have His servants try to establish the work at Vaugirard? At first M. Picoté altogether put aside the idea, but it gradually approved itself to his mind, enough to make him write about it to his brethren; and after many objections raised by all, especially by M. Olier, it pleased God to make the latter (while in Retreat expressly with the object of ascertaining His Will) see clearly that it was there God would have them go. Accordingly, a very small, poor house was taken in the village, and they began their new life, without any servant, depending upon Madame de Villeneuve, who used to send them some *potage* and *bouilli* daily for their dinner, and " a little roast mutton " at night for supper as their only food. They put themselves under the direction of the Superior of the Benedictines of Saint Maur—a very holy man; and M. Olier further consulted S. Vincent de Paul, the Père Saint Jure, Père Bataille, a Benedictine, and other persons of eminent wisdom and saintliness, as to their course. M. Bourdoise, too, entered with great ardour into their plans. " Oh, what a great thing it would be," he wrote to them, " if we could find even three priests full enough of love for Christ's Church to follow the leading of God's Holy Spirit, and make a stand against the world and its ways ! three priests who, when they are shewn what He through His Church has ordered, do not forthwith answer, 'It is not the custom—we do not so—what would be said?—it is inconvenient—the world would be offended—people would laugh at us—let us be content to take things as we find them, and not set up to be wiser than those who went before us!'" Nor must Marie Rousseau be overlooked. This woman, in spite of her humble condition in life, filled a very remarkable position among the more devout part of society at that time. "She is a light and a counsellor to many of the most illustrious as well as the holiest people in Paris," M. Olier wrote. And after enumerating princesses and duchesses, the Duchesse of Orléans, the Princesse de Condé, and others, he adds, "And apostolic men and missionaries are glad to learn God's Ways from her mouth. The Père Eudes, the greatest preacher of our day, often consults her, and so did Père de Condren. She has been the counsellor of M. du Coudray, raised up of God for our Eastern Missions;" and so he goes on with a long list of the good works which were forwarded by Marie Rousseau's prayers and counsels. All through M. Olier's troubles she had never questioned for a moment but that they were trials intended to lead him to greater heights of grace, and now she urged some of those who had taken a different view of the case to come to Vaugirard, and see what he was doing. All his mental gifts had returned, his preaching, speaking, whatever he undertook, was admirably done. It chanced that the Curé of Vaugirard was called away, and he left his parish in charge of the little Company, who worked it admirably. Priests began to flock in—some men of note, such as M. de Bassancourt, and M. de Gondrin, who in two years' time became coadjutor of Sens. They were soon twenty in number, and M. Olier was unanimously chosen as Superior, and thus at last the work which de Condren had looked upon as his "principal vocation" was fairly begun in spite of difficulties and hindrances. But M. Olier was not destined to remain at Vaugirard.

The frightful condition of the Faubourg Saint Germain, both moral and spiritual, has been already alluded to, as also the Mission held there by the priests of the Conférence de Saint Lazare; but it was an illustration of what all these holy men—de Bérulle, de Condren, Vincent de Paul, M. Olier, etc. etc., had ever said,—that no Mission can have more than a passing influence, where there is not a steady consistent work kept up by the local Clergy. The parish of Saint Sulpice—which was at that period of a vast extent, all subject to the jurisdiction, both civil and ecclesiastical, of the Abbé of Saint Germain—is described by all who speak of it as the very sink of Paris, for its utter irreligion and immorality, and the Mission seemed to the Curé M. de Fiesque merely to have stirred up and brought to light the hopelessness of the evil. In utter despair he determined to resign his post, and knowing M. Olier, and seeing how well he was supported by his company of priests, M. de Fiesque urged upon him to undertake the charge. At first the request was utterly rejected, but it was pressed by many whose opinion had great weight with M. Olier,—S. Vincent de Paul, Père Tarrisse, M. Bourdoise, and Marie Rousseau among others,—and at length he felt himself that it was a call from God, and once seeing that, he undertook the heavy burden cheerfully and gladly. Three points he set before himself as his work—the instruction and sanctification of the people, the sanctification of the Clergy, and the training of young men for Holy Orders. "I feel such boundless longings for the salvation of all men," he wrote, "and to infuse the zeal for God's Love and Glory into all hearts; I think what it would be to send forth a thousand disciples to carry abroad the Love of Jesus Christ, and to do honour to the Blessed Sacrament on all sides;—and then when I reflect that this charge offered me may set all this forward, I am overcome with happiness, and I desire nothing save to glorify my Master."

M. Olier's family took a different view of the matter. It was even worse than his rejection of the Bishopric of Châlons; they looked upon his taking the office of an obscure parish priest as a degradation to their house, and his mother and eldest brother came to Vaugirard and used every means in their power, coaxing and reviling alternately, to dissuade him from the step; and finding all in vain, his mother refused to see him again.

M. Olier went at once into Retreat as a preparation for the new undertaking, and on the Assumption 1642 he and his fellow-workers and their Seminary took possession of Saint Sulpice; the King, Cardinal Richelieu, the Princesse de Condé, the Duchesse d'Aiguillon, and numberless other great personages, testifying their hearty interest in the work,—which must have tended to modify Madame Olier's views as to the loss of social position she thought her son was incurring. Indeed, these great ladies, with several others, went to see the irate mother, and strove to appease her wounded vanity by the interest they testified in her son's noble work for the Church.

Saint Sulpice was no bed of roses. M. Olier and his Community (which ere long numbered fifty priests) devoted themselves not only to the active work of evangelizing the depraved wilderness which the parish presented, but they also studied in every way to make their own lives forward that work. In order to avert the possibility of scandal, no women were allowed to enter the Seminary;—all funds were common, each member of the Community receiving food and raiment, but no one appropriating anything, whether revenue or offerings, to himself. "It pertains to me," M.

Olier wrote, "to receive with one hand, and give with the other—to afford the rich an opportunity of giving to our Dear Lord through His Members, but to take nothing from the parish for myself—appropriating part of that which comes in to the poor, part to the maintenance of superannuated Clergy, and the rest to the wants of the Community." Nothing could be simpler than the fare provided for these last; nevertheless M. Bourdoise used to laugh at his friend for accustoming men who were intended to go forth as poor country curates to a manner of living far more plentiful than they would hereafter get in their village curacies. M. Olier wished all to wear the plainest dress possible; his own cassock was made of coarse serge, and he would not have any of their surplices trimmed with lace—a custom which has prevailed at Saint Sulpice to the present day. The rules of the house were simple; but M. Olier laid great stress on their being faithfully kept; and without absolute necessity no one was to miss keeping the Canonical Hours, or the morning meditation. He divided the huge parish into eight districts, over each of which a priest presided, who in his turn was aided by ten or twelve more, working under his direction. In every street some devout layman was to assist the Clergy, keep a list of the parishioners, report cases of sickness, and the like. Those who were dangerously ill were to be visited daily, and others less seriously sick were never to be left more than two days without care, and the opportunity used for giving some religious help. Certain priests were intrusted with the administration of the sick, others were to attend to the Sacraments of Baptism and Matrimony, giving heed that no one was neglected in those matters;—others were always ready to hear Confessions. Every day after the principal meal, all difficulties and cases of conscience were laid before the Superior, and if he could not resolve them, he used to send some member to the Sorbonne to ask counsel, and the answer was made known in the evening after supper. Such questions were continually arising, and the discussions and investigations consequent upon them proved a most valuable part of the training for the Community. M. Olier shared in everything with the rest, refusing to accept any privileges as Superior, save those of harder work and more anxiety than any one else; and with this intention he took a vow "to serve all Christians"[1]—by which he devoted his time, his property, himself, wholly to others; adding to this yet another vow— "In all things to seek the more perfect way."

One point of parochial labour to which M. Olier devoted special attention was teaching and catechising the children, whose deplorable ignorance bade fair

[1] "servitude à tous les Chrétiens."

to produce another generation of no better morals than their parents. He also arranged classes and instructions for domestic servants, a much neglected section of society; besides various others to meet the wants of all ranks and ages; and he set himself to stem, in every conceivable way, the tide of profligacy which ran strong on all sides—taking urgent measures among the rest to hinder the habit of duelling, which was carried at that period to an inconceivable extent in Paris.

On all sides the great work of Saint Sulpice was a matter of discussion and admiration. Statesmen and Bishops were found consulting its founder, who at this time was only thirty-four years of age, although his wisdom in spiritual things led men of double his years to turn to him for counsel. But he was not self-reliant, and one of his constant objects was to draw other men whom he knew to be stronger than himself, as theologians, controversialists, or preachers, into his society, and thus to strengthen his hands. He knew, too, how to use the help of good laymen; and indeed it cannot but strike one as a secret of M. Olier's success, that he was so quick in turning whatever came to hand to good account. For instance, finding that a sale of bad books and charms went on close to the church doors, he lost no time in setting up a rival library of good books, and to this day a certain bookseller is privileged to keep his bookstall against the walls of Saint Sulpice, though whether the Clergy still superintend and revise its contents we know not.

Again, coming suddenly one day upon a large assembly of people surrounding a juggler, who was carrying on sundry unseemly buffooneries, the Curé of Saint Sulpice (whose powers of preaching were attractive, if not specially learned) stationed himself at a little distance, and began to address the mob, who soon forsook the juggler to hearken, and before long, fascinated by his earnest and vigorous words, the whole assemblage was gathered round him.

A Confraternity of the Blessed Sacrament tended greatly to promote earnestness and devotion, and it is a characteristic anecdote of the times and persons, that one Thursday, at the weekly meeting of the Confraternity, when M. Olier was rebuking the upper classes for their irregularity in adoration of the Blessed Sacrament, Charlotte de Montmorenci, Princesse de Condé, stood up and said humbly, " Monsieur, I neglected it on Saturday, for I went to see the Queen instead ;"[1] to which M. Olier replied, " It would have been more to your credit, Madame, if you had come to the Court of the King of Kings."

S. Vincent de Paul's Confrérie de la Charité had

[1] " Monsieur, j'y ai manqué samedi, étant allée faire ma cour à la Reine."—Vie, pt. ii. p. 194.

once begun to work in the parish, but had almost died out. M. Olier re-established it, as well as Sisters of Charity, to minister among the poor and sick.

The old Church soon proved much too small for the worshippers, and on February 20, 1646, the Queen Mother, Anne of Austria, laid the first stone of the new Saint Sulpice, built by the great architect of his day, Gamard; and in spite of all the troubles of the Fronde, and various local disturbances raised up by the more profligate part of the parish, who found their profits hindered, the work went on bravely. It would be tedious to describe in detail all the different plans and works which M. Olier set on foot for the benefit of his large parish, some of which, called forth by the pressing necessities of the day, in consequence of the civil wars of the Fronde, were temporary only. It can scarcely be a matter of wonder that such ceaseless and anxious labours should have told upon any man's health. M. Olier had always believed that God only intended him to work the parish of Saint Sulpice for ten years, and had often said so to his intimate associates. One day early in the year 1652, one of these remarked to him that it was almost ten years since he entered the parish, and that there was no probability either that he would or could leave it at present. "All that will be as it pleases God," was the answer; "we have only to leave ourselves and everything wholly to Him, without any thought of self, and He will do as seems best to Him."

M. Olier knew even then that his health was failing—he was already under medical treatment; but the one most needful remedy—rest—he was not taking. In June, however, he succumbed to a severe fever, and on the 20th of the month the doctors declared that he could not live twenty-four hours. On being told this, M. Olier forthwith signed a document by which he resigned his cure unconditionally to the Abbot of Saint Germain, who (as has been said already) had supreme jurisdiction over it; and he also made his will. This time, however, it pleased God to restore his health, not however until one of his fellow-labourers, M. de Bretonvilliers, had been appointed Curé of Saint Sulpice.

That he left it himself without any vainglorious satisfaction in the great work he had done may be gathered from a circumstance recorded a few months later. When passing through Lyons, M. Olier went to the Church of the Feuillants, and having taken his place in the first vacant confessional, he was seen to make his confession with such tokens of visible sorrow and contrition, in the shape of tears and sighs, that the lookers on supposed him to be some specially notorious sinner graciously moved to penitence !

In the year 1645, M. Olier had begun to build a

college, which was a necessity under the circumstance of his rapidly increasing community. Various troubles had beset him in the process—among others a violent émeute kindled by the profligate people whose trade he had so greatly destroyed. It is a curious bit of contemporary history, illustrative of the times, to find a body of three hundred of the notoriously bad women living in the parish going first to the Luxembourg, and afterwards to the House of Parliament itself, to protest against their reformer! They were altogether repulsed, it is true; but M. Olier lived through stormy days at that period, and for long he was obliged to have a guard of soldiers posted in the Community house to keep off the rabble. The Bishop of Rodez had attempted just after this to induce M. Olier to let him resign his see in his, M. Olier's, favour; and, as on similar occasions, refusing to decide for himself, M. Olier had referred the decision to his Superior, the Abbot of Saint Germain, who, though originally opposed to the Seminary, now came entirely round, and entreated its founder to persevere. The Seminary was officially confirmed as an ecclesiastical community in October 1645, and this new building was entrusted to Jacques le Mercier, architect of the Palais Royal and of part of the Louvre;—the chapel was painted by le Brun. The keynote to the whole inner fabric was "Now I live, yet not I, but Christ liveth in me;"

and in harmony with this, the Hidden Life of Our Lord was made the special object of a weekly minor as of a yearly great festival. "If you can arouse the hidden life in our priests," M. Olier was wont to say, "we shall do;" and he continually quoted S. Ambrose: "*Omnia Christus est nobis, signaculum in fronte, ut semper confiteamur: signaculum in corde, ut semper diligamus: signaculum in brachio, ut semper operemur.*" "PER *Christum*, CUM *Christo*, IN *Christo.*"

Some of the members wanted to put the inscription "Collegium Apostolicum" over the entrance, but M. Olier observed that if they put anything it ought only to be "Séminaire de Saint Sulpice," the name by which the work was known. "But," he added, "I would rather put nothing, and let the institution be known more by its results than by its name. I would ask our Lord to let the thing speak for itself, and that our disciples may be known by their manner of life, by their conversation, and their work for love of God and of His Church, so that it may be fitly said of our House, '*Nomen habet quod vivat.*'"

Once a year he appointed a day on which all the Community publicly renewed their ecclesiastical vows, some Bishop, if possible, presiding at the ceremony. Out of affection for the memory of la Mère Agnes, to whom M. Olier always considered that he owed his vocation, he asked to be admitted into the Third

Order of Dominicans, which was gladly granted him shortly before he resigned the parochial charge of Saint Sulpice.

From that time all his time and thoughts were given to the work which had so long been foremost in his heart—training the Clergy; and his success was assuredly great. As the Bishop of Nevers remarked: "The external building is fine, but the inward building up of ecclesiastical life is far finer, and instead of saying with the Apostle, 'Behold what manner of stones are here!' we might well exclaim, 'Behold what manner of men are here!'" Freedom from worldliness, fraternal charity, lowliness and readiness for the humblest occupations, obedience and punctuality, are among the special characteristics of the Saint Sulpiciens, as mentioned by contemporary writers. M. Olier's personal influence with the Séminaristes must have been great. Many who came thinking themselves nearly ready for ordination, learnt to take a higher, truer view of the priesthood, and required to be urged and encouraged to proceed when the time came. Not all the students were young men. A certain M. de Sève, formerly Président aux enquêtes to the Parliament of Paris, came at sixty to be trained, and seems to have been mortified at being kept back from Holy Orders longer than he expected, in spite of his persevering exertions to prepare. A letter from M. Olier, written with a view to console this worthy man, concludes thus:—"Humble yourself utterly before God, be patient, and listen quietly to your Master's Voice, saying to you as to His disciples, 'In your patience possess ye your souls.' He will speak soon, but wait till He does; and from the bottom of your heart— which knows how far you are from the perfection of those Orders to which you aspire—tremble lest you approach them before He sees you confirmed in His Ways. All the future blessing and well-being of your life depends upon the spirit in which you go up for Ordination, and your obedience to your Divine Master's Law. He does not accept the service of any one who thrusts himself forward, who does not wait His Call reverently, humbly, and patiently."

One is glad to learn that M. de Sève in due time obtained his object and proved a valuable, earnest priest.

M. Olier pressed the importance of study with great urgency on his disciples, especially such as immediately concerned their office. "In the Confessional," he said, "you are called upon suddenly, and without time for consultation or reference, to give decisions on the most important of questions, decisions against which there is no appeal, and which will influence your fellow-men through all eternity. In the pulpit you have to deal alike with the learned and the ignorant, to maintain Gospel truth, to combat against vice, to resist the force of public opinion, to refute and expose heresy, so that the simplest can understand you; all of which necessarily requires a more than ordinary amount of knowledge—deeper and fuller than that men commonly acquire—of a stronger, more practical character." Day by day more men flocked in to obtain such teaching, and before long Seminaries were started on all sides, all of which M. Olier was glad to promote by sending members of his Society to start them, though he did not wish to take them permanently into the hands of that Society. He always maintained that Saint Sulpice could do more good by training priests who should return to their own dioceses, and themselves found and govern similar institutions. Wherever he went, he was beset with requests on behalf of Bishops or towns wanting to train Clergy, and Seminaries at Rodez, Limoges, Nantes, Aix, and many more, soon arose.

On two or three different occasions, after resigning his parochial charge, the missionary spirit rose so strongly in M. Olier, that in spite of his failing health he would fain have gone to China with Père de Rhodes, who however, believing that the Founder of Saint Sulpice was in his right place, declined to take him, a refusal which M. Olier attributed to his own unworthiness. He was offered the Bishopric of Babylon, with a view to the Persian Missions, but the Saint Sulpiciens unanimously declared that he must not leave them. The final result of all this was the establishment of the Séminaire des Missions Etrangères. M. Olier was also actively concerned in North American Missions, and a great promoter of the spiritual welfare of the French colonists.

This active life, spent so entirely in his Master's service, was however fast drawing to a close. M. Olier had never been really well since the illness which immediately led to the resignation of his parochial charge, and one malady after another laid hold of him with unrelenting tenacity. His doctors sent him to various places for change of air, or mineral waters, but a stroke of paralysis came, and deprived him of the use of his left side. This occurred at Peray, near Corbeil. He was removed as soon as it was practicable to Paris, and during the long illness that ensued, his remarkable cheerfulness and calmness impressed S. Vincent de Paul so strongly that he could not refrain from commenting on it to those who watched over the sick man. Yet some portion of the spiritual trials which had so harassed him formerly came again upon M. Olier, with this remarkable feature however, that now, even when most dry and powerless, as it seemed, he was always completely like his former self, overflowing with rich spiritual and mental stores when any one came to consult him. Some one noticed this to him, and the answer given, with a smile, was—that he seemed now to have two heads, one his own, which was in a sorry state—the other one provided by God for his neighbour's service. The Queen came to see him, and after his departure one of his attendant priests, who feared that he was no longer equal to the occasion, asked something concerning the interview? "God gave me some little matters to satisfy her with," was the answer.

Frequently M. Olier could neither read nor meditate, nor do anything to lighten the wearisomeness of his confinement, and just then it was that interior dryness would press heaviest. But he would only say, " Our Dear Lord will not have me find pleasure in anything. I must be satisfied, and submit willingly to His commands." It is touching to hear of his delight in a little tame bird, which would sit on his table and pick up crumbs, but one day the window was left carelessly open, and the bird flew away!

The doctors wished him to take the Eaux de Bourbon, and though not expecting any benefit himself, he obeyed, travelling thither by slow stages. There was some difficulty in arranging the journey so as to rest in hotels near to a church, and it was suggested that during the journey he should abstain from receiving Holy Communion. "Nay," the sick man exclaimed, "take what else you will away, but leave me that, the one only comfort I have."

M. Olier felt that his end was at hand; and he wished once more to visit Notre Dame du Puy, and Langeac, where his still well-loved friend the Mère Agnes rested. At the latter place he said, smiling, to the Prioress, pointing to the stick by help of which he walked painfully: "You see what I am brought to, *ma mère;* it is all thanks to *la Mère Agnes!*" meaning that she had foretold the many crosses which, in God's mercy and love, were to lead him heavenwards.

As death drew nearer those around were struck with his increasing delight in dwelling on the Resurrection, a mystery which had always had a peculiar attraction for him. He asked for a picture representing it, and feeble as he was, one day he remained for an hour on his knees before this picture. His nurse remonstrated at length, and was permitted to lift him back to his arm-chair; but M. Olier exclaimed, "Who could ever grow weary while thinking of that mystery!" From time to time he was heard murmuring to himself, "Ah, sweet Eternity,—not far off now!" He refrained from talking much of his coming death, seeing that it distressed his brethren, but on Ash-Wednesday 1657, he said to M. de Bretonvilliers, "Let us make ready, for we shall soon have to part. Easter will bring the parting." He then named M. de Bretonvilliers as his successor, and henceforward daily conferred at length with him concerning the working of their Seminaries. To the last he continued such ministrations as he was able to perform. A lady of high rank, long his penitent, asked him to fix the time most convenient to himself for hearing her confession. "It must be before Easter," he replied; and it was observed that as another person for whom he had a great regard left his room, he gave her his blessing unperceived by her. On Monday in Holy Week, March 26th, he had another slight stroke, without losing his consciousness, but henceforth he ceased to notice anything save that which had reference to God. On Easter Eve some one asked M. Olier to remember him when he entered upon the blessedness of the Saints, using some expressions of praise which roused the patient's humility. "You grieve me very much," he said earnestly. During Easter Day he had frequent attacks of unconsciousness, and the power of speech was entirely gone, but at intervals he was able to make signs of affection to his friends, and his countenance was beautifully calm. On Easter Monday, S. Vincent de Paul came to see him as usual, and remained beside his seemingly unconscious friend until he drew his last breath towards the evening. This was April 2, 1657.

The great work of revival among the Clergy in

France had now reached its climax, and if the more conspicuous share rests with the Lazarists and the Saint Sulpiciens, in whose hands the small seed grew to a mighty tree, we cannot forget that the seed itself was planted and watered by their brethren, the Oratorians, and especially by their faithful friends, Pierre de Bérulle and Charles de Condren. It was a favourite maxim of the latter that "a man should only love his own Congregation relatively to the whole body of the Church;" *i.e.* that no narrow party spirit savouring of "I am of Paul, and I of Apollos," should mar the breadth which says of all, "I am of Christ." Oratorians, Lazarists, and Seminarists all alike sought one end—the Glory of God; all combined, each after his own gift, to set it forth. Surely all, drawing round the Great White Throne hereafter, with the countless souls their loving labour has gathered in, will join in the same song of triumph, "Salvation is of our God Which sitteth upon the Throne, and of the Lamb!"

CHAPTER VII.

PRESENT TIMES.

THE Congregation of the Oratory was dispersed like others in the Great Revolution, and it was not till 1852 that, after much consideration and many prayers, a few earnest priests joined together to renew the work which their predecessors had begun, and which brought them the heritage of so many great names. They came forward to devote themselves to Christ's service, taking as their watchword, that their aim was to be the universal good of the church, "*Avoir un esprit universel de l'Eglise et non limité.*" Speaking of the way in which this aim is to be carried out, a living Oratorian says: "How great to the eye of faith, though oft hidden to human sight, is the mission of the shepherds of souls! But, at the same time, how awful their responsibility! What countless difficulties thwart their ministry, what need they have to be aided and upheld, lest they sink disheartened by the isolation in which they too often find themselves, beneath the unceasing struggles which they must never dare to relax! And what a sacred duty, to a body of priests who are really animated by the Spirit of Christ, to go forth and lighten the burden of such faithful labourers, and help them to reap a more abundant harvest for the Lord! Now this is precisely what the Oratory intends to do. Its constitution is altogether sacerdotal, its members are subject in all things to episcopal jurisdiction, just as the parochial clergy are, and their services can be called for wherever they are wanted; either in preliminary education preparing lads for the clerical life, or in the higher seminaries, training the future ministers of our altars more directly for their sacred calling; or later on, coming to the assistance of their former pupils either in parochial work, if called to such by the bishops, or in giving Retreats. The houses of the Oratory are ever open to priests who want a few days of retirement and recollection to renew their strength; in a word, the Oratorian is in constant contact with his brethren of the parochial clergy, helping those to whom God has given a desire for so much of the Community life as their circumstances will allow, by means of spiritual exercises, prayers, conferences, etc., which are all means of counteracting that fatal isolation which too often depresses and exhausts the most energetic spirits among us."[1]

[1] P. A. Perraud, Esprit du nouvel Oratoire, p. 392.

How keenly Père Gratry, that saintly Oratorian who has but so recently passed from among us, felt that this isolation was a great flaw in the organisation of the Clergy of to-day, he has told us forcibly in his life of Henri Perreyve.

"Surely," he says, "were such centres of intellectual and moral association more numerous, under the blessing of God's Holy Spirit they would do much towards the advancement of the priestly calling. How many brave men, crushed and saddened by their isolated positions, would find fresh strength in such a *point d'appui* for their toil. Might not such associations furnish strength, and mutual kindling of love to God and man, for the effecting of those mighty enterprises of zeal, love, and science of which we stand so sorely in need? Think what an enormous power is wielded by industrial association! How much more might intellectual association for moral and religious work effect! Would not such united efforts have power to overstep the moral and religious differences which sever the East, Africa, and Asia from our Western centres of civilisation? and might we not thereby look to see the harmony of the intellectual and religious world established for which we all so greatly yearn? Might not peace be restored thereby to the human mind, peace to the nations of the world? On all sides we find the workmen of Europe struggling to organise a free association among themselves, and when the day comes that God's labourers do the like, we shall see among them those great works which S. Bernard prophesied, " firmissima vi rectitudinis consistent !"[1]

There is a great deal said at the present time about the education of the Clergy. It is felt on all sides that while doubtless we need that our priesthood should be supplied from all classes, and that it should no longer be treated as a respectable way of providing for younger sons whose abilities are scarcely sufficient to get on in other professions, still that the men who are to come forward as teachers of Christ's flock must learn diligently themselves. Ignorance, theological or general, cannot hold its own against the tide of unbelief and rationalising inquiry which floods the world. In 1662 Bossuet wrote : " Preparation for the priesthood is not, as some men seem to think, a matter of some brief study, it is rather a life-long education—it is not a sudden effort to withdraw from evil, but a confirmed habit of abstinence therefrom; not a temporary fervour, but a devotion, rooted and established by long practice. Saint Gregory of Nazianzen used the striking expression concerning S. Basil, that 'he was a priest before entering the

[1] Henri Perreyve, p. 85.

priesthood;' meaning that he had learnt its graces before receiving its Order."[1]

And Mgr. Dupanloup wrote in 1850: "To bear the weight of the priesthood, that is to say to devote himself for his whole life, a man must either be born great, or become great :—a vulgar heart, a feeble character, a grovelling mind, an imperfect education, will not come up to the mark. In this day our people require something more of their Clergy, and they are right."

Our times are not given to unquestioning acquiescence in mere assertion. Everything, from the highest to the lowest subjects of faith, history, discipline, is a matter of discussion, criticism, and argument. Men do not receive truth as such simply because it is put before them by authority, and the most remote country curate is liable to be called on to give an answer for the hope that is in him, and to explain the grounds on which he teaches dogma to his people. Consequently, if they mean to serve God to their utmost, His priests must be prepared to meet the world and its arguments with well read, thoughtful, disciplined minds.

"We are passing through a period which is torn asunder in every direction by the most turbulent passions," says P. Adolphe Perraud.[2] "There was a time when the priest's position and influence in

---

[1] Œuvres, ed. Lachat, xii. 645.   [2] Oratoire de France, 416.

society were accepted as a matter of course, but now everything is subjected to doubt and criticism, above all, whatever concerns the rights, teaching, and government of the Church. The humblest parish priest must expect to encounter self-elected *esprits forts*, and many on all sides reject the authority of his ministry. Men have been told too often that they have no superiors—that all are equals, and they will not accept the superiority of the sanctuary any more than that of heraldry or position.

"If then, recognising this fact, and in spite of prejudice and estrangement, we yet would fain do good among men, and set forward the salvation of souls, it is obvious that we must seek elsewhere that authoritative *préstige* without which our words will be fruitless, our ministry ineffective. There may have been passing seasons of perversion and failure, but as a whole the Church has assuredly ever striven to be all things to all men, that she may win them to Christ. She has found the way of adapting herself to every need. . . . . But at the present time, fresh from the storm of revolution which casts men upon an unknown future, without guide or restraint, is it not evident that the Priesthood has new duties to fulfil, and that the necessity of the actual moment imposes a higher standard of duty than before on all priests who are worthy of the name?

"Everywhere, always, under all conditions, the priest must be a man of prayer and self-sacrifice. He is called to be a living commentary on the Gospel before the eyes of all men, and the Gospel sets before all eyes wisdom and justice only. The primary duties of the Priesthood are fixed, independent of all the changes and chances of social revolutions. And therefore the groundwork of all clerical education lies in Holy Scripture and the earliest tradition. The first laws of our apostolic ministry have not changed since the time when Andrew and Peter, James and John, left their nets to become fishers of men; and we still seek the first rules of ecclesiastical perfection among those primitive Fathers and first Councils, which breathe the very purest and healthiest spirit of Christianity.

"But if, above all and before all, the priest is called upon to be a man of Eternity, as God's representative, he must most assuredly also be a man of Time, seeing that his mission is to heal and enlighten the men of his own day. If our Lord Jesus Christ had become Incarnate in the present day, or if He had selected any other country rather than Judea for the scene of His Incarnation, He would—we cannot doubt it—have adopted the garb and spoken the language of the people among whom He manifested Himself. Even so, if we would be understood by our contemporaries, and carry the words of everlasting life to their hearts, we must learn to speak their language. They have shaken off the old tie of a privileged class, and they will only vouchsafe to negotiate the weighty matter of salvation with us on the basis of a common right. They no longer seek us out; but are we acting up to our standard as the priests of Jesus Christ if we refuse to go to them, to accept the existing state of things, and thus to purchase our right to minister to troubled minds and to aching hearts?

"But this keen appreciation of the times we live in, this delicate capacity for being all things to all men without ever ceasing to be one's-self, *i.e.* God's Priest; this minute knowledge of the passions, the errors, the intellectual and moral evils of the day,—all these are indispensable elements of modern ecclesiastical education, without which our ministry will fail to retain its hold over the faithful, or to win back the wandering sheep. Our soldiers are being armed with new weapons, and new machinery is adapted to the novel practices of modern war and modern tactics; and in like manner God's servants must be furnished with fitting arms for the novel warfare they have to encounter, if they are to contend successfully against the passions and weaknesses of the day. Our rising generation of priests must not be content only to seek a spirit of prayer, a habit of self-denial, or pure single-minded faith; they must seek also the keenest apprehension of the special needs of our times. If ever there was cause to warn our younger brethren against that fatal delusion of indolence or inexperience, which represents the ministry as a peaceful office in which a man may lead a tranquil, easy life, there is such cause now. . . .

"The priest of this day is often cast amid a population hostile to his teaching, mistrustful of his intentions, merciless to his weaknesses, incapable of being won otherwise than by the genuine ascendancy of his own character, combined with indefatigable devotion and the tenderest charity. We must expect daily, hourly contests—we must always be able to prove our right to be believed or even tolerated—we must give no loophole for blame, whether in the pulpit or the confessional, in our daily intercourse with the sick and poor, in our dealings with science and intellect,— down to the most trifling details of external conduct and manners. Sceptical as the age is concerning our dogmas, it is unflinching in its judgment as to all that concerns the virtue or dignity of a priest; it will not rest satisfied with commonplace decency in him. With a rigid severity which might indicate a hidden instinct of that faith he has forsaken in practice, the worldly man will not tolerate common worldliness among priests. He is not content with the low secular standard on their behalf; one might almost say that in proportion as he rejects the supernatural character of the priestly mission, so he seems jealous of the priest's personal dignity of life. We may indeed say with Mgr. d'Orléans, that 'vulgar hearts, feeble characters, grovelling minds, imperfect education,' will not suffice for the task which in the existing state of things is laid upon the Clergy, and that he who would meet it thoroughly needs to be either 'born great or become great.'"

Surely it behoves those who are charged with the education of the Clergy to form and cultivate this greatness of mind in those men who are preparing for the priesthood. They must teach our young men to aim at tenfold courage, a tenfold spirit of faith and sacrifice; to be real apostolic teachers, humble, charitable, ever ready to devote themselves to God's Work; but meanwhile they must learn to understand and see that social system amid which they will have to work in its true colours; they must become acquainted with its dangers as well as its advantages; its weak as well as its strong side, so as to learn how to make a good use of the one, without being disheartened by the other; in short, the very difficulties of the age must be brought to bear upon them, so as to form useful servants of the Church, intelligent fellow-workmen of Him Who is the Unchanging King of every age.

Men must realize that though the groundwork of

their ministerial labour is necessarily the same in every age, its superstructure must be modified and adapted to the actual wants, the peculiarities, the special imperfections, the spiritual cravings of the time in which it has pleased God to call them to work.

"The Gospel we preach in the nineteenth century is the same as that of the third, or the twelfth," it has been well said; "but it cannot be preached in the same manner; and an Italian and an English sermon, although preached on one subject and in time contemporaneous, will of necessity differ in method of composition, in style, in manner of delivery."[1] The same may be said of other parts of a priest's work. Probably there is not so much difference now in good earnest preaching as there was in the early days of the Oratory, when a laboured bombastic style, overflowing with classical quotations and allusions, with conceits and quips of all kinds, prevailed so largely. S. Francis de Sales was one of the foremost to make a move in this direction, and he has told us how his father used to lament over the simplicity of his sermons: "In my time it was very different; sermons were much rarer, but goodness knows what real preachments they were! so studied, so learned! more Latin and Greek in one than you stick into a dozen!"[2]

---

[1] L'Oratoire Moderne, P. Perraud, p. 423.
[2] Spirit of S. Francis de Sales, p. 328.

Cardinal de Bérulle put forward very earnestly before the men whom he had trained for their priestly functions, that there could be no good or profitable preaching without much preparatory prayer, above all else, and he urged them to make the subjects on which they were about to preach part of their daily meditation. Next to this he insisted upon constant study of Holy Scripture, and the Fathers of the Church, as models of simplicity and dignity of style. One of his Congregation, whose experience was great, wrote a book of counsels to preachers,[1] which in many respects are as applicable to the present day as to his own.

"My first counsel if you want to preach well" (he says) "is to pray well: my second to pray well: my third, fourth, and tenth is still pray much to God. Have but one aim in your sermons—God's Glory and the salvation of souls. Read Holy Scripture again and again diligently. Your calling in the pulpit is solely to preach God's Word, as our Lord Jesus Christ, Whose deputed officer you are, would do;—therefore all mere secular imagery and profane science must be banished. One single passage from the Holy Bible has more weight with Christian minds than a hundred human reasonings,—do not fear to preach it 'pure and undefiled.' If you need anything

[1] Avis aux Jeunes Prédicateurs, P. Le Jeune.

more, I should say read chiefly S. Augustine, S. Chrysostom, the Summa of S. Thomas, and the Lives of the Saints. When you are writing a sermon, always consider how far it is calculated to be useful to a mechanic, or a servant girl; but above all, aim at making it what no one can hear without some profit; —it may be that among those who hear you there will be some one person who will hear no other sermon in the whole year than yours, and who may be converted if you speak to his heart. Eloquence and studied emphasis may help to persuade men, but I cannot recommend you to use well-rounded periods and artificial points. That is not the way in which the Son of God preached. If you have to speak against heresy, let it be done with respect, compassion, tenderness and love; conceding all that you possibly can concede, consistently with truth. Above all, abstain from reproach, invective, or contemptuous words."

The Oratorians continued to inculcate simplicity and a devotional, loving tone as the real way to make preaching profitable. Another book on the subject, attributed for a time to Massillon (himself an Oratorian), but acknowledged afterwards as the work of Père Gaichiez, gives some very earnest practical instructions to the Clergy:—

"The chief study of every preacher should be the

Bible," he says.[1] "He must seek to understand it by the help of prayer, and to live up to its teaching in his daily course. He must meditate continually on it, seek light as to its mysteries, learn it by heart, become thoroughly familiar with its language, and mould his own upon its expressions. S. Chrysostom, S. Augustine, S. Gregory, and S. Bernard are the great models for preachers, and one should never cease drawing water from these wells. A mere rhetorician or sophist may preach his own imaginations, but a true preacher will prefer to use the thoughts of the Fathers. Religion is not a new thing he has to make,—he has received it, and he deals out to other men that which he has received.

"It is not enough that a preacher be merely a worthy man, he must be a devout man—it is earnestness which teaches most to those that hear. That springs from an inner appreciation of the things of God; but a dry cold heart will give out nought save lifeless, powerless words. If possible it would be a good thing never to write sermons except in those happy moments when, after prayerful study, a man's heart is full of glowing warmth. Then all his expressions flow from a sanctified source, and God uses such devout workers to grave His law upon men's hearts,—an unsanctified hand will not impress His true im-

[1] Maximes sur le Ministère de la Chaire.

pressions. There is no better means of cultivating talent, however great, than by prayer. The Fathers of the Church, heavily burdened as they were with responsible offices, prayed much and preached often.

"Living apart from the world in retirement, learning detachment from self through humility and mortification, uplifted by prayer and contemplation, a true preacher finds his chief delight in studying and practising God's Word. At the altar he pleads the interests of his people before God, that he may the better plead God's interests with the people in the pulpit. He is as the angels of Jacob's dream keeping up a mysterious intercourse between heaven and earth. He clasps the Cross to his inmost heart, ready if need be to bear outward witness to it, even to the death.

"Above all else, the preacher's duty is to make men know and love the Lord Jesus Christ. Therein lies the whole of our life's religion,—all things depend on our One Mediator. In preaching sometimes men dwell largely on God the Creator, His Providence, His Goodness, His Justice, while they do not give sufficient prominence to God our Redeemer. . . . .

"It is presumption to suppose that you can be listened to for more than an ordinary length of time, without wearying your hearers. They have a certain stock of patience, and beyond that you should not try them. A full vessel can hold no more, and if you persist in pouring in, it only causes waste. Men go away from an overlong sermon with the same sort of weariness and discomfort as is caused by a bad dream. It is always better to cut down rather than add to a sermon; and your constant aim should be brevity. True eloquence depends far more on the high tone than on the cleverness of your thoughts, and a noble soul is a better source of inspiration than a sharp wit.

"The best tribute to a sermon is thoughtful silence on the part of your hearers when they are dismissed. He who would move others must himself be moved. The burning wood which warms us is consumed itself. That which is false or unreal can never be truly touching. Thus imagination does not speak with a heartfelt tone. . . . It beseems the dignity of the pulpit to speak with purity, precision, elevation. That which has been well thought out should be happily expressed. An ill set diamond loses half its beauty. But a wise preacher cuts off all embellishment which interferes with his true aim. Our husbandmen root up the flowers which spring amid the corn, for they damage the harvest in spite of their beauty; and the gardener prunes away the over-abundant leafage, which would hinder his fruit from ripening. . . .

"There is a certain seemliness of style as well as of manner and appearance. It is expected of a preacher that he should speak as a man of God. A sermon is not mere conversation or club oratory; when you preach you speak TO the people, and OF God. Do not venture upon newly-coined words, or indulge in a fantastically antiquated diction. Your speech should be like your life, modest, pure, single-hearted: simple enough to be understood by all, without failing in dignity. Of old, all Grecian orators were prone to quote Homeric expressions. Homer was the type of Greek eloquence; and even so a Christian preacher should mould his words as well as his thoughts upon Holy Scripture, so as to give a dignified and reverent tone to his style. God's ambassador ought to speak the language of God. . . . .

"It is not the applause of men, not even the success of a sermon, which makes the preacher acceptable to God: it is his own earnest labour joined to a humble estimate of his own talent and power."

Bossuet's biographers tell us that that great preacher never went into the pulpit without having knelt in the deepest self-humiliation before his crucifix, seeking the light of God's Holy Spirit; and marvellous as were his facility and eloquence, he was singularly devoid of self-confidence, resting solely on the strength and inspiration to be won through prayer and study of Holy Scripture. Surely such had need be the habit of mind and practice of preachers in our times as much as in the seventeenth or eighteenth century; and there is great truth in what a living author says: "Simplicity, warmth, earnestness—these ought to be now, if ever, the characteristics of our apostolic preaching. Of late parliamentary debates have accustomed men to require close reasoning and conclusive evidence. They want to go straight to facts, and are impatient of the lengthy involutions which were the glory of bygone rhetoricians. Now-a-days neither speaker or hearers have leisure to linger thus on the threshold of a subject. Every one is speeding on, all around us is haste, and if we have the opportunity of commanding men's attention for a few brief moments amid their bewildering preoccupations, we owe it to their immortal souls and to our own ministry not to waste those scarce and precious seasons. Simplicity, precision, clearness, a distinct and lucid setting forth of doctrine,—holding in horror all mere phraseology, all empty rhetoric,—such should be the main features in our earthly rendering of our Divine message. But we must combine strength with our other qualities, and that because in these days perhaps there is no greater hindrance to the Kingdom of God than the weakness and slackness of convictions which we find everywhere. And this strength is only to be won by continual meditation on Holy Scripture: there it is that we can gather up

God's own strength. '*Ibi absconditta est fortitudo ejus*'[1] (Hab. iii. 5)."

And assuredly, too, there is no less need now than in the days of S. Philip Neri, of S. Vincent de Paul, or of M. Olier, to gather together the young men of all classes and destinations, whose lot is for the most part cast among manifold temptations, different it may be in kind, but no less perilous than those which beset their forerunners of the seventeenth and eighteenth centuries. If our Clergy are to gather in souls for the Great Harvest, must they not strive to gather our young men and boys around them, to attract them by higher and more intellectual pleasures from the grosser forms of self-indulgence, to supply them with social enjoyments free from debasing influences, to direct and share their reading and inquiry, to watch over their faith, and to arm them against the delusions of rationalistic self-conceit and "vain science falsely so called." Truly these are not the days for the pastors of the flock to sit down satisfied with looking at any one side of their vast and endless task! But if our Clergy are to be ready to cope with the learned unbeliever and the scientific rationalist, surely we need that some among them should be able, by means of Religious Communities and Brotherhoods, to give themselves up to deeper and more scientific study than the parish

[1] L'Oratoire Moderne, p. 434.

priest, once launched upon the endless and necessary cares of his flock, can possibly seek. "Formerly" (so wrote the present Archbishop of Paris, Mgr. Guibert, then Bishop of Viviers) "the most learned men of the day were found among the Clergy; men whose daily occupations admitted of profound study, or who, members of religious corporations, were able to give themselves up to literary work, which was made easy to them by the treasures they possessed in their libraries and scientific collections. But where shall we find priests now who do or can give their lives to this department of God's service?"

Modern science aims above all things at getting rid of the supernatural, and, as a modern writer says, "we must develop an altogether new system of intellectual perceptions."[1] In order to meet this need, the French Clergy have been urged by their rulers to extend the range of their studies, and to prepare themselves to grapple with the foe on his own ground. The Council of Paris in 1849 pressed strongly on the Clergy that nothing could be more fatal to their right influence than ignorance or incapacity to deal with general subjects.

"It is an absolutely indispensable necessity," so writes Balmès, "for the Clergy to be educated up to the level of their times, so as not to permit error to

[1] M. Littré.

wield weapons which are wanting to truth. We cannot press the importance of this duty too earnestly on the ministers of religion. Let them indeed live a life apart from the world in its purity and simplicity,—but let them beware of living apart from the intellectual movement going on around them; let them grasp firm hold of the truth that there is no antagonism between an enlightened intelligence and an upright heart; that science is not the enemy of virtue, and that the Clergy may keep their eyes fully open to the intellectual progress of the times without sullying themselves with the corruption which too often besets that progress.

"The man whose office it is to teach the weightiest of all truths to others ought not to be estranged from any form of knowledge. As it behoves him to be the example of all personal goodness in his moral life, so ought he to wield the sceptre of intelligence."[1]

S. Francis de Sales used to say that ignorance was almost as bad as malice in a priest, and that knowledge was a kind of eighth sacrament of the Church.

"They are really righteous," says S. Gregory, "who are furnished forth by the love of the Country above to meet all the ills of the present life;"[2] and it is in that Country only that we may dare to hope for an end to

[1] Mélanges Religieux et Philosophiques.
[2] Morals, bk. v. xvii.

the Church's woes and struggles. In our time, as in the times of the holy men gone before us, we need to raise the cry—

> "Our foes press on from every side,
> Thine Aid supply, Thy Strength bestow;"

and with them to pray,—

> "To Thy Great Name be endless praise,
> Immortal Godhead, One in Three!
> O grant us endless length of days
> In our true Native Land with Thee.
> Amen."

The bright shining lights set before us by the Father of us all, "lest we should faint or stray," are doubtless now pleading for the Church before His Face, as once they prayed and toiled for it here; and gladdened by the thought, let us dwell lovingly and thankfully on their examples, and say, in the words of the All Saints' Hymn,—

> "Exules
> Vocate nos in PATRIA."

NEW BOOKS

IN COURSE OF PUBLICATION BY

MESSRS. RIVINGTON

WATERLOO PLACE, LONDON

HIGH STREET, OXFORD; TRINITY STREET, CAMBRIDGE

May 1873

Some Elements of Religion. Lent

Lectures. By **Henry Parry Liddon**, D.D., D.C.L., Canon of St. Paul's, and Ireland Professor of Exegesis in the University of Oxford.

Crown 8vo. 5*s.*

Lectures on the Reunion of the

Churches. By **John J. Ign. von Döllinger**, D.D., D.C.L., Professor of Ecclesiastical History in the University of Munich, Provost of the Chapel-Royal, &c. &c. Authorized Translation, with Preface by **Henry Nutcombe Oxenham**, M.A., late Scholar of Balliol College, Oxford.

Crown 8vo. 5*s.*

The Holy Catholic Church: its

Divine Ideal, Ministry, and Institutions. A Short Treatise. With a Catechism on each Chapter, forming a Course of Methodical Instruction on the subject. By **Edward Meyrick Goulburn**, D.D., Dean of Norwich.

Crown 8vo. 6*s.* 6*d.*

· London · Oxford · Cambridge ·

MESSRS. RIVINGTON'S

The Book of Church Law. Being
an Exposition of the Legal Rights and Duties of the Clergy and Laity of the Church of England. By the Rev. **John Henry Blunt**, M.A., F.S.A. Revised by **Walter G. F. Phillimore**, B.C.L., Barrister-at-Law, and Chancellor of the Diocese of Lincoln.
Crown 8vo. 7s. 6d.

Henri Perreyve. By A. Gratry,
Prêtre de l'Oratoire, Professeur de Morale Evangélique à la Sorbonne, et Membre de l'Académie Française. Translated, by special permission, by the Author of "A Dominican Artist," "Life of S. Francis de Sales," &c., &c.
With Portrait. Crown 8vo. 7s. 6d.

Notitia Eucharistica. A Commentary,
Explanatory, Doctrinal and Historical, on the Order of the Administration of the Lord's Supper, or Holy Communion, according to the use of the Church of England. By **W. E. Scudamore**, M.A., Rector of Ditchingham, and formerly Fellow of St. John's College, Cambridge.
8vo. 28s.

The Spirit of S. Francis de Sales,
Bishop and Prince of Geneva. Translated from the French by the Author of "The Life of S. Francis de Sales," "A Dominican Artist," &c. &c.
Crown 8vo. 6s.

Our Mother Church: being Simple
Talk on High Topics. By **Anne Mercier**.
Crown 8vo. 7s. 6d.

· London · Oxford · Cambridge ·

New Publications

Selection from the Sermons preached

during the latter Years of his Life, in the Parish Church of Barnes, and in the Cathedral of St. Paul's. By Henry Melvill, B.D., late Canon of St. Paul's, and Chaplain in Ordinary to the Queen.

Two Volumes. Crown 8vo. 5s. each.

Life, Journals, and Letters of

Henry Alford, D.D., late Dean of Canterbury. Edited by his Widow.

With Portrait and Illustrations. 8vo. 16s.

The Guide to Heaven. A Book of

Prayers for every Want. (For the Working Classes.) Compiled by a Priest. Edited by the Rev. T. T. Carter, M.A., Rector of Clewer, Berks.

A New Edition. 16mo, *uniform in size with* "The Treasury of Devotion." 1s.

The Large Type Edition may be had. Crown 8vo. 1s. 6d., *or limp cloth,* 1s.

A Selection from the Spiritual

Letters of S. Francis de Sales, Bishop and Prince of Geneva. Translated by the Author of "The Life of S. Francis de Sales," "A Dominican Artist," &c. &c.

Crown 8vo. 6s.

Fifteen Sermons preached before

the University of Oxford, between A.D. 1826 and 1843. By John Henry Newman, B.D., sometime Fellow of Oriel College, Oxford.

New Edition. Crown 8vo. 5s.

London · Oxford · Cambridge

MESSRS. RIVINGTON'S

Words to Take with Us. A
Manual of Daily and Occasional Prayers, for Private and Common Use. With Plain Instructions and Counsels on Prayer. By **W. E. Scudamore**, M.A., Rector of Ditchingham, and formerly Fellow of St. John's College, Cambridge.

New Edition, Revised.   Small 8vo.   2s. 6d.

The Permanence of Christianity
Considered in Eight Lectures preached before the University of Oxford, in the Year MDCCCLXXII, on the Foundation of the late Rev. John Bampton, M.A. By **John Richard Turner Eaton**, M.A., late Fellow and Tutor of Merton College, Rector of Lapworth, Warwickshire.

8vo.   [*Nearly ready.*

Dictionary of Sects, Heresies, and
SCHOOLS OF THOUGHT. By various Writers. Edited by the Rev. **John Henry Blunt**, M.A., F.S.A., Editor of the "Dictionary of Doctrinal and Historical Theology."

(*Forming the Second Portion of the* "Summary of Theology and Ecclesiastical History," *which Messrs.* RIVINGTON *have in course of preparation as a* "Thesaurus Theologicus" *for the Clergy and Laity of the Church of England.*)

Imperial 8vo.   [*In the Press.*

The Thirty-nine Articles of the
CHURCH OF ENGLAND EXPLAINED IN A SERIES OF LECTURES. By the Rev. **R. W. Jelf**, D.D., late Canon of Christ Church, Oxford, and sometime Principal of King's College, London. Edited by the Rev. **J. R. King**, M.A., Vicar of St. Peter's in the East, Oxford, and formerly Fellow and Tutor of Merton College.

8vo.   [*Nearly ready.*

· London · Oxford · Cambridge ·

NEW PUBLICATIONS

Voices of Comfort. Edited by the
Rev. Thomas Vincent Fosbery, M.A., Hon. Chaplain to the Bishop of Winchester, and sometime Vicar of St. Giles's, Reading.

Small 8vo. [*In the Press.*

Ecclesiastes. The Authorized Version,
with a running Commentary and Paraphrase. By the Rev. Thos. Pelham Dale, M.A., Rector of St. Vedast with St. Michael City of London, and late Fellow of Sidney Sussex College, Cambridge.

8vo. [*In the Press.*

Litanies for Congregational Use.
Edited by the Compiler of "The Treasury of Devotion."

32mo. [*In the Press.*

The Gospel of the Childhood. A
Practical and Devotional Commentary on the Single Incident of our Blessed Lord's Childhood (St. Luke ii. 41, to the end); designed as a Help to Meditation on the Holy Scriptures, for Children and Young Persons. By **Edward Meyrick Goulburn**, D.D., Dean of Norwich.

Square 16mo. [*In the Press.*

The Chorister's Guide. By W. A.
Barrett, Mus. Bac. Oxon., of St. Paul's Cathedral, Author of "Flowers and Festivals."

Square 16mo. [*Nearly ready.*

· London · Oxford · Cambridge ·

MESSRS. RIVINGTON'S

A History of the Holy Eastern
Church. The Patriarchate of Antioch, to the Middle of the Fifth Century. By the Rev. **John Mason Neale**, D.D., late Warden of Sackville College, East Grinsted. Followed by a History of the Patriarchs of Antioch, translated from the Greek of Constantius I., Patriarch of Constantinople. Edited, with an Introduction, by **George Williams**, B.D., Vicar of Ringwood, late Fellow of King's College, Cambridge.

8vo. *[In the Press.*

The Annotated Book of Common
Prayer. Being an Historical, Ritual, and Theological Commentary on the Devotional System of the Church of England. Edited by **John Henry Blunt**, M.A., F.S.A.

Sixth Edition, Revised. Imperial 8vo. 36s.

The Hour of Prayer; being a
Manual of Devotion for the Use of Families and Schools.

Crown 8vo. *[Nearly ready.*

The Last Days of Père Gratry.
By **Père Adolphe Perraud**, of the Oratory, and Professor of La Sorbonne. Translated by special permission.

Crown 8vo. 3s. 6d.

The Knight of Intercession, and
other Poems. By the Rev. **S. J. Stone**, M.A., Pembroke College, Oxford.

Second Edition. Small 8vo. 6s.

· London · Oxford · Cambridge ·

New Publications

The Argument delivered before
the Judicial Committee of the Privy Council. By **Archibald John Stephens**, LL.D., one of Her Majesty's Counsel in the case of Thomas Byard Sheppard against William Early Bennett, Clerk. With an Appendix containing their Lordships' Judgment.

8vo. 9s.

Eight Lectures on the Miracles.
Being the Bampton Lectures for 1865. By **J. B. Mozley**, D.D., Regius Professor of Divinity, and Canon of Christ Church, Oxford.

Third Edition, Revised. Crown 8vo. 7s. 6d.

A Shadow of Dante. Being an
Essay towards studying Himself, his World, and his Pilgrimage. By **Maria Francesca Rossetti**.

With Illustrations. Second Edition. Crown 8vo. 10s. 6d.

A Handy Book on the Ecclesi-
astical Dilapidations Act, 1871. With Remarks on the Qualification and Practice of Diocesan Surveyors. By **Edward G. Bruton**, Fellow of the Royal Institute of British Architects, and Diocesan Surveyor, Oxford.

Crown 8vo. 3s. 6d.

Sermons on Certain of the Less
Prominent Facts and References in Sacred Story. By **Henry Melvill**, B.D., late Canon of St. Paul's, and Chaplain in Ordinary to the Queen.

New Edition. Two vols. Crown 8vo. 5s. each.

· London · Oxford · Cambridge ·

MESSRS. RIVINGTON'S

Aids to Prayer; or, Thoughts on the Practice of Devotion. With forms of Prayer for Private use, By **Daniel Moore**, M.A., Chaplain in Ordinary to the Queen, and Vicar of Holy Trinity, Paddington, Author of "Sermons on Special Occasions."

Second Edition. Square 32mo. 2s. 6d.

Church Organs: their Position and Construction. With an Appendix containing some Account of the Mediæval Organ Case still existing at Old Radnor, South Wales. By **Frederick Heathcote Sutton**, M.A., Vicar of Theddingworth.

With Illustrations. Imperial folio. 6s. 6d.

The Path of Holiness: a First Book of Prayers, with the Service of the Holy Communion, for the Young. Compiled by a Priest. Edited by the Rev. **T. T. Carter**, M.A., Rector of Clewer, Berks.

With Illustrations. Crown 16mo, 1s. 6d., or limp cloth, 1s.

The Athanasian Origin of the Athanasian Creed. By **J. S. Brewer**, M.A., Preacher at the Rolls, and Honorary Fellow of Queen's College, Oxford.

Crown 8vo. 3s. 6d.

Historical Narratives. From the Russian. By **H. C. Romanoff**, Author of "Sketches of the Rites and Customs of the Greco-Russian Church," &c.

Crown 8vo. 6s.

· London · Oxford · Cambridge ·

NEW PUBLICATIONS

The Way of Life.
A Book of Prayers and Instruction for the Young at School, with a Preparation for Confirmation. Compiled by a Priest. Edited by the Rev. **T. T. Carter**, M.A., Rector of Clewer, Berks.

Imperial 32mo. 1s. 6d.

Thoughts on Personal Religion.
Being a Treatise on the Christian Life in its Two Chief Elements, Devotion and Practice. By **Edward Meyrick Goulburn**, D.D., Dean of Norwich.

New Presentation Edition, elegantly printed on Toned Paper. Two vols. Small 8vo. 10s. 6d.

An Edition in one vol., 6s. 6d.; also a Cheap Edition, 3s. 6d.

Life in the World:
being a Selection from Sermons preached at St. Luke's, Berwick Street. By the Rev. **Harry Jones**, M.A., Incumbent of St. Luke's, Berwick Street, Soho.

Second Edition. Small 8vo. 5s.

The Perfect Man;
or, Jesus an Example of Godly Life. By the Rev. **Harry Jones**, M.A., Incumbent of St. Luke's, Berwick Street.

Second Edition. Crown 8vo. 3s. 6d.

Dictionary of Doctrinal and Historical Theology.
By Various Writers. Edited by the Rev. **John Henry Blunt**, M.A., F.S.A., Editor of the "The Annotated Book of Common Prayer."

Second Edition. Imperial 8vo. 42s.

MESSRS. RIVINGTON'S

The Psalms. Translated from the Hebrew. With Notes, chiefly Exegetical. By **William Kay**, D.D., Rector of Great Leighs, late Principal of Bishop's College, Calcutta.

8vo. 12s. 6d.

Sermons. By **Henry Melvill**, B.D., late Canon of St. Paul's, and Chaplain in Ordinary to the Queen.

New Edition. Two vols. Crown 8vo. 5s. each.

The Origin and Development of Religious Belief. By **S. Baring-Gould**, M.A., Author of "Curious Myths of the Middle Ages."

Vol. I. **MONOTHEISM AND POLYTHEISM.**
Second Edition. 8vo. 15s.

Vol. II. **CHRISTIANITY.**
8vo. 15s.

Parish Musings; or, Devotional Poems. By **John S. B. Monsell**, LL.D., Rural Dean, and Rector of St. Nicholas, Guildford.

Fine Edition. Small 8vo. 5s.

Cheap Edition, 18mo, limp cloth, 1s. 6d.; *or in cover,* 1s.

Sermons on Special Occasions. By **Daniel Moore**, M.A., Chaplain in Ordinary to the Queen, and Vicar of Holy Trinity, Paddington; Author of "Aids to Prayer," &c.

Crown 8vo, 7s. 6d.

· London · Oxford · Cambridge ·

New Publications

Prayers and Meditations for the
Holy Communion. With a Preface by **C. J. Ellicott, D.D.**, Lord Bishop of Gloucester and Bristol.

With Rubrics in red. Royal 32mo. 2s. 6d.

The Star of Childhood. A First
Book of Prayers and Instruction for Children. Compiled by a Priest. Edited by the Rev. **T. T. Carter, M.A.**, Rector of Clewer, Berks.

With Illustrations reduced from Engravings by **Fra Angelico**.
Royal 16mo. 2s. 6d.

Notes on Church Organs; their
Position and the Materials used in their Construction. By **C. K. K. Bishop.**

With Illustrations. Small 4to. 6s.

The Hidden Life of the Soul.
From the French. By the Author of "A Dominican Artist," "Life of Madame Louise de France," &c. &c.

Crown 8vo. 5s.

Ancient Hymns. From the Roman
Breviary. For domestic use every Morning and Evening of the Week, and on the Holy Days of the Church. To which are added, Original Hymns, principally of Commemoration and Thanksgiving for Christ's Holy Ordinances. By **Richard Mant, D.D.**, sometime Lord Bishop of Down and Connor.

New Edition. Small 8vo. 5s.

· London · Oxford · Cambridge ·

MESSRS. RIVINGTON'S

The Two Brothers, and other Poems.
By Edward Henry Bickersteth, M.A., Vicar of Christ Church, Hampstead, and Chaplain to the Bishop of Ripon; Author of "Yesterday, To-day, and for Ever."

Second Edition. Small 8vo. 6s.

The Life of Justification. A Series
of Lectures delivered in Substance at All Saints', Margaret Street, in Lent, 1870. By the Rev. **George Body**, B.A., Rector of Kirkby Misperton.

Second Edition. Crown 8vo. 4s. 6d.

The Life of Temptation: A Course
of Lectures delivered in Substance at S. Peter's, Eaton Square, in Lent, 1872; also at All Saints', Margaret Street, in Lent, 1869. By the Rev. **George Body**, B.A., Rector of Kirkby Misperton, Yorkshire.

Crown 8vo. 4s. 6d.

The "Damnatory Clauses" of the
Athanasian Creed Rationally Explained, in a Letter to the Right Hon. W. E. Gladstone, M.P. By the Rev. **Malcolm MacColl**, M.A., Rector of St. George, Botolph Lane.

Crown 8vo. 6s.

The Sayings of the Great Forty
Days, between the Resurrection and Ascension, regarded as the Outlines of the Kingdom of God. In Five Discourses. With an Examination of Dr. Newman's Theory of Development. By **George Moberly**, D.C.L., Bishop of Salisbury.

Fourth Edition. Crown 8vo. 7s. 6d.

· London · Oxford · Cambridge ·

New Publications

History of the Church under the
Roman Empire, A.D. 29-476. By the Rev. **A. D. Crake, B.A.**, Chaplain of All Saints' School, Bloxham.

Crown 8vo.   [*In the Press.*

The Pope and the Council. By
Janus. Authorized Translation from the German.

Third Edition, Revised. Crown 8vo. 7s. 6d.

Letters from Rome on the Council.
By **Quirinus.** Reprinted from the "Allgemeine Zeitung." Authorized Translation.

Crown 8vo. 12s.

Directorium Pastorale. The
Principles and Practice of Pastoral Work in the Church of England. By the Rev. **John Henry Blunt**, M.A., F.S.A., Editor of "The Annotated Book of Common Prayer," &c. &c.

Third Edition, Revised. Crown 8vo. 7s. 6d.

The Pursuit of Holiness. A
Sequel to "Thoughts on Personal Religion," intended to carry the Reader somewhat farther onward in the Spiritual Life. By **Edward Meyrick Goulburn**, D.D., Dean of Norwich.

Fourth Edition. Small 8vo. 5s.

· London · Oxford · Cambridge ·

MESSRS. RIVINGTON'S

Apostolical Succession in the
Church of England. By the Rev. **Arthur W. Haddan**, B.D., Rector of Barton-on-the-Heath, and late Fellow of Trinity College, Oxford.

8vo. 12*s.*

The First Book of Common
Prayer of Edward VI. and the Ordinal of 1549. Together with the Order of the Communion, 1548. Reprinted entire, and Edited by the Rev. **Henry Baskerville Walton**, M.A., late Fellow and Tutor of Merton College; with Introduction by the Rev. **Peter Goldsmith Medd**, M.A., Senior Fellow and Tutor of University College, Oxford.

Small 8vo. 6*s.*

Allegories and Tales. By the Rev.
W. E. Heygate, M.A., Rector of Brighstone.

Crown 8vo. [*In the Press.*

Twelve Addresses at his Visita-
tion of the Cathedral and Diocese of Lincoln, in the year MDCCCLXXIII. By the **Bishop of Lincoln**.

Crown 8vo. [*Nearly ready.*

Parochial and Plain Sermons.
By **John Henry Newman**, B.D., formerly Vicar of St. Mary's, Oxford. Edited by the Rev. **W. J. Copeland**, Rector of Farnham, Essex.

New Edition. Eight vols. Crown 8vo. 5*s. each.*

• London • Oxford • Cambridge •

New Publications

Sermons bearing on Subjects of
the Day. By **John Henry Newman**, B.D. Edited by the Rev. **W. J. Copeland**, Rector of Farnham, Essex.

New Edition. Crown 8vo. 5s.

Spiritual Guidance.
With an Introduction by the Rev. **T. T. Carter**, M.A., Rector of Clewer, Berks, and Honorary Canon of Christ Church Cathedral, Oxford.

Crown 8vo. 6s.

Self-Renunciation.
From the French. With Introduction by the Rev. **T. T. Carter**, M.A., Rector of Clewer, Berks.

Crown 8vo. 6s.

The Divinity of our Lord and
SAVIOUR JESUS CHRIST. Being the Bampton Lectures for 1866. By **Henry Parry Liddon**, D.D., D.C.L., Canon of St. Paul's, and Ireland Professor of Exegesis in the University of Oxford.

Sixth Edition. Crown 8vo. 5s.

Sermons Preached before the
University of Oxford. By **Henry Parry Liddon**, D.D., D.C.L., Canon of St. Paul's, and Ireland Professor of Exegesis in the University of Oxford.

Fourth Edition. Crown 8vo. 5s.

• London • Oxford • Cambridge •

MESSRS. RIVINGTON'S

Brighstone Sermons. By George Moberly, D.C.L., Bishop of Salisbury.

Second Edition. Crown 8vo. 7s. 6d.

A Manual for the Sick. With other Directions. By **Launcelot Andrewes**, D.D., sometime Lord Bishop of Winchester. Edited, with a Preface, by **Henry Parry Liddon**, D.D., D.C.L., Canon of St. Paul's.

With Portrait. Second Edition. Large type. 24mo. 2s. 6d.

The Apocalypse: with Notes and Reflections. By the Rev. **Isaac Williams**, B.D., late Fellow of Trinity College, Oxford.

Crown 8vo. [*In the Press.*

The Life of Madame Louise de France, Daughter of Louis XV., known also as the Mother Térèse de S. Augustin. By the Author of "A Dominican Artist," "The Life of S. Francis de Sales," &c.

Crown 8vo. 6s.

*Instructions for the Use of Can-*didates for Holy Orders, and of the Parochial Clergy; with Acts of Parliament relating to the same, and Forms proposed to be used. By **Christopher Hodgson**, M.A., Secretary to the Governors of Queen Anne's Bounty.

Ninth Edition, Revised and Enlarged. 8vo. 16s.

· London · Oxford · Cambridge ·

New Publications

The Treasury of Devotion.
A Manual of Prayers for General and Daily Use. Compiled by a Priest. Edited by the Rev. **T. T. Carter**, M.A., Rector of Clewer, Berks.
Sixth Edition. 16mo, 2s. 6d.; *Limp cloth,* 2s.
Bound with the Book of Common Prayer. 3s. 6d.

A Dominican Artist.
A Sketch of the Life of the Rev. Père Besson, of the Order of St. Dominic. By the Author of "The Life of Madame Louise de France," &c.
Second Edition. Crown 8vo. 6s.

The Reformation of the Church
of England. Its History, Principles, and Results. A.D. 1514-1547. By **John Henry Blunt**, M.A., Vicar of Kennington, Oxford, Editor of "The Annotated Book of Common Prayer," &c., &c.
Second Edition. 8vo. 16s.

Fables respecting the Popes of the
Middle Ages. A Contribution to Ecclesiastical History. By **John J. Ign. von Döllinger.** Translated, with Introduction and Appendices, by **Alfred Plummer**, M.A., Fellow and Tutor of Trinity College, Oxford.
8vo. 14s.

Sketches of the Rites and Customs
of the Greco-Russian Church. By **H. C. Romanoff.** With an Introductory Notice by the Author of "The Heir of Redclyffe."
Second Edition. Crown 8vo. 7s. 6d.

· London · Oxford · Cambridge ·

MESSRS. RIVINGTON'S

Household Theology. A Handbook

of Religious Information respecting the Holy Bible, the Prayer Book, the Church, the Ministry, Divine Worship, the Creeds, &c., &c. By **John Henry Blunt**, M.A.

New Edition. Small 8vo. 3s. 6d.

Curious Myths of the Middle

Ages. By **S. Baring-Gould**, M.A., Author of "Post-Mediæval Preachers," &c.

With Illustrations. New Edition. Crown 8vo. 6s.

The Prayer Book Interleaved.

With Historical Illustrations and Explanatory Notes, arranged parallel to the Text. By the Rev. **W. M. Campion**, D.D., Fellow and Tutor of Queen's College, and Rector of St. Botolph's, and the Rev. **W. J. Beamont**, M.A., late Fellow of Trinity College, Cambridge. With a Preface by the **Lord Bishop of Ely**.

Seventh Edition. Small 8vo. 7s. 6d.

Sickness; its Trials and Blessings.

New Edition. Small 8vo. 3s. 6d.

Also a Cheap Edition, 1s. 6d.; or in paper cover, 1s.

Hymns and Poems for the Sick

and Suffering. In connection with the Service for the Visitation of the Sick. Selected from Various Authors. Edited by **T. V. Fosbery**, M.A., Vicar of St. Giles's, Reading.

New Edition. Small 8vo. 3s. 6d.

· London · Oxford · Cambridge ·

New Publications

Miscellaneous Poems. By Henry Francis Lyte, M.A.

New Edition. Small 8vo. 5s.

The Happiness of the Blessed.

Considered as to the Particulars of their State; their Recognition of each other in that State; and its Differences of Degrees. To which are added, Musings on the Church and her Services. By **Richard Mant**, D.D., sometime Lord Bishop of Down and Connor.

New Edition. Small 8vo. 3s. 6d.

*Catechesis; or, Christian Instruc-*tion Preparatory to Confirmation and First Communion. By **Charles Wordsworth**, D.C.L., Bishop of St. Andrew's.

New Edition. Small 8vo. 2s.

Warnings of the Holy Week, etc.

Being a Course of Parochial Lectures for the Week before Easter and the Easter Festivals. By the Rev. **W. Adams**, M.A., Author of "Sacred Allegories."

Sixth Edition. Small 8vo. 4s. 6d.

Consolatio; or, Comfort for the Afflicted.

Edited by the Rev. **C. E. Kennaway**. With a Preface by **Samuel Wilberforce**, D.D., Lord Bishop of Winchester.

New Edition. Small 8vo. 3s. 6d.

· London · Oxford · Cambridge ·

MESSRS. RIVINGTON'S

Family Prayers. Compiled from Various Sources (chiefly from Bishop Hamilton's Manual), and arranged on the Liturgical Principle. By **Edward Meyrick Goulburn,** D.D., Dean of Norwich.

New Edition. Large Type. Crown 8vo. 3s. 6d.
Cheap Edition. 16mo. 1s.

The Annual Register. A Review of Public Events at Home and Abroad, for the Year 1872.

8vo. 18s.

The Volumes of the New Series, 1863 to 1871, may be had, 18s. each.

Yesterday, To-Day, and For Ever. A Poem in Twelve Books. By **Edward Henry Bicksteth,** M.A., Vicar of Christ's Church, Hampstead, and Chaplain to the Bishop of Ripon.

Seventh Edition. Small 8vo. 6s.

Bible Readings for Family Prayer. By the Rev. **W. H. Ridley,** M.A., Rector of Hambleden.

Crown 8vo.

Old Testament—Genesis and Exodus 2s.
New Testament, 3s. 6d. { St. Matthew and St. Mark. 2s.
{ St. Luke and St. John. 2s.

Liber Precum Publicarum Ecclesiæ Anglicanæ. A **Gulielmo Bright,** A.M., et **Petro Goldsmith Medd,** A.M., Presbyteris, Collegii Universitatis in Acad. Oxon. Sociis, Latine redditus.

New Edition, with all the Rubrics in red. Small 8vo. 6s.

· London · Oxford · Cambridge ·

New Publications

Sacred Allegories. The Shadow of
the Cross—The Distant Hills—The Old Man's Home—The King's Messengers. By the Rev. **W. Adams**, M.A., late Fellow of Merton College, Oxford.

With numerous Illustrations.

New Edition. One Vol. Crown 8vo. 5s.

The Four Allegories separately. Crown 8vo. 2s. 6d. each.

A Glossary of Ecclesiastical
Terms. Containing Brief Explanations of Words used in Theology, Liturgiology, Chronology, Law, Architecture, Antiquities, Symbolism, Greek Hierology and Mediæval Latin; together with some account of Titles of our Lord, Emblems of Saints, Hymns, Orders, Heresies, Ornaments, Offices, Vestments and Ceremonial, and Miscellaneous Subjects. By Various Writers. Edited by the Rev. **Orby Shipley**, M.A.

Crown 8vo. 18s.

Stones of the Temple; or Lessons
from the Fabric and Furniture of the Church. By **Walter Field**, M.A., F.S.A., Vicar of Godmersham.

With numerous Illustrations. Crown 8vo. 7s. 6d.

Strena Christiana; a Christian
New Year's Gift; or, Brief Exhortations to the Chief Outward Acts of Virtue. Translated from the Latin of Sir **Harbottle Grimston**, Bart., Member of Parliament, 1640. 32mo. 1s. 6d.

Or the Latin and English together. 32mo, 2s. 6d.

· London · Oxford · Cambridge ·

MESSRS. RIVINGTON'S

A Companion to the Old Testa-
ment. Being a Plain Commentary on Scripture History, down to the Birth of our Lord.

Small 8vo. 3s. 6d.

Latin Prose Exercises. Being
Easy Graduated English Sentences for Translation into Latin, with Rules, Explanations, a Vocabulary, and Index. Intended for the Use of Beginners and Junior Forms of Schools. By **R. Prowde Smith**, B.A., Assistant Master at the Grammar School, Henley-on-Thames.

Crown 8vo. 2s. 6d.

A Theory of Harmony. Founded
on the Tempered Scale. With Question and Exercises for the use of Students. By **John Stainer**, Mus. Doc., M.A., Magd. Coll., Oxon, Organist to St. Paul's Cathedral.

Second Edition. 8vo. 7s. 6d.

Selections from Lucian. With
English Notes. By **Evelyn Abbott**, Assistant Master in Clifton College.

Small 8vo. 3s. 6d.

Progressive Exercises in Latin
Elegiac Verse. By **C. G. Gepp**, B.A., late Junior Student of Christ Church, Oxford, and Assistant Master at Tonbridge School.

Second Edition, Revised. Crown 8vo. 3s. 6d.

· London · Oxford · Cambridge ·

New Publications

Examples of Conics and Curves.
By the Rev. **W. H. Laverty**, M.A., Fellow and Mathematical Lecturer of Queen's College, and Public Examiner in the University of Oxford.

Fcap. 4to. 2s. 6d.

Materials and Models for Greek
and Latin Prose Composition. Selected and arranged by **J. Y. Sargent**, M.A., Tutor, late Fellow of Magdalen College, Oxford; and **T. F. Dallin**, M.A., Fellow and Tutor of Queen's College, Oxford.

Crown 8vo. 7s. 6d.

The First Hebrew Book; on the
Plan of "Henry's First Latin Book." By the late **Thomas Kerchever Arnold**, M.A., formerly Fellow of Trinity College, Cambridge.

New Edition. 12mo. 7s. 6d.

Madvig's Syntax of the Greek
LANGUAGE, especially of the Attic Dialect, for the use of Schools. Translated by **Henry Browne**, M.A., and edited by the late **T. K. Arnold**, M.A.

New Edition. Imperial 16mo. 8s. 6d.

A Sketch of Grecian and Roman
History. By **A. H. Beesly**, M.A., Assistant Master at Marlborough College.

With Maps. Small 8vo. [Nearly ready.

· London · Oxford · Cambridge ·

New Pamphlets

English Church Defence Tracts.

No. 1. ROMAN MISQUOTATIONS.

No. 2. ARE CLERGYMEN OF THE ENGLISH CHURCH RIGHTLY ORDAINED?

No. 3. PAPAL INFALLIBILITY.

No. 4. MORE ABOUT "ROMAN MISQUOTATIONS:" IN REPLY TO A PAMPHLET ENTITLED "ANGLICAN MISREPRESENTATIONS."

8vo. 3d. each.

The Shortened Order for Morning and Evening Prayer daily throughout the Year except on Sunday, Christmas Day, Ash Wednesday, Good Friday, and Ascension Day. With "The Act of Uniformity Amendment Act."

Royal 32mo. 1d.

An Additional Order for Evening Prayer on Sundays and Holy-Days throughout the Year taken from the Holy Scriptures, and Book of Common Prayer, and approved by the Ordinary for use in the Diocese of Peterborough, with a Table of Occasional Psalms and Lessons as approved by the Ordinary.

Royal 32mo. 1d.

· London · Oxford · Cambridge ·

New Pamphlets

A Charge to the Clergy of the Diocese of St. David's. Delivered by **Connop, Lord Bishop of St. David's** at his Eleventh Visitation, October and November 1872. With an Appendix.

8vo. 2s. 6d.

*A Charge delivered to the Clergy of the Dio-*cese of Llandaff, at his Eighth Visitation, July 1872. By **Alfred Ollivant**, D.D., Bishop of Llandaff.

8vo. 2s.

*A Charge delivered to the Clergy of the Dio-*cese of Bangor at his Fifth Visitation, August 1872. By **J. C. Campbell**, D.D., Bishop of Bangor.

8vo. 1s.

Indian Missions. A Letter to His Grace the Archbishop of Canterbury. From **Henry Alexander Douglas**, D.D., Bishop of Bombay.

8vo. 1s.

The Great Commission. Meditations on Home and Foreign Missions. Designed originally for the December Ember Week of the Year 1872, in which falls the Appointed Day of Humble Supplication for an Increase of the Number of Missionaries, and for the Blessing of Almighty God upon their Labours. By **Edward Meyrick Goulburn**, D.D., Dean of Norwich.

Small 8vo. 6d.

· London · Oxford · Cambridge ·

New Pamphlets

The Life of Faith and the Athanasian Creed.
A Sermon preached before the University of Oxford in the Church of St. Mary the Virgin on the Twenty-First Sunday after Trinity, 1872. By H. P. Liddon, D.D., Ireland Professor of Exegesis and Canon of St. Paul's.

8vo. 1s.

A Common Sense View of the Athanasian Creed Question. By **Henry Arthur Woodgate**, B.D., Rector of Belbroughton.

Crown 8vo. 4d.

Our Position as Catholics in the Church of England. A Letter to a Friend. By the Rev. **Arthur Wollaston Hutton**, B.A., formerly Scholar of Exeter College, Assistant-Curate of St. Barnabas, Oxford.

8vo. 1s.

Defence of the English Ordinal. With some Observations upon Spiritual Jurisdiction and the Power of the Keys. By the Rev. **W. R. Churton**, M.A., Fellow of King's College, Cambridge, and Honorary Canon of Rochester Cathedral.

8vo, cloth. 3s.

The Colour of the Cross. An Allegory.
By **J. G. S. Nichol**, Head Master of King James's Grammar School, and Curate of Knaresborough.

Crown 8vo. 1s.

· London · Oxford · Cambridge ·

Commentary on the Gospels

Devotional Commentary on the Gospel Narrative. By the Rev. Isaac Williams, B.D., formerly Fellow of Trinity College, Oxford.

New Edition. Eight Volumes. Crown 8vo. 5s. each.

Thoughts on the Study of the Holy Gospels.
Characteristic Differences in the Four Gospels—Our Lord's Manifestations of Himself—The Rule of Scriptural Interpretation furnished by our Lord—Analogies of the Gospel—Mention of Angels in the Gospels—Places of Our Lord's Abode and Ministry—Our Lord's Mode of Dealing with His Apostles—Conclusion.

A Harmony of the Four Evangelists.
Our Lord's Nativity—Our Lord's Ministry (Second Year)—Our Lord's Ministry (Third Year)—The Holy Week—Our Lord's Resurrection.

Our Lord's Nativity.
The Birth at Bethlehem—The Baptism in Jordan—The First Passover.

Our Lord's Ministry. Second Year.
The Second Passover—Christ with the Twelve—The Twelve sent Forth.

Our Lord's Ministry. Third Year.
Teaching in Galilee—Teaching at Jerusalem—Last Journey from Galilee to Jerusalem.

The Holy Week.
The Approach to Jerusalem—The Teaching in the Temple—The Discourse on the Mount of Olives—The Last Supper.

Our Lord's Passion.
The Hour of Darkness—The Agony—The Apprehension—The Condemnation—The Day of Sorrows—The Hall of Judgment—The Crucifixion—The Sepulture.

Our Lord's Resurrection.
The Day of Days—The Grave Visited—Christ Appearing—The Going to Emmaus—The Forty Days—The Apostles Assembled—The Lake in Galilee—The Mountain in Galilee—The Return from Galilee.

Uniform with the above.

The Apocalypse, with Notes and Reflections.

[*In the Press.*

By the same Author.

The Characters of the Old Testament. A Series of Sermons. 5s.

Female Characters of Holy Scripture. A Series of Sermons. 5s.

· London · Oxford · Cambridge ·

Keys to Christian Knowledge

Small 8vo. 2s. 6d. each.

A Key to the Knowledge and Use of the Book of Common Prayer. By **John Henry Blunt**, M.A., F.S.A., Editor of "The Annotated Book of Common Prayer."

A Key to the Knowledge and Use of the Holy Bible. By **John Henry Blunt**, M.A.

A Key to the Knowledge of Church History (Ancient). Edited by **John Henry Blunt**, M.A.

A Key to the Knowledge of Church History (Modern). Edited by **John Henry Blunt**, M.A.

A Key to Christian Doctrine and Practice. (Founded on the Church Catechism.) By **John Henry Blunt**, M.A.

A Key to the Narrative of the Four Gospels. By **John Pilkington Norris**, M.A., Canon of Bristol, formerly one of Her Majesty's Inspectors of Schools.

A Key to the Narrative of the Acts of the Apostles. By **John Pilkington Norris**, M.A.

· London · Oxford · Cambridge ·

Rivington's Mathematical Series

12mo.

By J. HAMBLIN SMITH, M.A.,
OF GONVILLE AND CAIUS COLLEGE, AND LATE LECTURER AT ST. PETER'S COLLEGE, CAMBRIDGE.

Algebra.
Part I. 3s. Without Answers, 2s. 6d.

Exercises on Algebra.
Part I. 2s. 6d. [Copies may be had without the Answers.]

Elementary Trigonometry.
4s. 6d.

Elementary Hydrostatics.
3s.

Elements of Geometry.
Containing Books 1 to 6, and portions of Books 11 and 12 of Euclid, with Exercises and Notes. 3s. 6d.

Books 1 and 2; Books 3 and 4; Books 5 and 6; and portions of Books 11 and 12; 2s. each; or limp cloth, 1s. 6d.

Elementary Statics.
3s.

By E. J. GROSS, M.A.,
FELLOW OF GONVILLE AND CAIUS COLLEGE, CAMBRIDGE.

Algebra.
Part II. [*In the Press.*

By G. RICHARDSON, M.A.,
ASSISTANT MASTER AT WINCHESTER COLLEGE, AND LATE FELLOW OF ST. JOHN'S COLLEGE, CAMBRIDGE.

Geometrical Conic Sections.
[*In the Press.*

Other Works are in Preparation.

· London · Oxford · Cambridge ·

Catena Classicorum

A Series of Classical Authors. Edited by Members of both Universities, under the Direction of the Rev. **Arthur Holmes,** *M.A., Senior Fellow and Dean of Clare College, Cambridge, and late Preacher at the Chapel Royal, Whitehall; and the Rev.* **Charles Bigg,** *M.A., late Senior Student and Tutor of Christ Church, Oxford; Principal of Brighton College.*

Sophoclis Tragoediae.
  THE ELECTRA, 3s. 6d.   THE AJAX, 3s. 6d.
  Edited by **R. C. Jebb,** M.A., Fellow and Tutor of Trinity College, Cambridge, and Public Orator of the University.

Juvenalis Satirae.
  Edited by **G. A. Simcox,** M.A., Fellow and Classical Lecturer of Queen's College, Oxford. New Edition, revised. 5s.

Thucydidis Historia.
  Edited by **Chas. Bigg,** M.A., late Senior Student and Tutor of Christ Church, Oxford; Principal of Brighton College.
    Books I. and II., with Introductions. 6s.

Demosthenis Orationes Publicae.
  THE OLYNTHIACS, 2s. 6d.   THE PHILIPPICS, 3s.   DE FALSA LEGATIONE, 6s.
  Edited by **G. H. Heslop,** M.A., late Fellow and Assistant Tutor of Queen's College, Oxford; Head Master of St. Bees.

Aristophanis Comoediae.
  THE ACHARNIANS and THE KNIGHTS, 4s.   THE CLOUDS, 3s. 6d.   THE WASPS, 3s. 6d.
  Edited by **W. C. Green,** M.A., late Fellow of King's College, Cambridge; Assistant Master at Rugby School.
  An Edition of THE ACHARNIANS and THE KNIGHTS, Revised and especially adapted for Use in Schools. 4s.

Isocratis Orationes.
  AD DEMONICUM ET PANEGYRICUS. 4s. 6d.
  Edited by **John Edwin Sandys,** M.A., Fellow and Tutor of St. John's College, Classical Lecturer at Jesus College, Cambridge.

Persii Satirae.
  Edited by **A. Pretor,** M.A., Fellow of St. Catherine's College, Cambridge, Classical Lecturer of Trinity Hall. 3s. 6d.

Homeri Ilias.
  Edited by **S. H. Reynolds,** M.A., late Fellow and Tutor of Brasenose College, Oxford. Books I. to XII. 6s.

Terenti Comoediae.
  ANDRIA ET EUNUCHUS. 4s. 6d.
  Edited by **T. L. Papillon,** M.A., Fellow of New College, Oxford, late Fellow of Merton.

Demosthenis Orationes.
  DE CORONA. 5s.
  Edited by the Rev. **Arthur Holmes,** M.A., Senior Fellow and Dean of Clare College, Cambridge, and late Preacher at the Chapel Royal, Whitehall.

Herodoti Historia.
  Edited by **H. G. Woods,** Fellow and Tutor of Trinity College, Oxford.
    Book I. 6s.   Book II. 5s.

· London · Oxford · Cambridge ·

Select Plays of Shakspere

RUGBY EDITION. With an Introduction and Notes to each Play. Small 8vo.

As You Like It.   2s. ; paper cover, 1s. 6d.
Edited by the Rev. **Charles E. Moberly**, M.A., Assistant Master in Rugby School, formerly Scholar of Balliol College, Oxford.

Macbeth.   2s.; paper cover, 1s. 6d.
Edited by the same.

Coriolanus.   2s. 6d.; paper cover, 2s.
Edited by **Robert Whitelaw**, M.A., Assistant Master in Rugby School, formerly Fellow of Trinity College, Cambridge.

Hamlet.   2s. 6d. ; *paper covers*, 2s.
Edited by the Rev. **Charles E. Moberly**, M.A.

The Tempest.   [*In preparation.*
Edited by **J. Surtees Phillpotts**, M.A., Assistant Master in Rugby School, formerly Fellow of New College, Oxford.

Much Ado about Nothing.   [*In preparation.*
Edited by the same.

⁎⁎ *Other Plays are in Preparation.*

Scott's *Lay of the Last Minstrel.*

RUGBY EDITION. Edited, with an Introduction, Notes, and Glossary, by **J. Surtees Phillpotts**, M.A., Assistant Master in Rugby School, formerly Fellow of New College, Oxford.

Scenes from Greek Plays

RUGBY EDITION. Abridged and Adapted for the use of Schools, by **Arthur Sidgwick**, M.A., Assistant Master in Rugby School, and formerly Fellow of Trinity College, Cambridge.

Aristophanes.
THE CLOUDS.   THE FROGS.   THE KNIGHTS.   PLUTUS.

Euripides.
IPHIGENIA IN TAURIS.   THE CYCLOPS.   ION. ELECTRA.

Small 8vo.   *1s. 6d. each ; paper cover, 1s.*

⁎⁎ *Other Plays are in Preparation.*

· London · Oxford · Cambridge ·

Rivington's Devotional Series
Elegantly printed with red borders. 16mo. 2s. 6d.

Thomas à Kempis, Of the Imitation of Christ.
Introduction to the Devout Life.
From the French of S. Francis of Sales, Bishop and Prince of Geneva.

A Short and Plain Instruction for the Better
Understanding of the Lord's Supper: to which is annexed, the Office of the Holy Communion, with Proper Helps and Directions. By **Thomas Wilson, D.D.**, late Lord Bishop of Sodor and Man.
Complete Edition, in large type.

The Rule and Exercises of Holy Living.
By **Jeremy Taylor, D.D.**, Bishop of Down and Connor, and Dromore.

The Rule and Exercises of Holy Dying.
By **Jeremy Taylor, D.D.**, Bishop of Down and Connor, and Dromore.
The "Holy Living" and the "Holy Dying" may be had bound together in One Vol. 5s.

A Practical Treatise concerning Evil Thoughts.
By **William Chilcot**, M.A.

The English Poems of George Herbert.
Together with his Collection of Proverbs, entitled "Jacula Prudentum."

The Christian Year: Thoughts in Verse for
the Sundays and Holy Days throughout the Year.

CHEAP EDITION, WITHOUT THE RED BORDERS.

Thomas à Kempis, Of the Imitation of Christ.
Limp cloth, 1s.; or in cover, 6d.

Bishop Wilson's Holy Communion.
Large type. Limp cloth, 1s.; or in cover, 6d.

Jeremy Taylor's Holy Living. Limp cloth, 1s.
Jeremy Taylor's Holy Dying. Limp cloth, 1s.
Holy Living and Holy Dying. In One Vol, 2s. 6d.
The Christian Year. Limp cloth, 1s., or in cover, 6d.

· London · Oxford · Cambridge ·

www.ingramcontent.com/pod-product-compliance
Lightning Source LLC
Chambersburg PA
CBHW020318240426
43673CB00039B/844